CONTEMPORARY DIMENSIONS IN NIGERIAN MUSIC

A Festschrift for Arugha Aboyowa Ogisi

CONTEMPORARY DIMENSIONS IN NIGERIAN MUSIC

A Festschrift for Arugha Aboyowa Ogisi

Edited by

Charles Aluede   Albert Oikelome
Yemi Akperi   Oghenemudiakevwe Igbi

Malthouse Press Limited
Lagos, Benin, Ibadan, Jos, Port-Harcourt, Zaria

© Charles Aluede, Albert Oikelome, Yemi Akperi, Oghenemudiakevwe Igbi 2020
First Published 2021
ISBN: 978-978-58297-8-5

Published and manufactured in Nigeria by

Malthouse Press Limited
43 Onitana Street, Off Stadium Hotel Road,
Off Western Avenue, Lagos Mainland
E-mail: malthouselagos@gmail.com
Facebook:@malthouselagos
Twitter:@malthouselagos
Istagram:@malthouselagos
Tel: 0802 600 3203

All rights reserved. No part of this publication may be reproduced, transmitted, transcribed, stored in a retrieval system or translated into any language or computer language, in any form or by any means, electronic, mechanical, magnetic, chemical, thermal, manual or otherwise, without the prior consent in writing of Malthouse Press Limited, Lagos, Nigeria.

This book is sold subject to the condition that it shall not by way of trade, or otherwise, be lent, re-sold, hired out, or otherwise circulated without the publisher's prior consent in writing, in any form of binding or cover other than in which it is published and without a similar condition, including this condition, being imposed on the subsequent purchaser.

Distributors:
African Books Collective Ltd, Oxford, UK
Email: abc@africanbookscollective.com
Website: http://www.africanbookscollective.com

Acknowledgements

This festschrift was conceived to celebrate a sage of no mean repute, Dr. Arugha Aboyowa Ogisi, for the profundity of his immaculate research/creative output and manpower development in the field of music. It is also aimed at contributing to the advancement of knowledge in the music discipline. The cerebral, financial and moral contributions from the barrage of individuals who showed unending commitment to the actualization of this project have been superlative. Countless students/mentees, colleagues and friends were very supportive right from when the idea was conceived until it came to fruition. For space constraints, we may be unable to mention all the persons that facilitated the realization of this project, but such challenges notwithstanding, reference shall be made of the few who toiled day and night to ensure the success of the assignment.

We register our appreciation to the celebrant, Dr. Arugha Aboyowa Ogisi for later giving an approval for this project. When the plan was inchoate, Dr. Ogisi was tardy in giving assent. His tardiness stemmed from the fact that to him, it was too early to be counted among the respected leagues of scholars to be celebrated in such manner, because according to him, he still has a lot of contributions to make. From interactions with him, it was observed that he is an example of a man who believes in silent achievements. Good as his reasons may have been, a tacit approval to go ahead was given when he was reminded of the age-old tradition of giving honour to whom it is due. And today, his students and mentees whom he had groomed over the years look back to the springboard that shot them into the academic and sonic space with a word of gratitude. His mentees are immensely grateful to him, for without his acceptance, this project would not have come to fruition. This idea was first conceived by three of his students, Professor Charles Aluede, Rev. Dr. Yemi Akperi and Dr. Mudia Igbi; consequently, *Ogisi @ 65 Festschrift Committee* was formed with the three aforementioned persons.

Quite a number of individuals are highly appreciated for the huge monetary, material and other unquantifiable sacrifices made since the day the idea was conceived. In this segment, we show our gratitude to some mentees of Dr. Ogisi, who contributed various sums of money to aid the publication of the book with a reputable publisher. They are Professor Charles Aluede, Dr. Mudia Igbi, Dr. Yemi Akperi, Rev. Dr. Udoka Peace

Ossaiga, Dr. Mrs. Ereforo Dick-Duvwarovwo, Mrs. Rebecca Ogbeide, Dr. (Mrs.) Enoh Okafor, Mrs. Dora Okumbor and Mrs. Peace Onyenye. The committee is particularly grateful to the scholars who reviewed all the manuscripts in the book for their prompt response in reverting to us with the reviewed works. They are Professor Ovaborhene Idamoyibo, Professor Charles, Aluede, Dr. Albert Oikelome, Dr. Adeoluwa Okunade, Dr, Isaac Udoh, Dr. Kayode Samuel, Dr. Isaac Ibude, Dr. Peter Odogbor, Dr. Mudia Igbi, Dr. Yemi Akperi, Dr. Johnson James Akpakpan and Dr. Udoka Peace Ossaiga. The thorough and constructive criticisms given by these scholars are partly responsible for the quality of articles contained herein. We treasure the support received from erudite scholars and friends of Arugha Ogisi, like Professors Emurobome Idolor, 'Bode Omojola and 'Femi Adedeji. We also appreciate Professor Onyee Nwankpa for graciously accepting to write the foreword. We are indebted to all the contributors who sent papers for consideration in the book. To those whose papers scaled through the rigorous blind peer review and to the ones whose articles were rejected, we appreciate your interest in contributing to scholarship and celebrating a man of honour, Dr. Arugha Ogisi. The moral support received from the leadership of the Association of Nigerian Musicologists (ANIM), Conference of Music Educators in Nigeria (COMEN) and the Association of Dance Practitioners of Nigeria (ADSPON) is appreciated. We also specially thank our families for their patience during the entire duration the process of publishing this book lasted. Finally, we cannot thank God enough without whose guidance, wisdom and other manifold blessings, the project would have been a mirage: To God be the Glory!

Prof Charles O. Aluede
Chairman, Ogisi @ 65 Festschrift Committee

Dr Oghenemudiakevwe Igbi
Secretary, Ogisi @65 Festschrift Committee

Preface

This book, *Contemporary Dimensions in Nigerian Music,* is a compendium of twenty-one chapters in honour of a personage and teacher whose impacts can be felt in the moulding of a generation of music scholars in Nigeria who have grown to occupy notable spaces in different music faculties, globally. To give honour to whom it is due is an age-old tradition and is therefore considered appropriate that Dr. Arugha Aboyowa Ogisi be honoured in this form.

From ancient to contemporary times, Nigerian music has passed through different stages of transmutation. This music which has been primarily transmitted through oral means has in the last century received significant scholarly attention. Areas like folksong documentation, ethno-organological studies, popular music studies and art music have continued to feature in scholarly discourse. Societal dynamism allows room for scholarly reassessment and evaluation of aspects of Nigerian music; thus, reflecting change and continuity in the area. It is within this cusp that this book looks at contemporary trajectories in Nigerian music.

This festschrift which demonstrates high measure of originality, both in data gathering and presentation, is an effort by a team of reputable music scholars and budding ones out of whom are his former students, friends, admirers and contemporaries in providing new dimensions in the appreciation of Nigerian music. As a festschrift, the book starts with tributes and Ogisi's personality study. Beyond the tributes, the rest articles are calibrated into sections which cover diverse areas of music scholarship and they are: Ogisi's Contributions to Musicological Studies in Nigeria, Nigerian Musicology, Popular Music and Music Education, Nigerian Art and Church Music and General readings.

The first section of this book is on Arugha Aboyowa Ogisi's 'Contributions to Musicological Studies in Nigeria'. This segment, which has four chapters, hosts articles dwelling on different aspects of Arugha Ogisi. It starts with the duo, Charles Onomudo Aluede and Bruno Dafe Ekewenu, as they trace 'The Finger of Aboyowa Arugha Ogisi in Nigerian Music Education'. This is followed by that of Oghenemudiakevwe Igbi's 'An Exploration into the Genius of the Quintessential Nigerian Musicologist, Arugha Ogisi'. While Udoka Peace Ossaiga examines the 'Contributions of

Arugha Aboyowa Ogisi to the Development of Music in Bethel Baptist Church, Sapele,' David Bolaji looks beyond the church in his work entitled, 'Nigerian Art Music and Human Capital Development: the Unsung Contributions of Arugha Aboyowa Ogisi'.

In these chapters, the reader is likely going to discover that certain attributes of Ogisi are repeatedly mentioned. This is so because facts relating to his childhood, musical career and attributes will be probably the same and so presented by each author. But this should not dampen the enthusiasm of the reader because, without doubt, the account of three or more persons cannot be entirely the same, in that whatever characteristic features of the honouree that are not accommodated in one chapter may be found in the other. It is based on this understanding that we yielded to the principle of the more, the merrier.

Section II, which is on Nigerian Musicology, evoked much interest from contributors. Many manuscripts were received and after review, we were only able to accommodate seven. First among the essays in this section is that of Emurobome G. Idolor where he interrogated the 'Features of Orality in Okpẹ Disco Popular Music of the Niger Delta Region, Nigeria'. In their work, 'Songs for Living: Interrogating the Complexion of Song-Texts and Healing in Nigeria', 'Femi Adedeji and Charles Onomudo Aluede examine the music healing traditions of two adjacent communities in Western and Midwestern Nigeria. This section appears to have a good harvest of contributions from different communities within Nigeria. We say so because, judging from the first sets of essays therein, we observe that all the authors' thrusts of attention are on the musical traditions of different ethnic nationalities within Nigeria. For example, the chapter by Rotimi Peters Ologundudu is on 'The Role and Functions of Music in Odun Isu/Ijesu of Akokoland, Ondo State, Nigeria'; Peace Onyenye teases the 'Philosophical Aspects of Udje Performance in Delta State: A Study of Chief James Edah Towel Musical Ensemble'; John Aideloje Abolagba on the 'Textual Analysis of Owan Traditional and Religious Music as Educational Resources in Edo State, Nigeria'; Akin Joseph Osunniyi on 'Ogotun-Ekiti Bata Music: A Documentation of a Royal Music Ensemble'. And Margaret Akpevwoghene Efurhievwe explores 'Reconstructing *Opre* Indigenous Knowledge for Musicological Studies' including looking at the etymology of the genre that is peculiar to the Urhobo of Delta State Nigeria and traces how its name has metamorphosed into *Opiri.*

Sunday Ofuani's 'Applied Theory of Nigerian Highlife' is the opening chapter of this third section on Popular Music and Music Education. It is followed by Yemi Akperi's, titled 'Teach Children the Music they Enjoy: Incorporating Community Music into Basic Schools Music Programmes' and 'Popular Music and Skill Development in Tertiary Music Education' of Precious Omuku wraps up this section.

Section IV of this book deals with works on Nigerian Art and Church Music. In moving from Nigerian Musicology, one finds a smooth transition into Art and Church music in Nigeria. The chapters in this section are quite insightful and thought-provoking. The first, Isaac E. Udoh's, discusses 'Tensions between Ecclesiastical Authority and Musical Creativity in Nigeria: The Methodist Church, Nigeria Example.' Next, 'Bode Omojola's presentation, we see, evidently, the hand of Ekundayo Phillips in the 'Development of Modern Yoruba Music.' Still discussing some aspects of the music of the Yoruba, Opeyemi Adeyinka Asaolu reflects on the use of 'Traditional Music in the Anglican Communion from Churches in Iju-Ishaga Archdeaconry, Lagos West Anglican Diocese.' Moving from the question of Yoruba music in the church, Justina Enoh Okafor locates the Bible as an 'Invaluable Source and Inspirational Archive for Church Music Composition'.

Section V of this book dwells on general readings in and around music. Put aptly, it talks of music in societal transformation, music in films and music in African total theatre. These could be deduced from the contributions of Albert Oikelome on performance arts and societal transformation with emphasis on Footprints of David Academy, Bariga, Lagos, Nigeria, Philo Igue Okpeki on 'Relevance of Music in Nollywood' and Ayodele Samuel Adegboyega and Edward Oluwagbemiga Olusegun who did a bibliographic classification of music in African 'total theatre'.

Given the resumé of this text as stated above, its appeal cannot be over-emphasised. It is a good read for the musicologist, music director and music enthusiast. However, while the editors may share the blames of any possible slips in this text, the opinions canvassed in it are solely those of the authors.

Charles O. Aluede Ph.D   Yemi Akperi Ph.D
Albert Oikelome Ph.D   Oghenemudiakevwe Igbi Ph.D

Foreword

A musical giant is like a composition, indeed, a motet in a superb polyphonic texture which provides a device that gives a soft richness to the musical quality, as well as felicitous touches of craftsmanship reflecting the diversity that are most potently peculiar to the music profession. I, therefore, salute this day as one of us is compulsorily taking a formal bow on academic engagement.

I feel honoured and humbled to be asked to write a Foreword on a *festschrift* in honour of my much-respected senior, schoolmate and colleague, Dr. Arugha Aboyowa Ogisi. A *festschrift* in honour of Dr. Arugha A. Ogisi is a project of deservedly acuity. This book, *Contemporary Dimensions in Nigerian Music,* is aptly titled to reflect the various vectors and vistas in the development and evolutionary trends of Nigerian contemporary music in which he has played a significant role.

Graduating with the Bachelor of Arts degree in Music at the Nigeria's premier university, the University of Nigeria, Nsukka, in 1982, and also a holder of the Diploma in Music Education of the Department of Music, Dr. Ogisi did not leave anyone in doubt of what his passion and vision were. His opinions on African/Nigerian Music and Music in Africa/Nigeria (popular, indigenous, sacred or art music) were poignant, fearless and objective. His musical prowess, poise and drive were impressive. Ogisi was our one and only "professor". His musical activities were boundless, touching on the traditional African/Nigerian Music, Music Education, Western art music, and the Church, especially the Nsukka Baptist Church (now Holy Ghost Baptist Church) on Enugu Road, Nsukka. He would regularly dress up in suits and ties (like the conventional Professors), teaching us, as it were, the dressing ethics of undergraduates. Without a doubt, Arugha Ogisi was one of those few distinguished "elders" in the Department of Music, University of Nigeria, Nsukka.

Through this *festschrift*, the centrality of Arugha Ogisi as the *masquerade and dancer* is not in doubt. This is reflected on the theme and subthemes on which his friends, contemporaries, colleagues, former students, and admirers have written. This *festschrift*, coming during the world's most critical turning point in history, ravaged by the crippling effects of COVID-19 pandemic, exhibits "high measure of originality both in data gathering and presentation", offering new facets and insights into understanding and enjoyment of Nigerian music. Beginning with tributes, this book is designed into sections and chapters, covering diverse areas of music scholarship: Ogisi's Contributions to Musicological Studies in Nigeria, Nigerian Musicology, Popular Music and Music Education, Nigerian Art and Church Music, as well as General Readings. Charles Onomudo Aluede and Bruno Dafe Ekewenu trace "The Finger of Aboyowa Arugha Ogisi in Nigerian Music Education"; Oghenemudiakevwe Igbi engages the readers in "An Exploration into the Genius of the Quintessential Nigerian Musicologist, Arugha Ogisi"; Udoka Peace Ossaiga examines "The Contributions of Arugha Aboyowa Ogisi to the Development of Music in Bethel Baptist Church, Sapele"; David Bolaji looks into "Nigerian Art Music and Human Capital Development: The Unsung Contributions of Arugha Aboyowa Ogisi"; Emurobome G. Idolor interrogates the "Features of Orality in Okpẹ Disco Popular Music of the Niger Delta Region"; 'Femi Adedeji and Charles Onomudo Aluede examine the music healing traditions of two adjacent communities in Western and Midwestern Nigeria in their work titled "Songs for Living: Interrogating the Complexion of Song-Texts and Healing in Nigeria"; Peace Onyenye teases the readers on the "Philosophical Aspects of *Udje* Performance in Delta State"; Isaac E. Udoh discusses "Tensions between Ecclesiastical Authority and Musical Creativity in Nigeria: The Methodist Church, Nigeria Example", Precious Omuku looks at the importance of popular music and skill development in tertiary music education, while 'Bode Omojola's presentation vividly highlights the hand of "Ekundayo Phillips in the Development of Modern Yoruba Music", to mention just these few.

It is my avowed pleasure to Professor Charles O. Aluede and his team of editors, Dr. Albert Oikelome, Dr. Yemi Akperi, and Dr. Oghenemudiakevwe Igbi, for this honour bestowed on Dr. Arugha A. Ogisi in the form of a *festschrift*. I commend the various authors who have made this project possible through their friendships, contributions and scholarships. This book, *Contemporary Dimensions in Nigerian Music*, in honour of Dr. Arugha A. Ogisi, is sure to make an interesting read and an invaluable addition to your musical scholarship.

Professor Onyee N. Nwankpa, *Ph.D. (Calgary, Canada), KCW, ML, SFIARSA*
Professor of Composition, Theory and Conducting,
Department of Music, Faculty of Humanities,
University of Port Harcourt, Nigeria.

Editors

Charles Aluede is a Professor of Ethnomusicology and Music Therapy at Ambrose Alli University, Ekpoma, Nigeria. He has a Ph.D in Ethnomusicology from the University of Ibadan. Professor Aluede is a composer/arranger, performer, and an African music expert with emphasis on African Indigenous Knowledge Systems. He is the founder of Centre for Studies in Esan Music, a privately sponsored initiative aimed at the preservation of Esan musical mores. He has published widely on music healing in Nigeria, and is one of the leading African scholars of music therapy. A former Sub-Dean, Faculty of Arts, Ambrose Alli University, Ekpoma, Aluede is also an erstwhile National Secretary, Association of Nigerian Musicologists (ANIM), member of the International Trombone Association (ITA) and International Council for Traditional Music (ICTM).

Albert Oikelome is an Associate Professor of Music at the University of Lagos, Nigeria. He specialized in Choral Performance and Music Education as an undergraduate at the University of Nigeria, Nsukka, and later received M.A and Ph.D degrees in Ethnomusicology from University of Ibadan. Albert Oikelome has his specialty in choral conducting and vocal performance at the University of Lagos. He is the Director of the University Chorale and founder of *Africa Sings*, a concept dedicated to the promotion of choral music in African tertiary institutions. Over the years, he has been able to mentor young musicians who have risen to become stars in both classical and popular music streams. As a result of successful performances and teaching, Oikelome is a sought after teacher, clinician and adjudicator for solo vocal and choral workshops and competitions. Dr. Oikelome has to his credit, series of scholarly articles, books, lectures and choral works for small and large ensembles, many of these published in both local and international journals.

Yemi Akperi has a Ph.D in Music Education and Master of Divinity in Theology (M.Div.Th) from Delta State University, Abraka, and Nigerian Baptist Theological Seminary, Ogbomoso, respectively. He is a teacher, minister and administrator in the fields of education, music philosophy, theology, politics and cultural practice, with experience spanning both public and private sectors. Presently, he ministers at Shepherd Baptist Church, Benin City and is an Adjunct Lecturer of Worship Theology and Hymnody at Baptist Seminary, Benin City. He has published scholarly works on the philosophies of music education and programmes in Nigeria.

Oghenemudiakevwe Igbi currently teaches Music in the Department of Theatre Arts, University of Africa, Toru Orua, Bayelsa State, Nigeria. He holds a Ph.D in Music Composition from Delta State University, Abraka. A prolific composer and performer, Dr. Igbi has over eighty compositions to his credit and has performed in more than two hundred concerts. He is a skilled piano/organ accompanist and director of art music. He is the organist of First Baptist Church, Warri, and the Founder/Music Director, Cherub Voices of Warri. He conducts researches in the areas of music composition, performance, conducting/ensemble management, African musicology and music education, with paper contributions in local/international journals and referred books. Dr. 'Mudiakevwe Igbi is member, Association of Nigerian Musicologists (ANIM), Conference of Music Educators in Nigeria (COMEN) and Fellow, Ife Institute of Advanced Studies (IIAS).

Contributors

Abolagba, John Aideloje is a Chief Lecturer, Department of Music, College of Education, Ekiadolor, and an Adjunct Senior Lecturer in the Department of Theatre Arts, University of Benin. He obtained a Ph.D in Music Education from Delta State University, Abraka, and has published many articles in national and international journals.

Adedeji, Professor 'Femi holds a Ph.D in African Musicology from the University of Ibadan. He is a theologian, gospel music singer, prophet and pastor. He has researched extensively on Ifa music, Church music, gospel music and theology of music. He is a seasoned author, editor to many local and international journals and the immediate past President, Association of Nigerian Musicologists (ANIM).

Adegboyega, Samuel Ayodele holds an M.A in Theatre Arts and is a Principal Lecturer in the Department of Theatre Arts, College of Education, Ikere – Ekiti. He is currently studying for a Ph.D Degree in Theatre Arts at the Federal University, Oye.

Mus. Professor Emurobome G. Idolor read at the University of Nigeria, Nsukka, and University of Ibadan where he is credited as the first to earn a Ph.D degree in Music from a Nigerian University. An award winning scholar in African Music, Music Education with contributions to music composition and conducting, he, in 2006, became the first tenured Professor of Music in Delta State. In his over thirty years lecturing career at the Delta State University, Abraka, he developed the theory of Vertical Pentatonic Harmony (VPH) and has supervised many Master's and Ph.D. degree students. He is also a university system administrator with a track record of productive mentoring of young scholars.

Asaolu, Opeyemi Adeyinka holds a Ph.D in Ethnomusicology from Obafemi Awolowo University, Ile-Ife, Nigeria. He is a seasoned choral director, choir trainer, radio presenter and hymnologist. His research interest focuses on Church music specially choir management and development, elements in traditional Egungun festival in south west Nigeria, as well as music in politics. He lectures in the Department of Performing Arts, Olabisi Onabanjo University, Ago-Iwoye, Ogun State, Nigeria.

Bolaji, David holds a Ph.D in Music Composition from Delta State University, Abraka. He lectures in the Department of Music, University of Port Harcourt.

Efurhievwe, Margaret holds a Ph.D in Music Production from Delta State University (DELSU), Abraka. She is a lecturer of Music in DELSU, Abraka, and has madescholarly contributions to Music Production as an area of specialization in music.

Ekewenu, Bruno Dafe is a lecturer in the Department of Music, Delta State University (DELSU) Abraka. He has a Ph.D in African Musicology from DELSU and has done extensive research on the use of music in Igbe religion. He teaches double bass, band studies and piano.

Ofuani, Sunday lectures in the Department of Music, Delta State University (DELSU), Abraka, Nigeria. He holds a Ph.D in Music, specializing in Theory and Composition. He is a pianist, violinist, music researcher/writer and composer for many Churches and individuals. Dr. Ofuani is the founder and pioneer music director of Delta State Chorale and Orchestra, and the Asaba City Choral Society.

Okafor, Enoh holds a Ph.D in Music Theory and Composition from Nnamdi Azikiwe University, Awka. She is a principal lecturer in the Department of Music, College of Education, Agbor, Nigeria. She plays the piano and flute, and also teaches courses like orchestration and conducting.

Okpeki, Philo Igue is a lecturer in the Department of Music, Delta State University (DELSU), Abraka. She obtained a Ph.D in Music Media from DELSU in 2017, and has published some research papers in the areas of music media and African music.

Ologundudu, Rotimi Peters holds an M.A. in Music and is currently a doctoral student in African Musicology at Delta State University, Abraka.

He is also a senior lecturer in the Department of Music Technology, The Polytechnic, Ibadan.

Olusegun, Edward Oluwagbemiga graduated from DELSU, Abraka, with a Ph.D in African Musicology in 2019. He is a senior lecturer in the Department of Music, College of Education, Ikere – Ekiti.

Omojola, Professor Bode holds a Ph.D in Ethnomusicology from the University of Leicester, England, United Kingdom. He is a Five College Professor of Music at Mount Holyoke College and the Five College Consortium, Amherst, Hampshire, Smith College, and the University of Massachusetts, Amherst, in the United States of America (U.S.A). A highly skilled composer and seasoned author, Professor Omojola has contributed many scholarly articles in national and international journals of repute. He has held many positions in the academia including the Radcliffe Fellowship in musicology at Harvard University.

Omuku, Precious holds a Ph.D in Music Education from Nnamdi Azikiwe University, Awka. He is a seasoned performer and soloist with hundreds of performances in Nigeria and parts of Africa. He lectures in the Department of Music, University of Port Harcourt, Nigeria. He is also the Founder and Music Director of the Fused Ensemble, Port Harcourt.

Onyenye, Peace is a senior lecturer in the Department of Music, College of Education, Agbor, and a doctoral student at the University of Ibadan. Peace specializes in music media and African musicology.

Ossaiga, Udoka P. holds Bachelor of Church Music (B.C.M), Nigerian Theological Seminary, Ogbomoso, M.A, and Ph.D Degrees in Music Conducting and Directing from Delta State University, Abraka. He is the Music Minister, Unity Baptist Church, Ugbori-Warri.

Osunniyi, Akin Joseph has an M.A. in Music (Composition), and is a Ph.D student in the Department of Creative Arts, University of Lagos. He is a senior Lecturer in the Department of Music, College of Education, Ikere–Ekiti,an author of two books and many other publications.

Udoh, Isaac is an Associate Professor of Music and the current Head, Department of Music, University of Uyo, Nigeria. He holds a Ph.D in Music Theory and Composition from Nnamdi Azikiwe University, Awka.

Table of Contents

Acknowledgements
Preface
Foreword
Contributors
Tributes
Citation

Section I
ARUGHA ABOYOWA OGISI'S CONTRIBUTIONS TO MUSICOLOGICAL STUDIES IN NIGERIA

1. The Finger of Aboyowa Arugha Ogisi in Nigerian Music Education - *Professor Charles Onomudo Aluede & Dr. Bruno Dafe Ekewenu* - 1

2. An Exploration into the Genius of the Quintessential Nigerian Musicologist, Arugha Ogisi - *Dr. Oghenemudiakevwe Igbi* - 15

3. The Contributions of Arugha Aboyowa Ogisi to the Development of Music in Bethel Baptist Church, Sapele - *Dr. Udoka Peace Ossaiga* - 29

4. Nigerian Art Music and Human Capital Development: The Unsung Contributions of Arugha Aboyowa Ogisi - *Dr. David Bolaji* - 37

Section II
NIGERIAN MUSICOLOGY

5. Features of Orality in *Okpẹ Disco* Popular Music of the Niger Delta Region, Nigeria - *Professor Emurobome G. Idolor* - 55

6. Songs for Living: Interrogating the Complexion of Song-Texts and Healing in Nigeria - *Professor 'Femi Adedeji and Professor Charles Onomudo Aluede* - 75

7. The Role and Functions of Music in *Odun Isu/Ijesu* of Akokoland, Ondo State, Nigeria - *Rotimi Peters Ologundudu* - 91

8. Philosophical Aspects of Udje Performance in Delta State: A Study of Chief James Edah Towel Musical Ensemble - *Mrs. Peace Onyenye* - 103

9. Textual Analysis of Owan Traditional and Religious Music as Educational Resources in Edo State, Nigeria - *Dr. John Aideloje Abolagba* - 115

10. Ogotun- Ekiti Bata Music: A Documentation of a Royal Music Ensemble - *Akin Joseph Osunniyi* - 133

11. Reconstructing *Opre* Indigenous Knowledge for Musicological Studies - *Dr. Mrs. Margaret Akpevwoghene Efurhievwe* - 145

Section III
POPULAR MUSIC AND MUSIC EDUCATION

12. Applied Theory of Nigerian Highlife - *Dr. Sunday Ofuani* - 161

13. Teach Children the Music they Enjoy: Incorporating Community Music into Basic Schools' Music Programmes - *Dr. Yemi Akperi* - 175

14. Popular Music and Skill Development in Tertiary Music Education – *Dr Precious Omuku* - 195

Section IV
NIGERIAN ART AND CHURCH MUSIC

15. Tensions between Ecclesiastical Authority and Musical Creativity in Nigeria: The Methodist Church, Nigeria Example - *Dr. Isaac Udoh* - 202

16. Ekundayo Phillips and the Development of Modern Yoruba Music - *Professor 'Bode Omojola* - 213

17. Reflections of Traditional Music in the Anglican Communion: Samples from Churches in Iju-Ishaga Archdeaconry, Lagos West Anglican Diocese - *Dr. Opeyemi Adeyinka Asaolu* - 225

18. The Bible as an Invaluable Source and Inspirational Archive for Church Music Composition - *Dr. Mrs. Justina Enoh Okafor* - 238

Section V
GENERAL READINGS

19. Performance Arts and Societal Transformation: A Case Study of Footprints of David Academy, Bariga, Lagos, Nigeria - *Dr. Albert Oikelome* - 255

20. The Relevance of Music in Nollywood - *Dr. Mrs. Philo Igue Okpeki* - 269

21. A Bibliographic Classification of Music in African Total Theatre - *Ayodele Samuel Adegboyega & Dr. Edward Oluwagbemiga Olusegun* - 276

Index - 285

Tributes

Dr. Arugha Aboyowa Ogisi at 65

- Mus. Professor Emurobọmẹ G. Idọlọr

Age of sixty-five in life sojourn is reminiscent in stock taking. Such stock taking focuses on birth, level of education, employment, achievements, inter-human relations and societal impact. To attempt all these on Dr. Arugha Abayowa Ogisi is to embark on a full-length biographical exposition which is not only diversionary from the focus of a festschrift but also at variance with the subject matter of a tribute. In this context, the target is to briefly recount some of his humanitarian endeavours in these years under review especially as they concern this writer.

In the mid-1960s, I knew an elder female relation, Madam Utọrọ Ohwata, who, with unravelled commitment, comes from Adagbrassa-Ẹlumẹ to worship in the Baptist Church in Ogiedi. She regularly made brief stopovers in my father's compound to exchange pleasantries before proceeding for worship. Little did I know she was the paternal grandmother of Dr. Arugha Ogisi who, then lived in Sapẹlẹ. As my social network expanded beyond the local church to the Sapẹlẹ Baptist Association level in the early 1970s, the name, Deacon Francis E. Ogisi (Arugha's father) sounded homely with his exceptional benevolence in offering to host delegates from Ogiedi Baptist Church anytime the Bethel Baptist Church, Sapẹlẹ (where they worshipped) hosted the association in session. This church programme created a platform for me, being in the same age bracket with Arugha, to familiarise ourselves. In 1977, my uncle, Lt. Col. Timothy C. Eru who studied music told me that Arugha gained admission into the University of Nigeria, Nsukka, to study the same course. I was excited with the news as I was then the organist of the home church.

I opted to take after Timothy Eru and Arugha Ogisi in 1981 to study music. In response to my application, the Department of Music, University of Nigeria, Nsukka, invited me for an auditioning which was a prerequisite for admission. I sought Arugha's assistance to prepare me for the auditioning in music rudiments and aural perception. The weeklong exercise was very helpful in my examination performance.

We both met in Nsukka in the 1981/1982 academic session. While I was a first year Diploma student, he was in the final year degree level. A brilliant and multi-talented personality good in playing musical instruments such as the piano, violin, clarinet, flute and oboe, he doubled as the Conductor, Music Director and Organist in the Nsukka Baptist Church located in the university vicinity. In creative harmony, composition, conducting and research, his classmates called him 'Prof'. I keyed into this exceptional disposition by making him my complementary lecturer especially in the areas of theory, harmony, composition, general orientation on what the discipline entails and the bye-laws that governed the department.

On graduation, he joined the Department of Music, College of Education, and Warri, as a music lecturer where, after my Bachelor's degree in 1986, he absorbed me as a part-time lecturer. As the department was phasing out due to course rationalisation in all three Colleges of Education in the then Bendel State, he facilitated my employment in the Department of Music, College of Education, Agbor, in 1987. Eventually, the Department of Music in Warri phased out in 1988 and he was deployed to Agbor where, again, we both worked briefly before he immediately joined the staff membership of the Bendel State University, Abraka Campus in 1989. In his new employment in Abraka, he relocated me to join him in 1990 where we both worked and converted into the Delta State University (DELSU), Abraka, for thirty years before his retirement.

Collaboration with Dr. Arugha Ogisi is a pleasant experience. Achievements were recorded from mutual understanding, absorption of ideas and synthesis of opinions from relevant people. Albeit his wealth of professional experience, he neither paraded an all-knowing personality nor undermined inputs of younger colleagues. This disposition obliged his colleagues with unalloyed cooperation when he was Head of the Department of Music in Warri and Abraka at different tenures.

I cannot forget when in 1996, we requested the Senate of Delta State University, Abraka, to establish a Pre-degree music programme to beef up students' population in the department. It was a hectic struggle but our commitment and relentlessness earned successful approval. Admission quota thence, unimaginably populated the department that the increase became a competitive platform for students to improve academic quality – indeed, this development birthed first class products in the annals of the department.

At the undergraduate level, we collectively drew an entrepreneurially driven academic programme so designed to equip the products with practical music skills compliant with twenty-first century challenges. From the layout of the programme, the National Universities Commission (NUC) in its routine curriculum review exercises tapped into DELSU's innovative contents to update NUC Benchmark for the study of music in Nigerian universities. The strength of the programme has also been observed in its objective evaluation by curriculum designers of younger music departments in sister universities who toe the blueprint of the Abraka Music School.

Postgraduate music programmes in the Delta State University, Abraka, starting with the Doctor of Philosophy (Ph.D.) is the 5th, the Master of Arts Degree (M.A.) is the 6th, while the Postgraduate Diploma in Music (PGDM) is one of the first trail-blazing innovations in the Nigerian educational system. We synergised competences to design these music programmes comparatively in standard with global best practices of well-established universities in the world. Evidently, this effort positively paid off not only with updated contents in line with societal relevance but also provided a platform for internal upgrade of staff academic statuses in the department. It also offered opportunities for the production of high-level human capital to sister tertiary institutions.

We both synergised energies and expertise in the construction of the Music Performance Hall which houses a spacious performance stage, back stage, props room, stage lighting control room and allied facilities. Today, it is the pride of the department and indeed the university. In order to facilitate effective teaching/learning activities, he initiated the establishment of and created spaces for music media studios, music production studios, stage band studios, listening and viewing studios, purchased musical instruments and electronic equipment amongst many other achievements. A strategist and prudent resource manager of manpower, time and finance that are serially and systematically accounted for; indeed a hard worker who took after the dictum of hard work does not kill, rather it makes one stronger.

As his 65th birthday coincided with his official retirement from the public sector, it is obvious the Delta State University will miss his services. In times like these when the Department of Music more than ever needs his wisdom, proactive disposition, systemic administration, multi-specialisation trait in music and exploitation of inter-disciplinary relevance in subject matter delivery, he is retiring. To me, his leaving is a downright disconnection from a personality characterised with sincerity, hard work, companion, collaboration and at all times, he called me Mus. Certainly, I will deeply miss him but I am cheered up with his goodwill and priceless ideas from which I have eternally benefited.

People oftentimes ask why we are so close to one another; I guess, from the foregoing, the reason has become obvious. An Okpẹ adage reinforces this relationship thus: *Oborẹ ukeke oru rẹn ọwan, ọye ahaye kpanhẹn ikoko* (the magnitude of what an axe accomplished for the owner adjudged it to be carried with befitting regard on the shoulder). Truly, this write-up would have been a full-blown biography on him if it were not a part of a festschrift.

While I rejoice with Dr. Arugha Aboyowa Ogisi for career fulfilment and retiring from the Public Service hale and hearty, I wish him very many more years of good health to reap the fruits of his achievements and enjoy the reward of his humanitarian benevolence.

Happy 65th Birthday, My Brother! Happy Years of Partnership In Progress, My Wonderful Collaborator!! Happy Retirement from Public Service, Dear Colleague!!!

Tribute to a Detribalised Music Scholar

- Sunday Ofuani, Ph.D

The first time I met and knew Dr. A.A. Ogisi was on April 12, 2010, when I went to submit my application for post of lecturer in the Department of Music, Delta State University (DELSU), Abraka. As he was the then Head of Department, I submitted my application through him. Some of the characteristic challenges of contemporary Nigerian public office holders are selfishness, 'god-fatherism' and ethnicism. Since we never met nor knew each other beforehand, not forwarding my application would have been a normal thing. On the contrary, he forwarded it and I got the appointment. Save for my profile attached in the submitted Curriculum Vitae, he had no previous idea of my academic ability and skill in practical music. Official sincerity and zero tolerance for ethnic sentiment are constant characteristics of his. He is an excellent administrator who does not abuse, strategize or utilise official privileges for personal or ethnical benefit/politics. Apart from this, he read and reviewed some of my early writings, especially my articles on Church Music. He gave me no less than four reputable harmony and counterpoint books. And, several discussions that I had with him are academically inspiring. Although it pains me that some of my wishes for him as a lecturer did not come-through in DELSU, nevertheless, it is likely that tomorrow will bring-forth an opposite narrative, because he merits it. He is a practical musician and a musicologist to the core – a performer, composer, conductor, excellent reviewer/critique, editor, teacher, art and popular music director. And so, this tribute is dedicated to him.

Tribute to a Great Mentor, Dr. A. A. Ogisi

- Rotimi Peters Ologundudu

Good morning, *Oga*, Hmmm! 'How are you, when did you arrive from Ibadan?' Yesterday sir. *Oga*, we did not see you in Port Harcourt for the conference. "Yes! I could not make it. You see, I do not know what to write, I need ideas but they were not just flowing, not that I did not know what write, but you see…From that point, Dr. Arugha Aboyowa Ogisi continued to dish out his lecture on paper writing for one and half hours the "lecture" lasted. The foregoing was the conversation between me and Dr. Ogisi. That is the spirit Dr. Ogisi is made of, he could lecture you anywhere he meets you; that becomes his class as long as the student is willing to listen and of course you cannot walk away from him. I came to know Dr. Ogisi during my Postgraduate studies in 2013, and since then the bond grew and soared beyond teacher-student relationship. He is an astute, thoroughly bred and a methodical musicologist. He does not just gloss over the work of students given to him to supervise. He is a meticulous supervisor who pays attention to details until the work becomes archetypal and standard. I am privileged and elated to have passed through the tutelage of this erudite scholar. It is in appreciation of his sterling mentorship that I write this tribute in his honour.

Citation

The Man, Arugha Aboyowa Ogisi

Dr. Arugha Aboyowa Ogisi was born in Sapele on 3rd January 1955 to the family of Deacon F. E. and Deaconess O. Ogisi (*nee* Tonwe) who hailed from Ugbuwangue in Warri South and Ugbege in Warri North Local Government Areas of Delta State, respectively. His father was a merchant involved in the export of timber from the early 1950s to the early 1970s when he ventured into saw milling. He was also involved in haulage services in the 1960s and later went into transportation in the 1980s. He retired from active business in the early 1990s.

Ogisi attended Council Primary School, Sapele, (1961-1966), Baptist High School, Orerokpe (1967-1971), Obokun GCE/ACCA Courses, Ilesa (1972-1973). His foray into music began in 1964 when, as a boy soprano in the Choir of Bethel Baptist Church, Sapele, he was exposed to a number of choral works in the repertory of the music of the masters of Western Classical Music such as Mozart, Handel among others. Between February 1974 and August 1977 he taught Physics at Sapele Technical College, Sapele, and took music lessons from the late Mr. Green, Choirmaster/Organist of Saint Luke Anglican Church Sapele, Mr. John Omatsola, the distinguished Organist of Okotie-Eboh Memorial Baptist Church, Sapele and the conductor and impresario, the late Mr. R. P. I. Okerentie an alumnus of Sowande Music School, University of Nigeria, Nsukka. In 1975, Arugha Ogisi was appointed choirmaster, Bethel Baptist Church, Sapele, and in 1976 he established the Gospel Bells, a gospel band in Bethel Baptist Church, Sapele. Apart from the choir ministering in regular church Sunday services, he instituted an annual song service which held in 1976 and 1977. He also took the choir to record programmes for Bendel Radio (BDR), and the Nigerian Television Authority (NTA) both in Benin City. On a personal level he wrote scripts for music and other cultural programmes for BDR. In 1976, Mr. Okerentie enrolled him for the Grade 5 theory examination of the Associated Board of the Royal Schools of Music (ABRSM) which he passed. The success in the examination increased his interest in music and he became more active in musical activities in Churches in Sapele and its environs.

In 1977, Ogisi was admitted to the Department of Music, University of Nigeria, Nsukka, soon after he was appointed Choirmaster of Nsukka Baptist Church, Nsukka. He joined 'The Gospel Singers', an evangelistic gospel music band in the University in 1977 and became its Leader in 1979. During the long vacation of the 1979/80 session, Dr. A. A Ogisi taught music, part-time in the Colleges of Education in Benin, Agbor and Warri where he significantly contributed in raising the first set of music students.

While in the university, he maintained close contact with his professional Colleagues at BDR and the NTA Benin city. For BDR, he wrote and presented programmes like *'Folk Music International'* - a 15-minute weekly programme produced by one Mr. Charles O. and *From the Cotton Fields to the Concert Hall* - a 30-minute weekly programme produced by the late Cecilia Ordia. Each of these music programmes had 13 episodes that ran for an entire quarter of 13 weeks.

In his final year in 1982, Ogisi formed *The Friends of Music,* a show chorus that was dedicated to performing folk music from around the world. The group succeeded in recording nine 30-minute programmes for NTA Benin City under the oversight of the ace music producer, the late Mr. Sam Ehigie.

He obtained the Diploma in Music Education and the Bachelor of Arts degree in 1980 and 1982 respectively. He did his National Youth Service at the Department of Music, College of Education, Ikere-Ekiti and inspired many of the students to further their education beyond the NCE. One of such students recently obtained his doctorate in music, specializing in African musicology.

As a lecturer at the College of Education, Warri, he was able to rejuvenate the music programme of the College. He obtained the Master in African Studies (Music) and a Doctor of Philosophy in Ethnomusicology from the University of Ibadan in 1987 and 2009 respectively. His doctoral thesis is on *The Evolution of Popular Music in South-Western Nigeria 1900-1990.*

He had provided leadership in Department of Music at College of Education, Warri, in the 1980s and as acting Head of the Department of Music, Delta State University, Abraka for several years. He made unique contributions in both instances in the introduction of novel and innovative ideas in the development of music programmes in both institutions and some of them have been widely accepted in Nigerian music education by other tertiary institutions. He has taught several courses at undergraduate and at postgraduate levels and has also successfully supervised about thirty researches leading to the award of Master and Doctoral degrees in several areas of music.

His research interests include but not limited to popular music in Nigeria, continuity and change in Nigerian music, music and rites of passage in the western Niger Delta, Nigerian church music, music education in Nigeria, art music, Isekiri language and the musical arts. He has published over forty articles and book chapters in the areas. He is also a collector of folksongs and Nigerian Spirituals. He recently published a collection of Nigerian spirituals in the book *Praise the Lord* (2017).

He is also involved in creative activities in the form of composing/arranging of music and writing of poems. Some of his published compositions include *Dance of the Seven Spirit* a ballet, *Partum Opera 1* (a collection of some of his compositions and arrangements, and *Songs of the Wayfarers* a collection of some of his poems).

Dr. Ogisi has also been editor of journals like *Nigerian Music Journal* (2012), *Dance Journal of Nigeria* (from 2013 to 2017), and *Une: Abraka Music Journal* (1994 to 1997). In addition, he has reviewed several articles for many Nigerian and international journals. He is the editor of the book titled *Studies in Nigerian Music* (2015).

He is a member of International Council for Traditional Music, Association of Nigerian Musicologists (ANIM), Society of Music Educators of Nigeria (SOMEN), Composers Association of Nigeria, Association of Dance Scholars and Practitioners of Nigeria (ADSPON) and International Society for Music Education (ISME).

He is married with children.

SECTION I

Arugha Aboyowa Ogisi's Contributions to Musicological Studies in Nigeria

The Finger of Aboyowa Arugha Ogisi in Nigerian Music Education

Prof. Charles Onomudo Aluede[*] & Bruno Dafe Ekewenu, Ph.D[**]

Introduction

This chapter examines Arugha Aboyowa Ogisi's musical impetus, training and contributions to music education in Nigeria. In pursuit of this, the study relied on a mixture of methods to elicit data such as interviews and library search for relevant literature. The interviews were structured in such a manner that the inputs on Ogisi were obtained alongside those of his students at the College of Education, Warri, undergraduate and postgraduate students and colleagues at the Delta State University, Abraka and his contemporaries at the University of Nigeria, Nsukka. The study reveals Ogisi's unquantifiable impact on a cream of our present day music scholars in Nigeria at different levels of education. Consequently, it is recommended that periodically, studies on individual scholars should be investigated to generate a resource base on authors/composers. What we share at our fingertips currently may slip into oblivion if not properly documented for posterity.

Without any mien of contradiction, and judging from the title of this paper, the authors investigate the man, Arugha Aboyowa Ogisi whose musical career has spanned about four decades and still counting in the vineyard of music scholarship. To give honour to whom it is considered due is an age-old tradition which is by extension found in contemporary music scholarship. For example, Mokwunyei (2014) Aluede (2014) Idamoyibo (2014) and Dada and Dada (2014) have in the past paid tributes to Professor Mosunmola Ayinke Omibiyi-Obidike by referring to her as a formidable finger in the making of Nigerian musicologists, a woman of sterling relevance in contemporary music studies in Nigeria; with the duo, Dada and Dada examining her philosophies and ideologies of African music education. Shortly after this effort, the life, times and contributions of Professor D. C. C.

---

[*] Ambrose Alli University, Ekpoma
[**] Delta State University, Abraka

Agu was also captured in an impressive festschrift where Udoh (2017), Ibekwe (2017) Ajewole (2017) and Alvan-Ikoku interrogated issues bordering on his musicality, his music, his music scholarship and professionalism. It is very common in Africa for people's star to fall, their hearts stop to beat, hands feeble and bodies cold before suddenly being remembered for the contributions they have made. This is not exactly the case with Dr. A. A. Ogisi who we fondly call *Oga*. That he is still strong to watch us share our collective impressions of him is not only amazing but greatly inspiring.

Bureaucratic bottlenecks and inconsistent promotion yardsticks notwithstanding, when we talk of Ogisi, we talk of a great personage whose contributions to the development of musicological studies deserve an eminent space in contemporary musicological discourse within and outside Nigeria. In Nigeria where it is often customary to appreciate a personage, one notices sadly though that this idea is more of lip service. For example, while it is a standard world practice to find buildings and halls named after selected individuals who have distinguished themselves in their chosen fields and are honoured by others, in Nigeria, it is not that honorific titles are not given by dint of hard work but what we yet see are that they are primarily given to serving and retired military officers and members of the political class. Aside these categories, little or no recognition is often given to intellectuals in our society. This thought has been of grave concern and botheration to Aluede, (2012) when he queried that: "Why must our heroes die unsung? Why should they be forgotten even as they live? And why are there no foundations in memory of them? When good works are not praised, imaginative and creative energies are bound to eclipse into the oblivion". This study is therefore an effort in writing a story of someone whose creative ingenuity, musical scholarship/ activities and contributions are considered worthy of documentation for posterity.

Family Background

Arugha Aboyowa Ogisi was born on January 3rd 1955 to Mr. and Mrs. Ogisi of Ugbuwangue in Warri Kingdom, Delta State, Nigeria. He is the first born among six siblings. His love for music did not just come from the blues as his mother, Omawumi Ogisi (Nee Tonwe) was a chorister in First Baptist Church, Sapele. His mother's musical roles in the Baptist church influenced his musical career; he remarked that through his parents, he was exposed to the church music specifically Baptist at a tender age. There was a music atmosphere in the family and after going through some private music lessons generally with his mentors such as Lt. Col. Timothy Eru, Mr. Anirejuoritse John Omatsola, Mr. Papa Green an organist at St. Luke's Anglican Church, Sapele, between 60s and 70s and Mr. R. P. I. Okenrentie, he enlisted as a member of the choir with the Bethel Baptist Church, Sapele in 1964 and after a-one-year probation, he was finally robed in 1965. At this tender age, he took interest in the organ and promised himself to play for the church in the future.

His Educational Background

Arugha. A. Ogisi enrolled for his primary education between 1961– 1966 with the then Council Primary School, Sapele and by 1967 he attended the Baptist High School, Orerokpe for his Secondary education and finished in 1971. In 1972, he went for his Higher School Certificate programme for Advanced Level General Certificate in Education at Obokun Study Centre in Ilesha and finished in 1973. Between 1973 and 1977 he worked as a Tutor with the Sapele Technical College, Sapele. This was formerly a Trade Centre before it was converted to a Technical College. He taught physics, but was later drafted to teach English language because of his proficiency in the language and for want of manpower. While at Sapele Technical College (STC), he started to co-ordinate the school choir as part of extracurricular activities. He sat for and passed the Associated Board of Royal School of Music Examination (ABRSM) in 1976. It was at this point that his interest shifted from being a science student to become music aficionado. His love for music smudged on him especially after taking lessons in music theory and practice with Mr. R. P. I. Okenrentie. Similarly, because of his growing knowledge in music, various persons consulted and contacted him to teach music classes in and around Sapele.

His Early Contact with Music and Subsequent Education

Talking about the musical impetus which Ogisi had that influenced his music career, certain signposts stand out lucidly. First in the list is the British Broadcasting Corporation (BBC), Bush House, London. According to him, I was an avid listener of BBC from early 1970s till date. In the 1970s, this station had a lot of music programmes that were both educative and informative, such as 'talking about music', the pleasure is yours' 'Community hymn Singing', 'The King of Instruments' and several more. The radio played a significant part in my musical development. I still listen to the radio till date.

To him, another major and very significant contact with music was through Mr. Timothy Eru, who was the Senior Prefect at Baptist High School, Orerokpe. It is this Eru who tutored Ogisi on names of lines and spaces and elementary rudimentary music. It was he who also introduced Ogisi to sight reading of notes on the staff. This was limited to only key C major.

Elsewhere in his study of Raymond Primrose Itseoritse Okenrentie, Aluede (2012), averred that (R. P. I. Okenrentie) could be seen as the oil bean plant whose fruit exploded and burst open for its seeds to be dispersed far and wide. There is no gainsaying that he seeded music into the first generation of musicologists in Bendel State. The first of these is Timothy Eru. Eru's interest in music led him to study at the degree level at the University of Nigeria Nsukka. It was this Eru who first introduced A. A. Ogisi to the rudiments of music in 1968. Ogisi vividly recounts that he had genuine interest in music and wanted to learn the art of reading and writing music. As a result of this quest, in 1974 he was under the musical tutelage of Okenrentie where he further learnt music theory and sang in his choir. G.E. Idolor on the other hand also studied rudiments of music from Timothy Eru.

Nevertheless, in later years, he acquired more music lessons from Mr. Victor L. D. Green who hailed from Kalabari in Rivers State. He was the then Organist at St. Luke's Anglican Church, Sapele. On a contract of ten Naira (₦10) per month, Mr. Green taught Ogisi keys and time signatures in all the major and minor scales respectively. He also took lessons on sight reading and singing. He had a thorough drill on hymns from the Ancient and Modern and this programme lasted for a period of three months.

This background was the pivot which Mr. Green built on to introduce A. A. Ogisi to the basics in organ playing starting with the names of its parts, sitting and fingering positions as well as watching him (Mr. Green) play. Ogisi could not use the organ in the church for his practice since it was forbidden for anyone to do so except the church organist. In the course of looking for where to practice on the organ, he came across a bill board in Mr. John Anirejuoritse Omatsola's compound in Sapele, an advertisement calling on students to come for organ lessons with a little fee to be paid. On seeing this, Ogisi approached him and secured his lesson schedule. Mr. Omatsola who started playing organ since 1933 happily enrolled Ogisi as one of his students to enable him enhance his skills on the organ. This contract was at no cost because the paternal grandparents of Arugha Ogisi were related to the grandparents of Mr. Omatsola. More of Ogisi's music experience also came from Mr. R. P. I. Okenrentie, a music graduate from the University of Nigeria, Nsukka who was also a family relation to Ogisi. It all started when Mr. Okenrentie came back from his National Youth Service Corps in 1975, and took up a teaching appointment at the Institute of Continuous Education, Benin City. Ogisi then approached him for music lessons on theory and practice; this arrangement attracted a fee of ten Naira (₦10.00) only per month. After some months of intensive lectures, Mr. Okenrentie enrolled him for the Associated Board of Royal School of Music (ABRSM) examinations. Ogisi was successful in this first attempt. This certificate encouraged him to go into further music studies. According to Ogisi, his early contacts with choir masters many of whom were Yoruba influenced him musically. In his Primary School days, as a choir member, he learnt his parts by rote, and could also switch parts easily – Soprano to Alto and back to Soprano. During his secondary school days at the Baptist High School, Orerokpe he was part of the college choir. These earlier contacts greatly enhanced his interest in music.

By 1978, he was admitted into the Music Department for a Diploma certificate programme in music education at the University of Nigeria, Nsukka and had diploma certificate in 1980. He continued his studies at the same institution after the Diploma and completed a Bachelor of Arts (B.A. Hons.) degree programme in Music in 1982. Ever since his graduation from the University of Nigeria, Ogisi has maintained a high level of scholarship in his quest for musical knowledge. This statement is without contradiction when one considers the fact that he went further to the University of Ibadan, Ibadan for his postgraduate degrees- M.A. African Studies (Music) in 1987 and Ph.D. Ethnomusicology in 2009.

His Music Career

As we sat in his sitting room which is adorned with an upright piano at a corner, we observed myriads of piano books of different grades. We were informed that his children were budding pianists. Ogisi's teaching experience did not start with the National Service Year at the College of Education, Ikere-Ekiti. To be frank and with every sense of exactitude he testified that:

> Before my National Youth Service Corps assignment at the College of Education, Ikere-Ekiti, I already had a background in teaching. My interest in teaching arose while I was with the Sapele Technical College. At Ikere-Ekiti the work was enormous. Some of my fellow corps members then were Sam Chukwu, and Ngozi Okereke. At the completion of the exercise, efforts were made to retain me as a lecturer there but the process was tardy and I had to leave. I left due to family pressure (my parents) wanted me back home.

On his return home, he got a lecturing job opportunity with the College of Education, Warri. At the Music Department of the College, the academic staff composition was dominated by foreigners. Mr. Kwabena Owu and Mr. Ashton Spio were Ghanaians, Mrs. Adrin Czerwin a Russian lady and Mr. Adefala. The then Chairman of Governing Council, Professor Grace Alele-Williams wanted more Nigerians to be part of the staff list. This prompted Ogisi to apply for the lecturing job and he was immediately employed in 1983. Earlier on, he did part-time music teaching at the Colleges of Education, Agbor and Warri in 1980. By implication, his full-time appointment in Warri, three years later, was much of a home coming. As a lecturer and former Head of Department, Ogisi observed that majority of the students had challenges in terms of performance, particularly on their instruments as the single major music programme of the College did not equip them adequately. With the single major programme, the students

combined music with other teaching subjects like Religion, History, English, etc. In order to combat this among others, he took some decisive steps by:
i. introducing a one-year Pre-NCE programme to enhance their musicality.
ii. reviewing the music programme to make it more relevant to the needs of the society. In doing so, he introduced the course, general musicianship into the curriculum
iii. establishing the course, music and the mass media (music media) at the college of Education. He was motivated to do this because he observed that some of the foremost musicologists worked in the broadcasting and television stations across the country. Based on this, he felt that such a course should be incorporated into the music curriculum and this effort has been embraced by many tertiary institutions in the country.
iv. starting the "Town and Gown" concert in Warri which involved going on tour with his students to showcase their talents to the society. He went on performance tours with his students to the National Television Authority, Benin, Shell Hall, Ogunu, Warri, Delta Steel Complex, Steel town Ovwian-Aladja and Nigerian National Petroleum Corporation Hall, Edjeba, Warri. He exposed the students to the world of performance and this act motivated many others to come into the Department to read music.

He wanted to expand the frontiers of this performance tour to inter-state, but his experience with the "Town and Gown" experiment discouraged him. His discouragement actually came from the fact that proceeds in terms of monies realized from these tours were not remitted to the Department by the college administration for the upgrading of its facilities.
v. further reforming the curriculum to introduce operatic studies. This led to an operatic performance of "The Touch of Magic" which was held in the College Hall in 1983/1984 session. It was coordinated by Sam Ukwa, a graduate from the University of Nigeria, Nsukka who was then on national youth service programme at the Music Department of the College of Education, Warri.
vi. he also introduced dance into the programme and engaged the services of Mrs. Patricia Ogigirigi to teach stylized and classic dance. He brought in this innovation because as an African studies scholar he believes and sees dance as an integral part of music hence its incorporation. Ogisi is not alone in this stance. While Aluede (1999) shares a similar opinion that music is dance and dance is music in African worldview, the duo, Aluede and Eregare (2006) remark that to talk of dance without music is an academic fable and practical fallacy in Nigeria. Ogisi's days in Warri are replete with landmark achievements. As a very dedicated lecturer who later became Head of Department, he did not allow administrative responsibilities to blur his vision and mission. He taught a plethora of

courses which include: piano, voice, general musicianship, choral studies, band, dance, music media among others. He also supervised teaching practice and project supervision students, etc. He introduced the teaching of popular music as a theoretical course in the College as far back as 1985. In retrospect, while he considered the restructuring of the music curriculum by introducing new courses like general musicianship, operatic studies, dance and music media as great achievements which he is eternally proud of, he maintained that working at the College of Education at that time had its concomitant challenges. Prominently visible were lack of orchestral instruments and non-remittance of monies realized from the city tour organized by the Department for the purchase of orchestral and band instruments to enhance music studies by the College administration.

From the insightful narrative about his days in Warri, the story reeks of poor administration steeped on economic gains forgetting that the business of educating the citizenry is social service and not an economic construct. Although full of energy and drive to do more, Warri to Ogisi was obviously not the right place to be. In the month of November 1988, he joined the board of studies of the Department of Music, Bendel State University, Abraka Campus, now Delta State University (DELSU), Abraka. At the Delta State University, he taught both at the undergraduate and postgraduate levels the following courses: Music Media, Popular Music Studies, Orchestration, General Musicianship, Harmony, Band Studies, Operatic Studies, Dance, Acoustics, Advanced Music Technology, and Performance Practice. Worthy of note is his introduction of music into the university's Students Industrial Work Experience Scheme (SIWES), a move which Professor G. E. Idolor also supported as senior colleagues of the music Department. He has successfully supervised seventeen master's dissertations and eleven doctoral theses. In Delta State University, his teaching career in music reached an apogee as he served at different capacities as a lecturer, Coordinator of pre-degree programme, Head of Department and Coordinator, Postgraduate Programme to mention a few. Today, a good number of Dr. Ogisi's products are in the Nigerian Army, Nigerian Navy and the Air-force. When asked if he would like to list some of his outstanding products, he gave a litany of names and their current fields. The list is humongous but we have however, harvested a few in no particular order and they are captured in the table below with their affiliations.

S/N	NAME	ESTABLISHMENT
1	Professor Charles Aluede	Ambrose Alli University Ekpoma Edo State
2	Dr. Bruno Ekewenu	Lecturer, Delta State University Abraka
3	Dr. John Agbolagba	Lecturer, College of Education Ekiadolor Benin City, Edo State
4	Dr. Peter Odogbor	Lecturer, University of Benin
5	Dr. Yemi Akperi	A Pastor with the Nigerian Baptist Convention
6	Dr. Philomena Okpeki	Lecturer, Delta State University, Abraka
7	Dr. Margaret A. Efurhievwe	Lecturer, Delta State University, Abraka
8	Lt. Col. P.D. Oguegbulu	Nigerian Army School of Music, Ojo Cantonment, Ojo
9	Onokan Lynda	Delta Broadcasting Service, Warri
10	Dr. 'Mudiakevwe Igbi	University of Africa, Toru Orua, Bayelsa State
11	Okonji Faith	Nigerian Air force
12	Enoh Unueroh	Nigerian Navy
13	Captain Obibine Frank	Nigerian Army
14	Captain Obi Jude	Nigerian Army
15	Chief Jowa Joseph	Staff Delta State University (DELSU) Secondary School
16	Ofomeyor Blessing	Delta Broadcasting Service (DBS) Asaba
17	Dr. J. E. Okafor	Lecturer, College of Education Agbor
18	Mrs. Peace T. Abugu	Lecturer, College of Education Agbor
19	Henry Dafe Ivwurie	Head, Brand and Corporate Communications, Providus Bank
20	Tebitie, Uruemuesiri	Director, TsioTsio Band Ughelli
21	Zitu Benafa	Green Chamber Chorale, Warri
22	Major Tega Ighorhiohwunu	Nigerian Defence Academy, Kaduna
23	Major Aaron Edojah	Nigerian Army
24	Mrs. Mary Osuegbu	Post-Primary Education Board, Delta State.
25	Dr. Bolaji David	University of Port Harcourt
26	Dase, Emmanuel	Michael and Cecilia Ibru University, Agbarha - Otor
27	Dase, Clement	St. Brigid's Girls' Grammar Sch., Asaba

Beyond Teaching Music

Under this heading, we will examine the musical character of Dr. Ogisi through lens of the various musical instruments he plays, his musical compositions and his other contributions to religious and social activities outside the lecture hall.

To talk of Ogisi as a versatile instrumentalist is not an understatement. Apart from teaching which he does with much passion, he is a seasoned conductor, music director, tenor singer and a player of quite a number of Western orchestral instruments such as the piano, organ, clarinet, violin, trumpet, flute and guitar. It is very consequential to state here that his coming to play many musical instruments had to do with his untiring search for knowledge. It is this drive which led him into teaching himself to play a number of instruments, some of them without an instructor. Contingent of this musical pedigree, Ogisi at every given time was able to play different musical instruments singularly or in a group. This attribute has always made him outstanding in band, choral and orchestral performances and studies. He also has outstanding records of contributions in the social and religious circles. For example, during his days in the University of Nigeria, Nsukka, he served as the President of Itsekiri Students' Association between 1979– 1981. In a similar vein, while at the College of Education, Warri, and till date in Delta State University, Abraka he has always associated and still associates with the Itsekiri Association-A socio-political forum within and outside the university.

In the religious realm, Dr. Ogisi has been very committed and dedicated to the service of the Almighty. As a Baptist from birth, he remains an active member of the faith till date. He has also extended his "hands of fellowship" in impacting his spiritual knowledge to other denominations. It is an obvious fact which is well captured on record that Dr. Ogisi in company of some other members founded the Full Gospel Businessmen's Fellowship International (FGBMF) in Abraka in 1993. As part of his efforts towards the growth of the church, Dr. Ogisi occasionally fellowships with the Living Faith Church, Winners' Chapel in Abraka where he sometimes gives inspirational sermons to members when the need arises. However in recent times, precisely since 2001 till date, he participates and fellowships with the Redeemed Christian Church of God (RCCG), Abraka where his wife, Dicta Ogisi, a Professor of Agricultural Economics, Delta State University Abraka, serves as a branch Pastor following her ordination by the church's General Overseer, Pastor Enoch Adeboye.

Apart from being a highly cerebral personage and a scholar of high degree, Ogisi has composed and published works for different instrumental media and they are:

SN	Title	Medium	Scale/Category	Difficulty
1.	Memories of childhood	Piano	Small	
2.	A song of hope	Solo soprano, SATB chorus, Flute and Piano	Large	Challenging
3.	Sunset	Concert band	Medium	Simple
4.	Concertina for Clarinet	String orchestra	Medium	Moderate
5.	A new dispensation	Contralto and tenor soli, narrator, SATB chorus, and orchestra.	Large	Challenging
6.	Aghans'ode	SATB chorus	Medium	Moderate
7.	Voices in twain	SATB	Small	Simple
8.	OgheneOse	SATB	Small Small	Simple
9.	Lord keep us safe this night	SATB	Small	Simple
10.	Separated lovers	High male voices	Small	Moderate
11.	Seven etudes for violin	Violin	Small	Challenging
12.	Dance of the seven spirits (Ballet)	Orchestra	Medium	Challenging

Arrangements

SN	Title	Medium	Scale/Category	Difficulty
1.	Sarabande	Orchestra	Medium	Simple
2.	Frohlicherlandman	Orchestra	Medium	Simple
3.	Descant to six hymns	Boy sopranos	Small	Simple
4.	Iyo nene	High voice and piano	Small	Simple
5.	Erisi	High voice and piano	Small	Simple
6.	Tere o tere o	High voice	Small	Simple
7.	Se SeSe	SSATB	Medium	Moderate
8.	Habanera	Orchestra	Medium	Challenging

Ogisi's Reflections on the Abraka Music School (AMS) and Music Scholarship in Nigeria

Having taught music since 1988 at the then Bendel State University, Abraka Campus which later became the Delta State University, Abraka, Ogisi has quite a number of concerns over the challenges bedeviling music studies in Nigeria. At his fingertips, he names some of them.

The need for a functionally well equipped departmental building at the Delta State University, Abraka, in his view, is paramount. The block in Site I was not built according to specification. The building lacks studios (Dance, Production, Media, and Band etc.) and a functional library. In summary, the Department is in dire need of a standard departmental building. Beyond a well furnished building, the Department also needs human resources to man the equipment. This therefore makes it imperative for the recruitment of music technologists who should be in charge of repairs and maintenance of the musical instruments. The Department needs a complete set of orchestral instruments that students can rely on for both individual and group performances. Although much success has been achieved previously in relying on students to buy their personal instruments, the limitation of such a tendency is that there will always be an absence of expensive instruments which should have enhanced the tonal colour and overall musical production of the Department's ensembles-some of such instruments are the Double Bass, Grand Piano, Cello, Timpani, among others. Students can hardly afford to purchase these instruments. Ogisi further posits that the Department of Music also needs resident artistes most especially in the areas of teaching traditional dances and construction of African Traditional Musical Instruments. This will inspire students into these stress areas. He extends his thoughts to an observation that the method of selection of students into the music programme is deficient. That is, the process of testing is based on cognition only; emphasis is not given on the testing of psychomotor skills. He suggests that after testing students in cognition by the university examination body, the Department should be allowed to conduct auditioning examinations to test psychomotor and aural skills among others. If this is done, the right calibre of students will always be admitted into the music programme-this will in no small measure enhance the standard of musicality of the products.

As part of his reflection on music scholarship in Nigeria, he observes that the curriculum NUC has imposed on the universities, does not reflect the societal needs. He emphasizes the need for the music institutions to reflect on what they teach music students, that there should be a balance between practical and theory. This will make the students to be more functional and relevant in the society after graduation. Corroborating this opinion, he cites an example by observing that in the Nigerian popular music industry, there is the absence of academic musicians. Instead, many of the academic musicians end up in the classroom while those making waves in the music industry were not even trained in the universities[i]. This therefore calls for the need for academic musicians to make their impacts felt in the Nigerian music industry. Dr. Ogisi suggests that music companies should be set up to publish compositions, various performances, and academic musicians should also go into performances and waxing of their records. Sharing his thoughts further, he also suggests that we should train our products to be technologically savvy in the departments of music in the country; so that students', individuals' or group performances should be recorded and put in Compact Disc and sold to the general public.

Quite insightful is his stand on the "publish or perish syndrome" which has characterized lectureship in Nigerian universities and which has blurred into music studies- a course which ought to be theory and practice based. He observes that this tendency has made most lecturers not to be committed to their teaching instead; they place their emphasis on publications. Arising from this he submits that the method of assessment of lecturers should be more embracing and that there should be a percentage given for performance, community impact by the lecturer, teaching effectiveness and publications. If this method of assessment is employed, lecturers will not only concentrate on self but also on the effective teaching of their students will be their utmost concern, thereby enhancing the quality of our music products[ii]. While urging the various university authorities to improve on power supply by exploring alternative means such as solar power to generate power to drive the system and make lecturers to work in a convenient environment, he suggests that university management should make it a priority to connect every lecturer to the internet at the expense of the system and the library should be well equipped with recent books/journals and a very functional E-library for students.

Dr. Ogisi advocates that music education should be formerly rooted in the primary through secondary school curriculum. It should be made compulsory at these levels of education. This done, we will be able to have a crop of very good materials for the tertiary music programmes. He strongly believes that African music should be the basis of our music education not what we are operating now where emphasis is placed on Western music. Our compositions and academic contents of what we teach should reflect the needs of the society. In addition to this, the stress areas should be connected to the needs of the society.

In all of these, A. A. Ogisi finds time to fulfil his family obligations. He is a very committed husband to his wife, Professor Ovuevuraye Dicta Akatugba-Ogisi with whom he has two children, Oyomire (female) and Oyoyila (male).

Conclusion

In this paper, we examined the family and educational background of Dr. Arugha Aboyowa Ogisi. We stretched the discussion to when he had his early contact with music and his subsequent musical career. In the course of this investigation, we discovered that aside BBC, Dr. Ogisi owes his musicality to a quadruplet of muses and they are- Timothy Eru, Raymond Okenrentie, Papa Green and Anirejuoritse Omatsola. Having spent many decades teaching music in tertiary institutions, he draws inferences from his experiences in postulating that the Abraka Music School (AMS) should be well equipped with musical instruments, studio and laboratory equipment. And speaking critically about music scholarship in Nigeria, he maintained that because of the present style of promotion mechanisms of lecturers in Nigerian universities, most lecturers no longer have the commitment to teaching instead; much emphasis is placed on publications. To him, this has adversely affected the quality of our music products. He therefore suggests that a rethink be done by the various university authorities in addressing these grey areas. Added to these is the issue of improving alternative means of electric power supply such as solar power installation in music departments so that the man hours and information constantly lost as a result of power outage will be resolved. No doubt, as Dr. Ogisi retires from University teaching, he leaves his successors with important notes on the enhancement of music scholarship in Nigeria.

References

Aluede, C. O. (1999). 'African Music and Dance: Any Difference?' *Nigerian Journal of Advanced Research in Education* Vol. 3 (1) 87 –96.

Aluede, C.O. & Eregare, E.A. (2006). 'Dance without Music: An Academic Fable and Practical Fallacy in Nigeria' *The Anthropologist* 8 (2) 93-97.

Aluede, C. O. (2012). 'R. P. I. Okenrentie and his Contribution to Art Music in Bendel State, Nigeria'. *Tribal Tribune Journal India.* Volume 5 (2) 1-9.

Aluede, C.O. (2014). 'M.A. Omibiyi-obidike: A Formidable Finger in the Making of Nigerian Musicologists'. In C. Aluede, K. Samuel & S.O. Adedeji (Eds.) *African Musicology: Past, Present and Future.* Ile-Ife: Association of Nigerian Musicologists. 55-66.

Monkwunyei, J. N. (2014). 'A Tribute to Omibiyi – Obidike at Seventy'. In C. Aluede, K. Samuel & S.O. Adedeji (Eds.) *African Musicology: Past, Present and Future.* Ile-Ife: Association of Nigerian Musicologists. 21-26

Idamoyibo, A. A. (2014) 'Mosunmola Ayinke Omibiyi-Obidike: A Woman of Sterling Relevance in Contemporary Music Studies in Nigeria'. In C. Aluede, K. Samuel & S.O. Adedeji (Eds.) *African Musicology: Past, Present and Future.* Ile-Ife: Association of Nigerian Musicologists.75-84.

Dada, O. A. & Dada, B. O. (2014). 'Mosunmola Omibiyi-Obidike: Philosophies and Ideologies of African Music Education'. In C. Aluede, K. Samuel & S.O.

Adedeji (Eds.) *African Musicology: Past, Present and Future.* Ile-Ife: Association of Nigerian Musicologists. 151-158.

Udoh, I. E. (2017). 'Dan Agu: The Man and His Music'. In Adedeji, S.O., Onyeji, C. &Onoura-Oguno, N. (Eds.) *Musical Horizons in Africa: Essays and Perspectives* Ife: Association of Nigerian Musicologists. 63-69.

Ibekwe, E. U. (2017). 'The Man, Professor Dan Christian Chikpezie Agu: A Reflection. In Adedeji, S.O., Onyeji, C. & Onoura-Oguno, N. (Eds.) *Musical Horizons in Africa: Essays and Perspectives* Ife: Association of Nigerian Musicologists. 32-38.

Ajewole, J. (2017). 'An Appraisal of Dan Agu's Music Scholarship and Professionalism'. in Adedeji, S.O., Onyeji, C. & Onoura-Oguno, N. (Eds.) *Musical Horizons in Africa: Essays and Perspectives* Ife: Association of Nigerian Musicologists. 20-23.

Alvan-Ikoku, O. N. (2017). 'How Musical is Dan?' In Adedeji, S.O., Onyeji, C. &Onoura-Oguno, N. (Eds.) *Musical Horizons in Africa: Essays and Perspectives.* Ile-Ife: Association of Nigerian Musicologists. 3-11.

---

[i] In many fields of human endeavour in Nigeria, practice in the society and the classroom have different structures. It happens in almost all professions except a few that are highly regulated like medicine. and teaching. Many people who make waves in automobile industry are not the engineers trained in the universities and this also applies to those making wave in the movie, restaurant, hotel/hospitality, fashion and textile industries.

[ii] As if his voice has been heard, in Nigerian Colleges of Education and universities currently, the basis for promotion of academic staff in music is publication and creative works which include compositions and performances. This is a welcome development as many use their creative works as resources for teaching the students.

2

An Exploration into the Genius of the Quintessential Nigerian Musicologist, ARUGHA OGISI

Oghenemudiakevwe Igbi, Ph.D[*]

Introduction

In the last five decades, there has been a surge in the number of Nigerians who received formal training in music. A number of these individuals went on to make remarkable contributions to the profession. There is no gainsaying that some of them have become role models to many others in the field of music as a result of certain striking qualities that they possess. These well-meaning personalities have left indelible footprints in their chosen profession and contributed significantly to the advancement of music practice and formal education through their research outputs and manpower development. Dr. Arugha Ogisi is one of such scholars who despite some of life's challenges he has had to grapple with, takes impartation of knowledge and research sacrosanct – an act that has culminated in the production of countless manpower in the music profession. This chapter seeks to capture some of the sterling qualities and musical contributions of this rare breed of a scholar to music scholarship and creativity. Utilizing data mainly sourced from interviews with Ogisi, his students, colleagues, and personal experiences that were garnered during the period of being a student at Delta State University (DELSU), Abraka, the paper avails readers the opportunity of getting firsthand information on this genius, and in the process document such data for posterity. Findings from the study reveal that Arugha Ogisi is a scholar of the finest grade, a writer who insists on finesse in scripting and reporting research findings, a teacher who expertly uses appropriate methods to impart knowledge, a fatherly figure and role model whose legacies in the Abraka Music School (A.M.S) will remain indelible. The paper recommends that his mentees should make further efforts to upload his scholarly publications and creative works online in order to guarantee wider readership and effortless accessibility by researchers.

---

[*] University of Africa, Toru – Orua

In recent times, it has become a vogue to publish festschrifts in honour of deserving individuals who have devoted significant parts of their sojourn on earth to the advancement of research and scholarship. In the field of music in Nigeria, a number of distinguished personalities have been honoured in this regard. They include Professors Fela Sowande, Meki Nzewi, Mosunmola Omibiyi-Obidike, Emurobome Idolor, Dan Agu, Femi Adedeji, Anthony Mereni, and now Dr. Arugha Ogisi. Indeed, none of the aforementioned names are undeserving of such honours. Aside celebrating a scholar's intellectual contributions through festschrift publications, festschrifts afford those who had not the opportunity of being so close to the honouree the chance of reading hidden facts about him/her. It brings to bear other knowledge about the individual that will directly or indirectly serve as motivation to budding scholars within and outside the profession.

There is barely anyone who has come in contact with Dr. Arugha Ogisi that will not testify positively of his uncommon intellectual prowess and creative ingenuity. That Ogisi is very intelligent is no wonder to this author; the puzzle lies in how vast he is in virtually all aspects of music, thus making it tough to believe he actually studied African Studies at the postgraduate level, with specialization in popular musicology. His contributions to the field of music as an academic discipline will remain ineffaceable for generations to come. These enduring legacies include quality scholarly publications, compositions, performances and human capital development. The paper which is largely descriptive and narrative, aims to make vivid some of these contributions, with a view to educating readers about the unforgettable trails left by this unsung hero, having bowed out of active service, at least for the time being. With Arugha Ogisi's teaching, creative and research experience spanning about forty years, the paper will be of enormous value to up-and-coming music scholars, as some of his unique attributes will be unearthed, with a view to getting newer insights into some aspects of his personality, teaching methods, depth of research in music and creativity. Data for the study were gleaned from interviews with the honouree/music students, perusal of Ogisi's publications/compositions and personal experiences. While Arugha Ogisi and his mentees relish the moment, other music scholars who have carved a niche for themselves should also be celebrated so as to enable others benefit from testimonies and research data emanating from the scholarly endeavors of such individuals.

Educational Background and Work Experience of Arugha Ogisi

Dr. Arugha Ogisi hails from Ugbuwangue – Warri, in Warri South Local Government Area of Delta State. He was born on 3rd January, 1955 in the city of Sapele, Delta State, Nigeria. He attended Council Primary School, Sapele, from 1961 to 1966 and Baptist High School, Orerokpe, between 1966 and 1971. Having served as Music Director and organist to some Baptist

Churches in Sapele and Warri, he developed interest to acquire formal education in Music by proceeding to the University of Nigeria, Nsukka (UNN). After completing his diploma course in Music Education at UNN, he enrolled for his first degree, and graduated in 1982 with a Bachelor's Degree in Music (Second Class Honours, Upper Division) majoring in theory and composition. Upon the completion of his National Youth Service in the Department of Music, College of Education, Ikere-Ekiti in 1983, he took up permanent appointment in the Department of Music, College of Education, Warri. Before then, he had worked in the same Department at College of Education, Agbor, as part time lecturer in 1980. But with the establishment of Bendel State University (BENSU), Abraka Campus, Ogisi relinquished the job at College of Education, Warri, shortly after the completion of his Master of Arts (M.A) Degree in Ethnomusicology at the University of Ibadan, in 1987, to accept an offer of appointment as Lecturer II at BENSU, Abraka Campus, in 1988. Prior to his appointment in Abraka, he had enrolled for a Doctor of Philosophy Degree programme at the University of Ibadan in 1987. The Abraka Campus of BENSU was later upgraded to a full University with the creation of Delta State in 1992; Ogisi remained there, but had risen to the position of Lecturer I, and started getting appointments to serve the University in different capacities, including the headship of the Department of Music. It is noteworthy that since the inception of DELSU, Dr. Arugha Ogisi has served a record seven times as head of department, member to several committees and boards, and as the postgraduate programme coordinator in the Department of Music. He has been external examiner a number of times, and is a member of several learned societies such as The Association of Nigerian Musicologists (ANIM), Conference of Music Educators in Nigeria (COMEN), International Council for Traditional Music (ICTM), International Society for Music Education (ISME), and others. He has also served as editor to some reputable journals and assessed papers for a number of local and international journals, including *Journal of the Association of Nigerian Musicologists, Nigerian Music Review, Dance Journal of Nigeria, Studies on Ethnomedicine (EM)*, African Musicology Online, and many others. Dr. Ogisi has also assessed academic staff of various colleges of education for promotion to the ranks of principal and Chief Lecturers. He has attended over thirty academic conferences and symposia and presented high quality articles including lead papers. He plays various musical instruments like the pianoforte, flute, violin, clarinet, trumpet, and trombone. He is a beautiful tenor singer, a fine conductor and music director. Ogisi is contemporaneous with individuals like Professors Bode Omojola, Emurobome Idolor, Young-Sook Onyiuke, Onyee Nwankpa, Drs. Sam Chukwu, Patience Oguoma, Emmanuel Aniwene, Sam Amusan, Chuma Chukwuka, Ijeoma Fuchianga, Sir Emeka Nwokedi, Mr. Ayo Bankole (Jnr) and several others. The abovementioned were either his classmates, immediate seniors or juniors while in the university.

He was mainly taught by British, Americans, and some of the best Nigerian music scholars. The foreigners who taught him include Elsa Tofolon (Italian), L. J. New (British), J. Cutliff (African-American), J. Furze (British), Mrs. Rocheska (Polish), D. Gomper (American), Mrs. Brassine (Belgian), and Tim Race (British). The Nigerian contingents that taught him include Meki Nzewi, Azubuike Ifionu, Wilberforce Echezona, Okechukwu Ndubuisi, Kanu Achinuvu, Samuel Akpabot and Mosunmola Omibiyi-Obidike. Others also taught him that were in cognate disciplines. They are Professors Tekena Tamuno, Adepegba Shyllon and others. The experiences he garnered from these fine scholars of international repute have been central to shaping his thoughts and increasing his penchant for perfection in music research and performance. He is married to Professor (Mrs.) Dicta Ogisi, and blessed with two children.

Arugha Ogisi in the Area of Popular Musicology

Popular music remains the most patronized of the musical styles performed in the Nigeria. The music has blossomed not only partly because of its satirical suitability, but its ability to convey emotive ideas. According to Okafor, (2005:327), 'it is understood and accepted by a lot of people not as a final solution to their problems but as a topical reflection of their sentiments and current world view'. But despite its very high patronage, formal studies in popular music in Nigeria is yet to receive the sort of attention other areas of musicology have received. This is due to some reasons that are not within the purview of this paper.

Ogisi's admission into the doctorate degree programme of the University of Ibadan in 1987 meant he is one of the earliest to begin serious researches in the area of popular musicology in Nigeria, which eventually culminated in the award of a Ph.D in the area. Aside the terminal degree in popular musicology and his highly educative thesis, he has impressively published thirty journal articles and book chapters bothering on different aspects of popular music in Nigeria (as at the time of this study). As a result, his works have become regular reference materials for those researching on popular music in Nigeria. With thirty articles in the field of popular music alone, he is without doubt among the most authoritative names and prolific Nigerian writers in the area. Ogisi's studies in this area cover a wide spectrum, with profound work in popular music history, practice, composition, periodization, origin, and the factors that impacted the development of the style in Nigeria. He relies on extensive data sourced from the field through interviews of practitioners, observation of musical performances, visits to the national archives and audio-visual recordings. This has resulted in well researched articles that center on different aspects of popular music in

Nigeria. His book, *Praise the Lord,* is one of the marks of his commitment to using his musical training to address specific needs of musicians. In the book, Dr. Arugha Ogisi took painstaking efforts to transcribe and notate two hundred and forty-eight (248) Nigerian spirituals frequently sung in Nigerian Churches and often referred to as 'praise and worship songs'. He did not end there – he went further to provide appropriate chordal progressions for the keyboard and sourced for suitable Bible scriptures that are in consonance with the text of the spirituals. This makes the book very suitable for use by choirmasters and music enthusiasts that are interested in gospel music.

The book which consists of praise and worship songs, fall under the category of 'religious pop music' (Agu, 2017:39). Remarking on religious pop music in Nigeria, Agu (2017:39) gives a very illuminative perspective on the genre.

> ...religious pop music has very strong rhythmic and melodic attractions. The songs are also characterized by antiphony, short melodic motifs (which makes it easy for Christians to quickly learn and memorize). They are usually songs of praise, adoration and supplication. The lyrics are sourced from Biblical stories and texts, verses and at times, incorporating human problems which are brought before God for spiritual solutions. The language is popular and understandable. The songs are performed in all Nigerian ethnic languages, as well as in the English language and Pidgin English. Consequently, their messages are clearly received and imbibed.

Commenting on the book by Arugha Ogisi, Agu (2017:vi) goes further to state that 'the songs in this collection are classified under 'The Improvised Vocal Music Types'. They are so classified because they are usually created and learnt by rote, hence they are not notated in music scores'.

It is for the high patronage of the religious pop songs and their unavailability in staff notation that stirred Arugha Ogisi to publish the book. The first copies that were printed got exhausted in a very short time owing to the huge demand by music graduates, Church musicians and music enthusiasts. Aside the creative aspect of popular music and as noted earlier, Ogisi is a prolific researcher and writer in the area. His works are always captivating even from the titles (see the following research titles that were randomly selected from some of his publications):

1. The Significance of the Niger Coast Constabulary Band of Calabar in Nigerian Highlife Music. Popular Music Studies in Nigeria: Accounting for the Neglect.
2. Socio-economic factors in the Evolution of Popular Music in South Western Nigeria.
3. The Bustling Fifties and Popular Music in Nigeria.
4. The Origin and Development of Nigerian Highlife Music.

5. Afro-Fusion Genres in Nigerian Popular Music.
6. The State of Popular music Studies in Nigeria.
7. Sourcing Data in Popular Music Research in Nigeria.
8. The Impact of Soul Music in Nigeria and several others.
9. The Impact of Hotels/Night Clubs in the Development of Popular Music in Nigeria
10. Composition, Rehearsals, Engagements and Performance Practices among Nigerian Popular Musicians

His works are not only rich in content, but cover a gamut of issues with their scope sometimes dating to colonial eras and the eighteenth century. Commenting on one of Arugha Ogisi's publications, Vidal (2012:218) unequivocally notes that 'the significance of the Niger Coast Constabulary Band of Calabar in Nigeria [a published article by Arugha Ogisi], is a great asset for anyone engaged in the history of one of Nigeria's popular music genres, the highlife'. In his study of popular music, Ogisi relishes identifying gaps in previous researches by other authors and makes painstaking efforts to fill those detected cavities that other studies did not address. He depends on extensive fieldwork to garner data rather than hinge his arguments on mere assumptions. He has carried out studies on *Juju*, *Soul music*, *Nigerian Highlife*, Popular dance, Palm wine music, music recording, and Gospel music. His publications on these topics can be found in reputable journals spread across different parts of Nigeria and abroad. He has also presented many of these scholarly works on popular music in academic conferences in different parts of Nigeria.

Arugha Ogisi's Style of Scholarly Writing

Every scholar has a style of writing that is unique to them. Reporting research data in the form of a paper or dissertation can be very tricky. This is because, 'the inability to accurately communicate research findings in ways that are comprehensible can jeopardize an entire research endeavour' Igbi (2017:60). In the work quoted above, the author identifies three styles of writing among Nigerian music scholars, wherein Dr. Arugha Ogisi is grouped in the second category. The group includes 'those who construct sentences in ways one would not think is possible. They write stylishly, treat words fashionably, and make the titles of their works very attractive. There is never a boring moment reading through their publications' (Igbi, 2017:61). The ability to sustain the interest of the reader throughout a paper involves a certain level of skill in the use of English or any other language utilized for such research. It is even more complex when writing a historical research or describing a phenomenon. Ogisi can be described as a 'master' in the art of reporting findings of a research. His grammatical constructions, captivating titles, and manner of presentation are usually top class. He treats words stylishly, uses tenses modishly, crafts enchanting titles for his papers and connects his ideas with unusual delight. Like fine wine, Ogisi's papers seem to get better each time one reads through; there is never the feeling of boredom. He presents his findings with exact dates of when events occurred and traces the factors that must have been responsible for such happenings. Another interesting aspect of Dr. Ogisi's style of scholarly writing is his refrainment from indiscriminate and unwarranted quotation of others' works. As has become the vogue in recent times, most writers seem to flood their articles with unnecessary quotations that have no relevance to their work, other than increasing the words in the paper. This academic defect can never be found in the works of Ogisi. He understands that the aim of literature is to know the extent of work done in an area, identify gaps in other studies, buttress facts, interrogate others' positions on related issues, give credence to those who may have done similar researches before, and to sharpen the focus of a study. After identifying gaps that other studies may not have filled, he (Ogisi) elects appropriate research methods that will enable him garner as much data as possible, and devotes majority of the paper to reporting findings gleaned from the field. Ogisi believes that for a research work to be good, the findings should constitute between 60-70% of the entire work. He believes the 'findings' is the section where the scholar should display his in-depth knowledge of the work, a part wherein the investigator unravels all his discoveries from the investigation, and 'goes to town'[1] by exhibiting all the stuff that may have been concealed prior to the research. But in carrying out this task, many writers are unable to keep the discourse lively. This is where Dr. Ogisi thrives. He reports data in such a way that the reader, does not lose interest perusing the work.

In buttressing some of the observations made in this section of the paper about Ogisi, below are twelve captivating titles of articles and a few delightful quotes randomly selected from some of his publications that are evident of his uncommon cerebral knack. The titles and quotes are so fascinating that it is almost impossible for a reader to flip when reading them.

S/N	Title of Paper
1	The Bustling Fifties and Popular Music in Nigeria
2	Palm wine Music in Nigeria
3	Conceptualizing and Facilitating African Music through Akin Euba's Lens
4	Nigerian Composers and the Search for National Identity
5	Prolegomena to Nigerian Music Historiography
6	Social factors and Music Change in 20th Century Nigeria
7	Rethinking the Visual Dimension of Music
8	Three Evidence Explicating the Visual Dimension of Music
9	Optimizing Postgraduate Music Studies in Nigeria
10	Phonic and Tonal Identities in Nigerian Literary Art Music
11	The Transformation of Popular Music from Adult to Youth Based

Art in Nigeria
12 Landmarks in the Sixty Year History of the Recording Industry and Popular Music in Nigeria

Quote

Although the recording industry is the lifeline of popular music in Nigeria, its dominant role only came to the fore during the decade of oil boom in the 1970s. Then the industry blossomed and brought to the limelight several genres and musicians. But as the phenomenon was tied to the state of the economy, the economic decline adversely affected and saw the structures that were in place during the boom years collapse. However, the challenge that resulted there from stimulated the ingenuity of Nigerians who made efforts to keep the sickening industry parsimoniously alive.

Quote

The exploitation of rhythm which resulted in several popular dances took the entire country by storm and created dance vogues. The phenomenon of dance vogue was a new experience in Nigeria, a multi-ethnic country where music and dance are ethnic based...

From inception, juju was a contemplative music that did not lend itself to dancing. However, in the 1950s, it began to transform into dance music, thus setting the stage for a dance vogue...

There is a yawning gap in the technical competence of Nigerians in the music video business that some jobs are outsourced to South Africa, not just for the scenic preferences but for the availability of more advanced recording equipment and expertise that exist there.

Quote

By the late 1920s, there was a drastic fall in the price of palm oil produce in the world market and Calabar whose prosperity, fame and musical vibrancy due to the export trade began to experience difficult times. The economic downturn reached a recession with accompanying unemployment and an exodus from Calabar to other towns with better employment prospects. Economy factor apart, the silting of the waterways that required expensive periodic dredging to make it navigate all year round bedeviled the Calabar harbour.

Quote

Several music types and genres exist simultaneously in society and some become dominant, resulting in vogues which often last a few months or even shorter and thereafter recede to the background. It is noteworthy that most genres remain undercurrents with slim possibility of taking the centre stage in becoming a vogue. For example, when highlife music was in vogue (1949-1966) in Nigeria, it completely dominated the Nigerian music scene and overshadowed other genres that they appeared to be undercurrents literarily waiting in the wings to break-forth. However, the dislocation of the social fabric upon which highlife depended led to its decline thus providing opportunity for other genres that hitherto had been sidelined to come into the limelight.

Ogisi in the Realm of Art Music Composition and Performance Praxis

Creative abilities in music (both composition and performance) come in different ways. It is 'a natural endowment which varies from one individual to another' (Nwamara, 2015: 176). Arugha Ogisi is a composer, arranger and performer with a very high sense of creativity and musicianship. He relies mainly on features sourced from African traditional music to compose most of his works, with a few elements drawn from European musical resources. Commenting on some Nigerian composers and their compositional techniques, Omojola (1995:78) notes that Arugha Ogisi is among those who have 'synthesized elements of European and African elements in their works'. Ogisi's compositions like *Memories of Childhood* and *Dance of the Seven Spirits* are testimonies of his profound understanding of African musical craftsmanship despite his exposure to Western music. His compositions include piano pieces, large orchestral works, and vocal works for S.A.T.B. He has also written for solo instruments and an opera titled *Partum Opera* published in 2018. He is a talented arranger of folk tunes for different mediums.

Ogisi is also a skilled pianist with very good sight reading ability. He served as choirmaster and organist in some Baptist Churches during his early musical years. As a conductor and organist, Dr. Ogisi has featured in over fifty major performances in different parts of Nigeria, especially in Nsukka, Benin, Sapele and Warri. As a performer, he is vast in the performance of art and popular music, and a brilliant interpreter of music scores. Ogisi can play various musical instruments like the piano, flute, clarinet, and violin.

Some of Arugha Ogisi's Contributions and Legacies in the Abraka Music School

Dr. Arugha Ogisi meritoriously served in the Department of Music, Delta State University (DELSU), Abraka, for over three decades. During this time, he was actively involved in the drawing of programmes and formulation of policies that were central to the feats achieved by the department since its inception. For example, in 2005, he and Professor Emurobome Idolor played vital roles in the development of a postgraduate programme in the

Department of Music. They also ensured that areas of specialization that were hitherto considered 'unscholarly' and unsuitable for serious academic studies by some Nigerian music scholars were introduced to the DELSU postgraduate programme in music. Through their efforts, DELSU, Abraka's Department of Music pioneered many areas of specialization at the postgraduate level including music media, music conducting and directing, music performance (with options in voice, dance and several Western orchestral instruments), sacred musicology, music technology, etc. As Head of the Department of Music for seven different tenures, he provided the needed leadership that led to the production of quality manpower for the music profession at the undergraduate and postgraduate levels. He is also reputed to be a multi-instrumentalist, beautiful singer, vocal coach and versatile scholar who could teach and supervise virtually all the areas of specialization in the department. Furthermore, as Head of Department, he always ensured that accreditation exercises were successful. He also created an atmosphere of harmony for staff.

Ogisi is an exemplary scholar and teacher who is always ready to go any length in addressing the academic challenges of his students and colleagues. He does not shy from constructively criticizing articles of colleagues or students who come to him for guidance before they are sent to journal editors for reviews. His desire to replicate himself in his students paid off with the turnout of not less than twenty-eight postgraduate students at DELSU, Abraka, as supervisor. There is no doubt that Dr. Ogisi's landmark achievements in the Abraka Music School will remain indelible for many years to come.

Personal Experience of Ogisi's Method of Teaching/Thesis Supervision, Academic Mentorship, Sense of Humour and Fatherly Attributes

There is no naysaying that not everybody in the academia has the ability to effectively impart knowledge on others. Even with profound knowledge of the subject matter, some teachers and thesis supervisors lack the appropriate teaching methods, techniques and procedures to explain phenomena to students or guide them in conducting researches. But Ogisi as an experienced teacher and supervisor, understands the abilities, needs, strengths and weaknesses of his students. This helps him elect appropriate approaches and tactics to employ in teaching a topic, passing instruction or supervising a students' researches. This author recalls how Dr, Ogisi expertly taught him how to write an introduction to a scholarly work. He (the author) had submitted the 'Background to the Study' part of his PhD thesis to Arugha Ogisi to peruse about five times without any improvement from the student despite the corrections made. In fact, what was submitted on each of the five occasions seemed worse than the previous. The work was replete with comments in red. Ogisi who must have been very disappointed, came up with an ingenious idea that not only solved the problem at the time, but served as a guide to this author in writing introductions to his papers. Ogisi said: 'the background to the study of any scholarly work is like a "story before the story". He went further to say: 'you initiate a story or write in a manner that leads your reader to what you are about to do… you do not rush to jump into the work without creating a background discussion that will lead to the crux of the discourse. Ogisi did not stop there, he went on to liken the background/introduction of a scholarly work to how relationships are built between individuals of the opposite sex. He said: 'it is like wooing a girl; you do not just walk up to a lady you have not met before and say 'I want to marry you'. No! 'You first of all create an enabling environment by exchanging pleasantries, asking a few friendly questions, showing some care, knowing some important aspects of the person, like family background, education, likes/dislikes, and so on. It is after this has been done before the wooer hits the nail on the head'. Ogisi went on: 'that is how to write the background… you are expected to set the tone for the discourse and gradually lead your reader to the research problem'. This clever method and example used by Dr. Ogisi was one of the turning points in this author's postgraduate studies.

It is difficult to be an unserious person and still have all the musical abilities and scholarly endowments of Arugha Ogisi that have been highlighted in the paper. From my experience, it is quite clear that without hard work, it will be impossible to write fifty scholarly articles and the barrage of creative works that Ogisi has. But despite being a workaholic, Dr. Ogisi still spends time with his students cracking jokes and making humorous comments. But a unique quality about his jokes is the deep wisdom and knowledge that are imbedded in them. As shown from the above narrative on thesis supervision and writing of 'background to the study', his jokes are although amusing, but full of wisdom, musical knowledge, or other lessons that could be applied in other life's situations. In other words, he uses comic stories and witty illustrations as methods of passing knowledge that may be more difficult to acquire under a normal learning condition.

In addition, many students who passed through the A.M.S will testify to Ogisi's extraordinary work rate. This writer recalls how he submits his thesis of over three hundred pages to him and it was ready in less than a week. Yet, despite the short time of returning the thesis, virtually all pages are awash with very critical and constructive comments in red. How was it then possible for him to read such a voluminous work in less than a week? The answer is simple; Dr. Ogisi had read through the nights! This is very uncharacteristic of many contemporary Nigerian lecturers. But Ogisi understands the fact that the primary aim of him being a lecturer is to teach students. He labours himself to attend to all undergraduate and postgraduate students despite the workload of having to teach and supervise research projects at all levels. He is always determined to help budding scholars grow even if it is at his detriment. He leaves his own works to attend to students' needs. It is noteworthy that he has supervised countless undergraduate projects, twenty Master Degree dissertations and eight Ph.D theses. In addition, Arugha Ogisi has published about fifty scholarly works including four creative and academic books. These impressive numbers and contributions are indeed worthwhile and are useful to both students and other researchers.

As a father, he is always willing to support and give the necessary advice that will make his students excel in academics and life generally. Regardless of the unfortunate setback to his postgraduate studies that had a lasting toll on him in terms of prompt promotions in his place of work, he still remains a progressive teacher who wants his mentees to outdo his achievements. As it is with every human being, Dr. Arugha Ogisi may have made some mistakes in life. But he is always quick to caution and counsel his students, for them not to risk making some of the mistakes he may have made in time past. He gives good advice regarding publications, job opportunities, availability of grants/scholarships in foreign universities, and information bothering on music practice in general. He shares his vast experiences with a view to making his students learn the positives and shun the negatives. Dr. Ogisi also makes books available to students from his very rich personal library. This author recalls how on the 8th of August, 2017, Ogisi called him to dole out a total of forty books to him. Apart from this author, Dr. Ogisi extended the kind gesture to nearly all his postgraduate students and most of his junior colleagues. It was later discovered that he had given out over four hundred books to different individuals. Such magnanimity is typical of a loving teacher and father; to have given out books that must have been bought with huge amounts of money to not just his supervisees but other postgraduate students and junior colleagues. Dr. Arugha Ogisi is indeed a living legend, hero, superman and a detribalized Nigerian who lived most of his life attending to others' challenges and rendering academic assistance to those in need of it. Even though some of his wishes may not have come to fruition as at the time of retirement, this author is still optimistic that someday, he shall receive his well-deserved reward and the ultimate prize for a scholar of his stature.

Conclusion and Recommendations

It will be impossible to discuss all the contributions of Dr. Arugha Ogisi to music scholarship in Nigeria in a study as this. The paper showed that he is an academic doyen among his peers, colleagues, students, and remains one of the unsung heroes of music scholarship in Nigeria. Despite some of the unfortunate circumstances that may partly have deprived him accelerated promotion in the university system, he still continued to make his contributions in the area of research and teaching of students. In light of the findings from the paper, it is recommended that his mentees consider having his scholarly and creative works compiled, published in different volumes, and made available in the cyberspace to guarantee broader readership and easy accessibility. The leadership of the Association of Nigerian Musicologists (ANIM) and Conference of Music Educators in Nigeria (COMEN) should also consider honouring this great musicologist and educator of no mean acclaim with an award/fellowship that are befitting of his invaluable contributions to music scholarship and practice in Nigeria.

References

Agu, D.C.C (2017). 'Utilizing the Power of Music in Contemporary Nigeria'. *An Inaugural Lecture of Nnamdi Azikiwe University, Awka*. Onitsha: Noben Press Ltd.

Agu, D.C.C (2017). 'Foreword' to *Praise the Lord: A Collection of Nigerian Spirituals*. Lagos: Amfitop Book Company.

Igbi, O. (2017). 'Reminiscences of a Legendary Nigerian Music Scholar and Composer, Dan Agu'. In Adedeji, F., Onyeji, C., and Onuora-Oguno, N., (Eds.). *Musical Horizons in Africa: Essays and Perspectives, a Festschrift in Honour of Daniel Chikpezie Christian Agu*. Ile-Ife: Timade Ventures Nigeria Ltd. Pp: 55-62.

Nwamara, A. O. (2015). 'Advancing Ensemble Music Pedagogy in Nigeria through the Application of Indigenous Knowledge Systems and Approaches: A Composer's View on CollaborativeCreativity'. *Journal of Nigerian Music Education*. No. 7. Pp: 173-178.

Ogisi, A. A. (2004). 'The Significance of the Niger Coast Constabulary Band of Calabar in Nigerian Highlife Music: An Historical Perspective'. *Nigerian Music Review*. No. 5: 37-50.

(2015). 'The Sono-kinetic Interface of Popular Dance in Nigeria: 1945-2015'.*Dance Journal of Nigeria*. Vol. 2: 201-227.

(2017). 'Landmarks in the Sixty Year History of the Recording Industry and Popular Music in Nigeria'. In Femi Adedeji, Christian Onyeji and Nnamdi Onuora-Oguno (Eds.)*Musical Horizons in Africa: Essays and Perspectives, a Festschrift in Honour of Daniel Chikpezie Christian Agu*. Ile-Ife: Timade Ventures Nigeria Ltd. Pp: 489-505.

(2018). 'The Impact of Soul Music in Nigeria'. Kenya: *African Musicology Online*.Vol. 8(1): 64-89.

Okafor, R. C. (2005). *Music in Nigerian Society*. Enugu: New Generation Books.

Omojola, B. (1995). *Nigerian Art Music*. Ibadan: IFRA

Vidal, A. O. (2012). *Selected Topics on Nigerian Music*. Femi Adedeji (Ed.). Ile-Ife: Obafemi Awolowo University Press.

B

The Contributions of Arugha Aboyowa Ogisi to the Development of Music in Bethel Baptist Church, Sapele

Udoka Peace Ossaiga, Ph.D[*]

Introduction

Dr. Arugha Aboyowa Ogisi, a musicologist, composer, conductor, and church musician of great competence and artistic versatility impacted on the development of music in Bethel Baptist Church, Sapele, Delta State. He achieved this through innovative musicianship, expansion of the church's hymn repertoire, and improvement of her choral music with systematic introduction of gospel music. These were made popular in Midwestern Nigeria via several television recordings, appearances, and broadcasts in the Nigerian Television Authority (NTA), Benin. However, there seems to be palpable silence in academic fora on his immense contributions to the development of music within the church. It is in this connection that this chapter discusses Ogisi's contributions to music in Bethel Baptist Church, Sapele. The work utilised biographic research method as well as personal communication with Ogisi. Conclusively, while noting the challenges of innovative musicianship to the development of church music in twenty-first century Nigeria, it recommends that budding church musicians need to learn from the experiences of such a personage.

Sapele is an urban community in Delta State, Nigeria. In the Midwestern Nigeria, Sapele was host to several churches amongst them was the Bethel Baptist Church, Sapele where Dr. Arugha Aboyowa Ogisi with his parents attended as a child. There, he was a chorister, and later served as choirmaster. In the Church, vital musical developments that underscored trends in church music towards fourth quarter of the twentieth century

---

[*] Music Minister, Unity Baptist Church, Warri. This is in celebration of Dr. Arugha Aboyowa Ogisi, My tutor who became my friend, My M.A and Ph.D supervisor who became my mentor. On the occasion of his retirement from fruitful service at the Department of Music, Delta State University, Abraka, where he contributed immensely in raising me and many others. To the glory of God.

Nigeria manifested through the musical activities of Dr. Ogisi. While the developments remain in the memory of surviving witnesses, not discussing them in scholarly writings does not enhance their accurate preservation, and promotion. This paper, utilising biographic research method, and data obtained through personal communication, discusses Dr. Ogisi's early musical exposure, music education, and contribution to music in Bethel Baptist Church, Sapele.

In the past few years, few music scholars have executed studies on the nature of church music; and the contribution of musicians to the developments of church music, especially, in Southern Nigeria. While the studies point at the contribution of musicians to the development of church in parts of Southern Nigeria, literature is scant on the contribution of church musicians from South-south geo-political zone to church musicianship in the area, especially, in the Nigerian Baptist Denomination. In the views of Eniolawun and Abolagba (2012), church music involves the sonic expression of Christians in their functions; and in pursuit of their religious objectives. Although the expression is not without cultural indicators, Thikan (2012) is of the view that church music in Nigeria needs national identity in tandem with cultural indicators of Nigerians. While nationality in Nigerian church music will ultimately point to the ethnic groupings that constitute the Nigerian state, his view resonates the need to promote more Nigerian traditional musical practices in the church services. It could be said that church music is an amalgam of musical arts that is performed by a congregation of Christian adherents in pursuit of their religious objectives, such as, worship, education, and mission. Among its performers are singers, instrumentalists, choirmasters, music directors, and priests.

In a study about church musicians in Asaba, Delta State, Ofuani (2015a) reports that Christian Mordi contributed to the development of music in the Anglican Communion as organist, and composer. He states that Mordi was an all-round musician who performed hymns, chants, and anthems on the organ, and served as gateway to contemporary church music and as the bridge between the pioneer, and contemporary church musicians in the Communion. The study presents the input of Christian Mordi to the performance and composition of Western music in the Anglican Communion. In another study Ofuani (2015b) focused on Anglican Church musicians among Igbos west of the Niger from 1905 to 2015 chronicling the roles of church musicians in the missionary (1905-1977), developmental (1977-1999), and contemporary (2000-2015) periods of the Anglican Communion in Igbo West of the Niger. He reports the contributions of several Deltan Igbo church musicians of the Anglican Communion who served as choirmasters, music directors, and organists of different parishes. While the study focused on Anglican Church musicians, Igbo West of the Niger from 1905 to 2015, the report involves the musical activities of the musicians beyond Igbo territories west of the Niger. The reviewed literature indicate the nature of church music as essentially a choral, and instrumental art with scant scholarly reports on the contribution of church musicians to the development of church music in Delta State.

Dr. Arugha Aboyowa Ogisi's Early Musical Exposure

Dr. Arugha A. Ogisi was born on 3rd January, 1955 at Sapele General Hospital into the family of Deacon. Francis and Deaconess. Omawumi Ogisi of Bethel Baptist Church, Sapele; of the Nigerian Baptist Convention (NBC). Each Christian denomination has its programmes through which its religious objectives are pursued. Thus, the Baptist denomination of his parents was known with graded training programmes that were designed for mental, social, and spiritual development of members from cradle to grave. Among the programmes were the Sun Beam Band (SBB), Royal Ambassador (RA), and the Youth Fellowship (YF) of the Nigerian Baptist Convention (NBC). Although these groups exist for the stated developmental objectives of the denomination, however, they also provide platforms for musicianship as each of the groups has its songs/hymns; and involve music in each of its meetings. At the age of four (4), Ogisi was enrolled into the Sun Beam Band (SBB). He grew through the programme and graduated to the Royal Ambassadors (RA) as was required of male adherents. The young Ogisi utilised the programmes to inculcate the virtues of discipline, commitment, hard-work, and spirituality. While these programmes were beneficial to his development, they could not satisfy a musical desire that has been aroused by several factors.

Dr. Ogisi was exposed to music through the church, television music programmes, and high school. It is noteworthy that services in Bethel Baptist Church, Sapele were profusely musical. Most elements of the services were powered by music which were performed by the church choir and congregants. These services exposed Ogisi to church music. Furthermore, music programmes that were broadcasted by the British Broadcasting Corporation (BBC) exposed him to developments in European music. In his words:

> Among what influenced my music career was the British Broadcasting Corporation (BBC) which I was an avid listener to from the early 1970s. They had a lot of music programmes that were both educative, and informative. They were "Talking about Music", "The Pleasure Is Yours", "Community Hymn Singing", "The King of Instruments", and several more. Radio played a significant part in my musical development. I still listen to radio till this day.

To express himself musically in the service of God, Dr. Ogisi joined the Bethel Baptist Church, Sapele's choir at the age of nine (9) in 1964. As a young boy, he sang soprano, and contralto parts in the SATB choir of the

Church. As was required of intending choristers, prior to featuring with the church choir in services, he underwent a one (1) year probation programme. This exposed him to the workings of the choir, and enabled him to familiarise closely with several anthems, hymns, processional, and recessional songs that were performed by the choir. According to Dr. Ogisi, he "rehearsed the songs to the point where he could sing many of them off-hand during the probation".

His quest for high education took him to Orerokpe in 1967, where he was admitted into Baptist High School, Orerokpe, Delta State. Although, his high school education temporarily disconnected him from music at Bethel Baptist Church, Sapele, it could not disconnect him from music in general. For at the high school, there was a choir whose membership was open to desiring members of the school community. Thus, he joined the school's choir wherein he also sang soprano, and contralto parts, intermittently. Between 1967 and 1968 while in the high school choir, Dr. Ogisi underwent biological maturation that broke his voice as typical of teenage males. Thus, he could no longer sing soprano, and contralto parts in the high school choir, so, he switched to tenor part. While at the high school, Ogisi identified with Christ, and His Church through his baptism at Orerokpe Baptist Church, Orerokpe in 1969 by an American missionary.

Dr. Arugha Aboyowa Ogisi's Music Education

While Dr. Ogisi has been involved in church and high school music, he knew there was need to obtain a measure of education in music. To this end, he combined both informal and formal approaches in pursuit of music knowledge. Thus, in 1968, when Lt. Col. T. C. Eru (1943-2013) started music classes at the premises of Baptist High School, Orerokpe, he learnt how to read music; this began his journey into music education. Along the line, his activities in church music declined as he focused on increasing academic tasks during his secondary school years through his "A" level; however, his path with music had just begun. After completing his Higher School Certificate (HSC), Dr. Ogisi sought opportunities to further his music education by looking for an instructor who could teach him how to play the organ. In the personal communication, he recalled that:

> after completing my Higher School Certificate (HSC), I decided to resume musical activities starting a music theory lesson in 1974 under Mr. Green who was an organist and choirmaster at St. Andrew Anglican Church, Sapele, as a prelude to knowing how to play the organ which was my major interest. I was attending music class three (3) times a week (Monday, Wednesday, and Friday) between 3pm-4pm each day at ten naira (₦10) per month (Ogisi, 2019).

It is noteworthy that his foray into music was a product of his personal decision, and effort. Although, Mr. Green was able to introduce him to music theory that enabled him to sight read at a good pace, he was not able to practice how to play the organ under him for lack of access to the instrument. Thus, at the end of the class, Mr. Victor L. D. Green advised him to look for an organ to practice with; this took him to many churches without success.

Around 1974, Deacon J. A. Omatsola (1911-1985) who was an organist at an Anglican Church in Sapele, and a music teacher at the church's owned school advertised for students who want to learn organ at his place in Sapele. The sight of the advert was a prayer answered as Dr. Ogisi responded and began practicing the organ haven learnt a measure of music theory. According to Dr. Ogisi: "I attended the organ practice whenever I had time, from there my organ playing skills were learnt. In October1974 while practicing the organ with Deacon Omatsola, Mr. R. P. I. Okerentie (1938-2000) returned to Sapele from the National Youth Service Corps (NYSC)."

Mr. Okerentie was a musician with notable theoretical, and practical skills, he was a foremost musically literate musician in Sapele and environ. Dr. Ogisi approached him for more lessons in music theory; and he obliged. Under Mr. Okerentie, Dr. Ogisi learnt advanced music theory; Mr. Okerentie also allowed him unhindered access to the organ at Okotie-Eboh Memorial Baptist Church, Sapele. The decision to switch from Deacon Omatsolato Mr. Okerentie was partly informed by distance for practicing with Mr. Okerentie halved the distance hitherto covered going to Mr. Omatsola's place for practice. The class continued till 1976 when Mr. Okerentie enrolled Dr. Ogisi to the Associated Board of the Royal School of Music (ABRSM) Grade Five (5) examination with him surpassing the per cent (80%) pass mark.

Engaging in the Royal School of Music Grade Five (5) examination points to a desire for formal music education which took him to the University of Nigeria, Nsukka (UNN), Enugu State; and University of Ibadan, Oyo State. His admission into the University of Nigeria, Nsukka (UNN) where he studied and graduated with Diploma in Music Education (Dip.Mus.Ed.) in 1980, Bachelor of Arts (B.A) degree in Music (Composition) in 1982; University of Ibadan where he graduated with Master of Arts (M.A) Degree in Music (African Musicology) in 1987, and Doctor of Philosophy (Ph.D.) Degree in Ethnomusicology (Popular Musicology) in 2009 capped his music certification.

Dr. Arugha Aboyowa Ogisi's Contributions to Music in Bethel Baptist Church, Sapele

In 1975 after Bethel Baptist Church Sapele overcame a protracted crisis, Dr. Ogisi began to assist the church's choirmaster unofficially. His dedication, and knowledge-based musical practice in the choir immediately caught the attention of the church who through committee nomination, and congregational approval appointed him the substantive choirmaster in 1976.

Under Dr. Ogisi's leadership as choirmaster, the choir did a lot of recordings, and had a lot of appearances at the Nigerian Television Authority (NTA), Benin, Edo State, through its programme: Church Choirs. The church's choir also featured severally with Rev J. E. Amromare (1940-) through his programme on the NTA. Two vital contributions of Dr. Ogisi to music in Bethel Baptist Church are the expansion of the church's hymns repertoire; and the introduction of gospel music.

Dr. Arugha Aboyowa Ogisi and Improvement of Hymn Repertoire in Bethel Baptist Church

In the 1970s, church music in Sapele and environs consisted of hymns that were learnt from foreign missionaries, and Nigerian church leaders. As a result, hymns repertory in the churches was mostly limited in number, and theme. Thus, few hymns were recycled in the weekly services of the churches. However, the *Broadman Hymnal* in use at Bethel Baptist Church contained several hymns that were not known by members of the church; thus, most of the hymns were not performed in the church. Dr.Ogisi saw the need to improve the hymns repertory of Bethel Baptist Church.

As choirmaster, Ogisi improved the church's hymn repertoire by leading the church choir to attempt learning, and singing through the *Broadman Hymnal* in S.A.T.B. In each rehearsal, he made hymn singing a vital task. He ensured choristers learnt the lines correctly; and gradually introduced the hymns into Sunday services of the church. While the choir could not go through all the hymns in the hymnal, the exercise exposed the choir to many hymns, and increased the church's knowledge of hymns as church members learnt to sing many hymns from the choir. Ogisi's improvement to Bethel Baptist Church hymn repertory was notably systematic.

Dr. Arugha Aboyowa Ogisi and Gospel Music in Bethel Baptist Church

Hymns and anthems were the major forms of music performed in Bethel Baptist Church in the early 1970s. While there were opening and closing hymns, and benedictions performed by the congregation at different points in the services, choral works were mainly limited to anthems. However, there was a vogue of gospel music around the world, which was also resonating in Sapele through the mass media. The "new music" came with performance practices that could be tagged immoral, noisy, and unacceptable by conservative members of the church. Thus, its introduction to churches in the area required wisdom. Thus, Dr. Ogisi introduced gospel music to Bethel Baptist Church, systematically. He sang and accompanied early gospels with guitar during weekly services, except Sunday services, to the admiration of members. Thereafter, he gradually introduced gospel music to Sunday services of the church. Gospel music goes with guitars, and drums, in addition to keyboard; most of which were not in the church for they were not used to perform the hymns, and anthems that were the mainstay of music in the church. Through his gospel music performances in the church, members saw the need to donate bass and lead guitars, drum-set, and other instruments to the Church. These were used to accompany gospel music, and airs.

To sustain the performance of gospel music in Bethel Baptist Church, Ogisi also formed a gospel music band in the church in 1978. The band was called *Gospel Bells*. This featured every Sunday during offering. This was around same time Bishop Benson Idahosa (1938-1998) was promoting gospel music through his Church of God Mission Gospel Band in Benin, Edo State.

Bethel Baptist Church in the 1970s was a significant church in the Nigerian Baptist Convention (NBC) for it was a leading church in then Sapele Baptist Association which consisted of churches of the Nigerian Baptist Convention (NBC) in Sapele, Okpe, Warri, Udu, Uvwie, and the environs. Thus, musical developments in Bethel Baptist Church easily spread to other parts of the Association. Till date, it can be observed that music in most Baptist churches in the area tilts towards gospel music. While other factors such as developments in information communication technology may be contributing to the dominance of gospel in the area, the role of Dr. Ogisi in introducing and spreading gospel music to the area is noteworthy.

Conclusion

The paper focused on Dr. Arugha Aboyowa Ogisi, his early music exposure, music education, and contribution to music in Bethel Baptist Church as a chorister, and choirmaster. Through the discourse, it could be deduced that Ogisi's musicianship was hone at home, church, and schools. For in them, he listened to, learnt, and performed music. His path with music in Bethel Baptist Church challenges church musicians to be innovative in their musicianship. While gospel music has become a component of church music practice in Sapele and environs, twenty-first century church musicians in the terrain have other opportunities to expand the scope of church music beyond the bounds of hymns, anthems, gospel music, and airs.

References

Eniolawun, I. O., and J. A. Abolagba (2012). 'Music's Mission in Worship and Evangelism'. *Nigerian Music Journal Vol 1,* 45-63.

Ofuani, S. (2015a). 'A Study of Musicians in Igbo West of the River Niger: 1905-2015'.In Arugha A. Ogisi (Ed.)*Studies in Nigerian Music Book 1.* Pp: 1-11.

Ofuani, S. (2015b). 'Christian Mordi and Church Music in Asaba Diocese of the Anglican Communion'. In Arugha A. Ogisi (Ed.)*Studies in Nigerian Music Book 1.* PP: 20-29.

Thikan, N. D. D. (2012). 'Church Music and National Identity in Nigeria'. *Nigerian Music Journal.* Vol 1,11-21.

Informant

Ogisi, A. A. (65). Personal Communication on Dr. Arugha Aboyowa Ogisi's Contributions to Music in Bethel Baptist Church, Sapele on 27th November, 2019.

4

Nigerian Art Music and Human Capital Development: the Unsung Contributions of Arugha Aboyowa Ogisi

David Bolaji, Ph.D[*]

Introduction

The sustainability of any field of academic study partly lies within the strength of its human capital development. Worthy of note are the unsung contributions of the erudite scholar, Arugha Aboyowa Ogisi on human capital development, spanning four decades in the field of Nigerian art music. On this premise, this chapter highlights and discusses some of the contributions of Ogisi to Nigerian art music. Relevant information was elicited from his mentees and supervisees through oral interviews. Additionally, bibliographic method was employed using abstractive procedures to review his selected published articles. Findings reveal that the intellectual expressionistic skills of Ogisi present him as a multi-faceted musicologist; an educator, composer, performer *par excellence*, and ethnomusicologist. Finally, his consistent mentoring and unquantifiable teaching within the academic milieu has contributed immensely to the birth of a plethora of modern art musicians in Nigeria.

Arugha Aboyowa Ogisi is a teacher who has made unique landmarks on his students and colleagues. Standing beside his contemporaries, Ogisi is a giant and selfless teacher, mentor and friend to his students. Having spent almost four decades in the academia, he has become an outstanding personage and erudite scholar. His selfless services call for acknowledgment, honor, and celebration in the world of Nigerian art music. One of the major attributes of Ogisi is his consistency in promoting Africanism which he achieved through ingenuous teaching skills that redirected the cognition of

---

[*] University of Port Harcourt, Port Harcourt, Nigeria

his students and mentees toward exploring the musical heritages of their communities and of Africa. Under Ogisi's supervision, a rich harvest of effectual African scholars have emerged, thereby continuing the spread and production of African Art Music.

Undoubtedly, the aforementioned testifies of Ogisi's prowess as a: teacher, supervisor and mentor; he is outstanding amongst music teachers of his generation. Similarly, his students and mentees testify that through self-sacrifice, Ogisi promoted and sustained the teaching profession as a divine calling and medium of giving knowledge back to humanity. He perceived the impartation of knowledge as a sacred phenomenon and blessing to humanity within the African setting. Thus, the ideological perspective of knowledge impartation through effective teaching and supervision serves as a means for sustainable development and not a mere means of livelihood. Hamm, (1989), White (2007) and Balogun, (2008), posit that knowledge impartation in the context of education generally stands as the developmental means of goodness to humanities. Basically, all of these facts reveal that Ogisi's philosophy is built on the sustainable development of humanity through education. Ogisi's teaching of Nigerian art music, is driven by this principle.

Modern Nigerian Art music, has been defined as musical artistic works of Nigerian art composers that are predominantly influenced by the traditions of Western classical music (Omojola, 2001). In line with this submission, the efforts of Ogisi towards the development of modern Nigerian art music are unquantifiable. This study is appreciative and acclamatory of Arugha Aboyowa Ogisi undeniable selfless services on human capital development in Nigerian art music.

Picture 1. Dr. Arugha Aboyowa Ogisi in his office

Brief Background of Arugha Aboyowa Ogisi

In a quest to give a detailed biography of Arugha Aboyowa Ogisi, this paper adopted his biography as captured in the National Conference proceedings of the Conference of Music Educators in Nigeria, (COMEN, 2019), held at the University of Port Harcourt, Faculty of Humanities, Department of Music.

Arugha Aboyowa Ogisi was born in Sapele to the family of Deacon F. E. and Deaconess O. Ogisi (*Nee* Tonwe) from Ugbuwangue in Warri South Local Government Area and Ugbege in Warri North Local Government Area respectively. His father was a timber merchant involved in the export of timber from the early 1950s to the early 1970s when he ventured into saw milling. He was also involved in haulage services in the 1960s, and later delved into transportation in the 1980s. He retired from active business in the early 1990s.

Ogisi started his formal education when he attended Council Primary School, Sapele, in 1961-1966. He proceeded to Baptist High School, Orerokpe in 1967-1971 and enrolled for Obokun GCE/ACCA Courses, at Ilesa between1972-1973 respectively. His foray into music began in 1964 when, as a boy soprano in the Choir of Bethel Baptist Church, Sapele, he was exposed to a number of choral works in the repertory of the music of the masters of Western Classical Music including Mozart, and Handel.

Between February 1974 and August 1977, he taught Physics at Sapele Technical College, Sapele and took music lessons from the late Mr. Green, Choirmaster/Organist of Saint Luke's Anglican Church Sapele, Mr. John Omatsola, then Organist of Okotie-Eboh Memorial Baptist Church, Sapele, and the conductor and impresario Mr. R. P. I. Okerentie. In 1975, he was appointed choirmaster, Bethel Baptist Church, Sapele and in 1976 he established the Gospel Bells, a gospel band in Bethel Baptist Church, Sapele. In addition to the choir ministering in the regular church Sunday services, he instituted an Annual song service which held in 1976 and 1977. He took the choir to record programmes with the then Bendel Radio, and the Nigerian Television Authority (NTA) both in Benin City. On a personal level he wrote scripts for music and other cultural programmes for the station. In 1976 he enrolled for the Grade 5 theory examination of the Associated Board of the Royal Schools of Music (ABRSM) and passed. The success in the examination increased his interest in music and he became more active in musical activities in Churches in Sapele.

In 1977 he was admitted to the Department of Music, University of Nigeria, Nsukka. Soon after this, he was appointed Choirmaster of Nsukka Baptist Church, Nsukka. He joined 'The Gospel Singers', an evangelistic gospel music band in the University in 1977 and became its Leader in 1979. During the long vacation of the 1979/80 session, Ogisi taught music part-time in the Colleges of Education in Benin, Agbor and Warri where he contributed in raising the first set of music students.

While in the university of Nigeria, Nsukka, he maintained close contact with his professional colleagues at Radio Bendel and the Nigerian Television Authority (NTA). For Radio Bendel, he wrote and presented the programmes titled Folk Music International, a 15-minute weekly programme produced by Charles Okp and From the Cotton Fields to the Concert Hall, a 30 minute weekly programme produced by the late Cecilia Ordia. Each of these music programmes had 13 episodes that ran for an entire quarter of 13 weeks. In his final year in 1982, he founded "The Friends of Music", a chorus group that was dedicated to performing folk music from around the world. The group succeeded in recording 9-minute programmes for NTA Benin City under the oversight of the ace music producer, the late Mr. Sam Ehigie.

Ogisi obtained the Diploma in Music Education and the Bachelor of Arts degree in 1980 and 1982 respectively. He did his National Youth Service at the Department of Music, College of Education, Ikere-Ekiti, and inspired many of the students to further their education beyond the Nigeria Certificate in Education (NCE). One of such students has recently obtained his doctorate in music, specializing in African musicology. Ever since Ogisi's graduation from the University of Nigeria, Nsukka, he has been deeply involved in teaching music in tertiary institutions in many capacities. Furthermore, after the completion of his National Youth Service, he was appointed lecturer at the College of Education Warri. While in Warri, he transformed the Music Department programme by introducing new series of musical performances that projected the department within and outside the college community. He obtained the Master in African Studies (Music) and a Doctor of Philosophy in Ethnomusicology from the University of Ibadan in 1987 and 2009 respectively. His doctoral thesis is on The Evolution of Popular Music in South-Western Nigeria 1900-1990.

He provided leadership in the Department of Music at College of Education, Warri, in the 1980s and as acting Head, Department of Music, Delta State University, Abraka for several years. He made unique contributions, in both instances, in the introduction of novel and innovative ideas in the development of music programmes, such as the introduction of music media as stress area, music broadcasting and journalism, Church music at post graduate level; some of which have been widely accepted and imbibed in other department of music programmes across Nigeria. Ogisi, has taught several courses at the undergraduate and postgraduate levels, and has also successfully supervised researches leading to the award of Bachelors, Masters and Doctoral degrees of music. His research interests include, but are not limited to, popular music in Nigeria, continuity and change in Nigerian music, music and rites of passage in the western Niger Delta,

Nigerian church music, music education in Nigeria, Itsekiri language and musical arts. Ogisi has published articles and chapters in books in these areas. He is also a collector of folk songs and Nigerian Spirituals. He has recently published a collection of Nigerian spirituals in the book, Praise the Lord.

Ogisi is involved in creative activities in the form of composing/arranging of music and writing of poems. Some of his published compositions include *Dance of the Seven Spirit* a ballet, *Partum Opera* (a collection of some of his compositions and arrangements, and *Songs of the Wayfarers* a collection of some of his poems). Beyond the creative attribute of composing music, he has edited high quality journals and some of which are *Dance Journal of Nigeria* (from 2013 to 2017), *Une: Abraka Music Journal* (1994 to 1997) and *Studies in Nigeria Music* (2015).

Aboyowa Ogisi is a member of many learned and professional bodies among which are the International Council for Traditional Music, (ICTM) the Association of Nigerian Musicologists (ANIM), Conference of Music Educators in Nigeria (COMEN), Composers Association of Nigeria, Association of Dance Scholars and Practitioners of Nigeria (ADSPON) and International Society for Music Education (ISME).

Ogisi's Effective Contributions to Human Capital Development
Ogisi's is highly distinguished as a scholar; his versatility and contributions to knowledge are palpable and potent in the personages that have evolved from his tutelage. Indisputably, Ogisi's contributions have added to the historical landmarks established by some early music educators in the then Bendel State, in the likes of Mr. Raymond Primrose Itseoritse Okenrentie and Dr. Emeka Nwanbuoku. Though, it is a fact in the academia that scholars approach the issue(s) of research based on the subject matter within the context and locale of the study. There are no common standards that could be used to measure equitably the contribution(s) of a scholar within his/her capacity. Agawu (2008: 1) argues that there are:

No standard or objective criteria existing for valuing scholarly work; indeed, the academic study of music worldwide has in recent decades developed a startlingly diversified profile. Moreover, questions of value, be they about kinds of repertoire, analytical and critical methodologies, or standards of writing, are not answerable outside specific ideological contexts.

Hence, it is necessary to state that Ogisi has established a landmark that speaks loudly of itself with tangible pieces of evidence in the sphere of Nigerian art music, as most of his scholarly writing border on breaking the silence of new scholastic discourse as it affects and benefits human capital development in the circle of Nigerian art music. The major factor that is evidenced in most of Ogisi's works and knowledge impartation is the profound insight and the need to exploit new ideological concepts in

Nigerian art music. Additionally, his resilient acts and efforts have unravelled new frontiers of knowledge in Nigerian art music.

Speaking on the contributions of Ogisi on the human capital development in the Nigerian art music, Idolor (2019) adopted a parody that "the way forward is the way backward." He reiterated that the genesis of Ogisi's academic journey and disclosed that, the road map of being a lecturer at the College of Education Warri in the 1980s was his starting point. He further reveals that the contributions of Ogisi are outstanding in the development of manpower, and have nurtured human capital development in the field of Nigerian art music. He states that having long outstanding years of experience in the teaching of art music and turning out numerous students from the level of the Nigeria Certificate of Education, (NCE programmes), First degree programmes, B.A/B.A (Ed), Master's degree programmes, (M.A), and Doctor of Philosophy programmes, (Ph.D) in different tertiary institutions in Nigeria, reveals that, Ogisi's contributions have acquired a prominent stance in Nigeria art music. This is because his high level of relevance has added to the social-cultural and educational ambience of Nigerian art music.

It is important as well to mention that, all of these achievements of Ogisi and his contributions to human capital development and art music, were alongside the cooperative efforts of his colleagues that served at the aforementioned departments of music. Some of these colleagues include, Professor Richard Okafor, Professor Dan Agu, Professor Ojo Rasaki Bakare, Professor Emuronome Idolor, Professor Charles Aluede, Professor Isaac Idamoyibo, Dr. Atinuke Layade, Late Dr. Joseph Ofori Ofosu, Mr. Opong, Dr. Ekewenu Bruno, Mr. Ogheneruemu Ehwre, Dr. Margaret Efurhievwe, Dr. Philo Okpeki, Dr. Justice Okoro, Dr. Sunday Ofuani and Mrs. Rebecca. Ogbeide It is necessary to state that, Professor Emurobome Idolor was tutored by Ogisi, in preparation for his music audition into the University of Nigeria, Nsukka. In the same vein, Professor Charles Aluede, Dr. Ekewenu Bruno, Dr. Mrs. Margaret Efurhievwe, Dr. Mrs. Philo Okpeki, Mr. Ogheneruemu Ehwre, Mrs. Rebecca Ogbeide, Dr. David Bolaji, Dr. 'Mudiakevwe Igbi, Dr. Udo Peace Ossaiga, Dr. Yemi Akperi, Dr. Olusegun Edward Oluwagbemiga, Dr. John Abolagba, Dr. Nathan Thikan, and Dr. Peter Odogbor were at one point or the other students of Ogisi.

Odogbor (2019) reiterates Ogisi's contribution to human capital development in the field of Nigerian art music, stating that the rigorous and passionate imputes of Ogisi through the rightful use of his skills in order to impact knowledge into students stands as part of his major distinguished contributions to Nigerian art music. On his part, Agbolagba Abolagba (2019), affirmed that the contributions of Ogisi to human capital development could be seen through the intellectual challenges and liberations given to his students, supervisees and mentees in order to exhume new areas of research for the advancement of knowledge in Nigerian art music. He adduced that, "this stands as one of the driving forces and philosophical school of thought of Ogisi". He added that, through this medium, many intellectual and profound scholars have emanated with outstanding researches carried out in diverse areas, through the insightful suggestions, intellectual tutelage, and assistance of Ogisi. Equally, Igbi (2019) notes that the vast knowledge of Ogisi in almost all the areas of music stands as a great asset in the academia. He adds that, the procedural pattern of Ogisi's teaching in any classroom activity can never be tied to a particular course as it were. Rather, he approaches his teachings through diverse models and principles. Thus, through his method of teaching, he broadens the knowledge horizon of his students, supervisee and mentees in order to reshape them to achieve their desired academic goals.

One could say that Ogisi, has addressed diverse issues and challenges using the logical ability in the field of academia. In the same vein, Idamoyobo (2011), acknowledges that Meki Nzewi, belongs to the aforementioned school of thought. Thus, the ingenuity of Ogisi's attribute is as well peculiar to Nzewi's school of thought that accepts faces and resolves intellectual challenges that may emanate from his creative perspective and scholarly writing within the academia.

Abstractive Review of Selected Scholarly Articles of Arugha Ogisi on Modern Nigerian Art Music

The voice of Arugha Aboyowa Ogisi rings distinctively loud and clear among numerous voices that have contributed to the discourse of Nigerian popular music. The in-depth clarity, accuracy, and holistic scholarly spiritism that he gives in investigating divergent areas of Nigerian popular music as a genre is unique. Some of these areas range from the origin, historical perspective, characteristics, socio-cultural influences, political and economic influences of Nigerian popular music. Putting all of these together, Ogisi's works stand tall among other works in this genre. Though drawing some of his resource materials from the existing studies, one would say that the efforts and contributions of Ogisi remain unadulterated in Nigerian popular music genre. Likewise, his frequent emergence of different shapes of studies in the said genre has added to the immense, detailed knowledge and understanding as well as the availability of instructional materials in the genre, globally. To this end, the abstractive reviews of three projective studies of Ogisi were considered in this study. These include: The Origin of Concert Music in Nigeria, 1850 – 1920; Sourcing Data in Popular Music Research in Nigeria and The Origin and Development of Juju music: 1900-1990.

Ogisi on 'The Origin of Concert Music in Nigeria'

The definitive thrust of the origin of concert music in Nigeria, 1850 – 1920, stands as a potent and detailed study that Arugha Ogisi used to present the historical antecedent behind the emergence of concert music in Nigeria. In the opening preface of the study, the polemical tone of Ogisi affirms that the current practices and the advancement of modern technology in Nigeria's musical entertainment does not present and represent the past worldview of the genre. In tracing and establishing the evolution of concert music in Nigeria, Ogisi notes that before the invention of a sound recording by Thomas Edison in 1877, the practices of concert music in Nigeria has been part of the performative genre used in enhancing the entertainment world. Tracing the birth of this genre to the musical involvement of the Sierra Leonean returnees and the divergent musical entertainment, spurred the emergence of concert music in Nigeria. Ogisi acknowledges the profound investigative and chronicle studies, which viewed concert music in Nigeria from the mid-nineteenth century, but however failed to untie and link the beginning of the genre to the present (Leonard 1967, Aig-Imuohuede 1975, Echeruo 1977, Omojola 1995). Thus, Ogisi used this study to ameliorate the historical precursor of concert music in Nigeria from its inception to the twentieth century. It is important to mention at this juncture, that the study is highly significant, not just because of its comprehensive knowledge and clarity on concert music in Nigeria. The study gives insight that reveals the attribute and passion of Ogisi on the proliferation of Africanism. The scholarly mannerism of Ogisi in promoting Africanism via his reach, perspective, and robust intent studies, has afforded him the altitude of presenting the state of Africanism in its content and practices within the worldview of Nigerian popular music.

Nevertheless, in the encompassing pattern of the study, Ogisi propounded four distinctive segments to which concert music in Nigeria could be investigated. These are: (i) the introduction and golden age of performance; (ii) the intense nationalism and distinct nationality identity; (iii) the emergence of Nigerians composers; and (iv) the emergence of a Nigerian concert music tradition. Despite the four promulgated segments on concert music in Nigeria in Ogisi's narrative, he, however, limited the compass of his study to the origin of concert music in Nigeria, 1850 – 1920. As part of the ingenuity in carrying out comprehensive research on concert music in Nigeria, the span of twelve (12) years was used for the fieldwork experience. (1988-2000). Nonetheless, the four distinctive sectionalism of the concert music in Nigeria as established by Ogisi was also used to complete the introductory section of the study. Ogisi, (2005) proposes that:

> The first period, 1866 to 1920, covers the period of its introduction and golden age of performance. The second period, 1920 to 1945, is characterized by intense nationalism and attempts at creating distinct national musical identity. The third period, 1945 - 1970, marks the emergence of Nigerians as composers. The fourth period, 1970 – present, represents the emergence of a Nigerian concert music

tradition, a period marked by significant increase in the number of active composers and experimentations in styles and idioms.

In an effort to untie the basic history behind the birth and practices of concert music in Nigeria, Ogisi recapitulates the activities of the Europeans and the introduction of Christianity as contributing factors that totally reshaped the lifestyle of Nigerians. The establishment of different types of Western musical genres was revealed as part of the dominant activities of that time. Likewise, the identification of the significant influence of Latin America and Sierra Leone returnees as a result of the abolition of slave trade, are institutions that gave birth to the practices of concert music in Nigeria. Specifically, in his painstaking historical study, Ogisi acknowledges Abeokuta as the birthplace for concert music in Nigeria this was due to the performances of various musical concerts by the returnees between 1850 and 1956. He buttressed this fact as Abeokuta had experienced the first concert earlier in 1852, before the recorded concert that was captured in Lagos in 1961.

However, in his quest to get to the genesis of concert music in Nigeria, Ogisi traced the first settlement community of the returnees to Badagry in 1839. To this end, he argued that the Badagry community stands the chance to be the first, birthplace of concert music in Nigeria, since the relocation of these returnees to Abeokuta came much later in 1852. Putting it clearly, he notes that thirteen years difference is enough to organize and stage the first concert music. Ogisi affirms that the contributive experiences of the genre which spans through diverse developmental movements before it got transformed into a well-defined artistic form were all witnessed in Lagos. Conclusively, Lagos stands as the expansion of concert music in Nigeria. The listed activities of the different musical associations that were founded via concert music in Nigeria were unravelled in the embodiment of Ogisi's study. The sub-heading of this includes the "Context and Content", Performance and the audience, the Rise of Musical Nationalism, and The Decline of Concert. Through all of these, Ogisi laid a detailed historical evolution and continuum music concert activities in Nigeria.

The conclusive part of the study mirrors the "the rise of musical nationalism and the decline of concerts." Through his historical compendium of facts on the study of the origin of concert music in Nigeria 1820 – 1950, Ogisi asserts that the dehumanization of the Nigerian clergy, Bishop Ajayi Crowther, stands as the pivot factor that led to the declining activity of concert music in Nigeria. Thus, he identifies that the endpoint of this resulted in the potent schism that was witnessed and recorded in the history of the evangelical churches in Nigeria, which eventually birthed the new dawn of independent churches in Nigeria. In addition, the establishment and huge patronization of cinemas in Lagos from 1905 added to the total decline of concert music in Nigeria.

Finally, the study of the origin of concert music in Nigeria proves to be an excellent article that gives outstanding historical evolution and the performance of concert music in Nigeria from its inception till the twentieth century. The integration of the cultural and linguistic mechanism by Ogisi, as well as the Africanism influence through the activities of the returnees, was captured with dates. The overall content of this study has proven to be invaluable with the proliferated knowledge that Ogisi has embedded in it. To this end, the article stands as an outstanding resource material for the study of Nigeria's popular music.

Nevertheless, the aforementioned phenomenon is premised on the established fact that, the advent of Western Educational system and Western art music in Nigeria contributed immensely to the developmental growth, sustainability strength and the globalization awareness of indigenous music and its narratives in Nigeria. Issues on this subject matter have been dealt with extensively by different researchers in Nigeria. Agu (1984), Ajirire, and Alabi, (1992), Idolor (2002), Bolaji, (2016) and Adeogun (2018). Similarly, Ogisi (2019) states that it is an undeniable fact that the effective influence and the acceptability ambience of Western art music in the Western world has a strong and saturated atmospheric fledging strength in comparison to what it is in Nigeria societies. Emphatically, the formidable practices and per-formative expression of this genre is not new to every average person in the Western world. One could say that, Western arts music has developed over the years from one institution to the other and serves as part of their way of life. Ogisi (2019), recognizes that, the teaching, learning and practices of Western art music have been imbedded in the curriculum of the educational system of the West. Thus, in the Western world, the knowing and expressive performance of the genre either through a vocal or instrumental medium has been seen as forming an integral part of humanity, from cradle through adulthood to old age.

In the Nigerian contexts, Ogisi, (2019) through his scholarly writing advocated strongly that despite the wide range of performances of art music that started from the platform of diverse concerts in Nigeria, and the performative acts of art music within the University community where music department is domiciled, huge gaps still exist between an average Nigerian child and the understanding, performance and appreciation of Western art music within the context of Nigeria society. In his argument, he stated that, the performances and practices of Western art music in Nigeria and Nigerian art music, has not been able to find a solid and connective ambience that is well rooted in the cognitive faculty of Nigeria's society. To a large extent, the identification, appreciation and value of art music, has not yet received appreciable recognition at the fundamental stages of education in Nigeria. He noted that the teachings and trainings of arts music have gained some acknowledgment to an extent in religious bodies and educational institutions in Nigeria. However, Ogisi posits, that the mere teaching of the genre as part of the curriculum is not the issue; does the act of taking it as a recreational subject for whiling away time drive home the core value of the genre. Rather, the need to see, use and promote the musical genre as a connecting paradigm to the indigenous level of the society in Nigeria is lacking. As a result of this, knowing the difference between art music and popular music and their musicians in Nigeria is a huge challenge. Ogisi (2019), states that the use of Western art music has not been able to address properly the needs and demands of average Nigerians. This is because there is a disconnection between the Nigerian society and the acceptability and usage of Western art music at the indigenous stage. It is of importance at this juncture to state the significant effect and influence of Western art music in Nigeria's Christian worship. Consequently, the use and performance of Western art music stands as the basic primordial musical style and principle that characterizes every worship service in most Orthodox churches. Basically, this has helped and contributed to the spread of arts music in the country.

Looking at the acceptability of Western art music within the general platform in the Nigeria society, Ogisi, (2020), opines that, Nigeria's music curriculum needs to be revisited, if a strong, positive and effective headway will be achieved. Furthermore, he stated that the learning, usage and performance of indigenous African music and Western art music have to be inculcated into the curriculum at every level of education in Nigeria. He hinged his submission on the fact that music is a phenomenon that forms an integral part of life in every Africa society. To this effect, learning indigenous music as a child within the four-walls of a classroom can never be out of place. He emphasizes that more attention should be given to the learning of indigenous music first, before the introduction of Western art music. Restating that both indigenous and Western art music should be carried out side-by-side within the classroom without the imposition of Western art music on indigenous Nigerian/African music. In the same vein, he stresses that the aftermath of learning both indigenous and Western art music should be tailored towards the propagation and sustainability of indigenous music in Nigeria. Stating that the knowledge gained from Western art music should be used as a paradigm in presenting and preserving indigenous music in Nigeria, and globally.

Furthermore, Ogisi noted that the correction of the huge misconception of most Nigerians in knowing and stating the difference between a Nigerian pop musician and a modern Nigerian art musician will be in proper perspective. This is because, the notion and concept of arts musician has been an intricate phenomenon for most Nigerians. Only some elites and educated persons could really differentiate the basic differences between the two genres. This singular reason has made the performative extension of art music and modern Nigeria art music not to be generally accepted in the Nigerian society.

While it is thoughtful to note and acknowledge the contributions of Ogisi in modern Nigerian art music, the necessity of not leaving behind the remarkable landmark that he established within the research parameter of the Nigerian popular music cannot be underestimated, rather it should be brought to the limelight as well. Ogisi has passionately proven his depth of knowledge for the promotion of African identity through what I call 'Neo-Indigenous Nigeria Popular Music. Reflective of this is the evidence that could be clearly seen in the rigorous propagations of outstanding research work 'The Evolution of Popular Music in South-Western Nigeria 1900-1990'. This work has acquired significant acclamations on the phase of Neo-indigenous Nigeria Popular music because of its relevance to the socio-cultural sphere of Nigerian art music. Likewise, the view of Ogisi, (2008) in unravelling the historical antecedents of Nigeria's popular music in South-Western Nigeria is that, the fundamental sympathetic view of African indigenous system of knowledge stands as a bedrock and microscope that must be used while launching into the systemic institution of Nigeria's indigenous popular music. He stated emphatically that, the popular music of any culture has a connective link to the indigenous knowledge of such culture in order to transmit the value system that are imbedded in the cultural heritage through popular music. Thus, indigenous popular music in Nigeria, displayed the Africanism and identity in each of its popular music. In view of this, the wide continuum investigation carried out in popular music in southern Nigeria, the historical source and inevitable documentation of various styles of popular music were scripted by Ogisi to include, Fuji music, Juju Music, Apala music, Afro-juju music and popular music. At this juncture it is necessary to note that one or two research has been carried out on Nigerian poplar music before the advent of Ogisi's work. However, it is notable to mention that "the Evolution of Popular Music in South-Western Nigeria stand as a major research work and valuable compendium introducing popular music in Nigeria. As a result of Ogisi's research, diverse researches have emanated thereby expanding the corpus of Neo-Nigerian popular music.

An Abstractive Review of 'Sourcing Data in Popular Music Research in Nigeria.' As part of the remarkable efforts of Arugha Aboyowa Ogisi on the scholarly trend of Nigerian popular music, the retrospective and propounded strategies of sourcing data in popular music research in Nigeria has added to the train of his scholarly prints. In the opening preface of the study, Ogisi acknowledged that distinct to other areas of music studies, researches into popular music via numerous applicable procedures to source for primary data, prove to be unknown and untapped. His practical experience along his doctoral thesis journey, gave birth to the proposed measure of sourcing data in popular music research in Nigeria. Ogisi's cognitive and logical presentation, reiterates the inadequate attention of data sourced by most Nigerian scholars. Adding that as of the time of his study, the expense of Nzewi's (1980) narrative on this subject matter, and the study Sourcing Data in Popular Music in Nigeria stands as the relative print materials on this subject. This implies that most Nigerian music scholars have not investigated the prospective challenges in fieldwork, as it concerns Nigerian popular music. Thus, he notes that though some universal fieldwork experience still remains the same, the place of peculiarities is inevitable to various fields of study. Ogisi unravels divergent sources, where scholars could tap relative and relevant materials on primary and secondary data for popular music studies.

Ogisi sub-divides and presents his intellectual property on *Sourcing Data in Popular Music Research in Nigeria* under thirteen different sections. All of these come under the Sources of Data, explaining his own philosophical fount as: primary, secondary, literary sources, published literary sources, journals, government publications, newspapers and magazines, unpublished literary sources, projects, dissertations and theses, reports/white papers, audio, and audio-visual sources, records, radio/TV music programmes, film, information and communication technologies (ICT) sources. In the sphere of each fountain, Ogisi presents his narrative in relation to how it could be of great benefit to any kind of study in Nigerian popular music. However, he reaffirms and projects the necessity of using and embracing the primary data fount in carrying out studies in Nigerian popular music. Due to the fact that the endpoint of it will certainly unravel original and new numerous facts in the investigative subject matter, in the field studies.

Ogisi on 'The Origin and Development of Juju Music: 1900-1990'

Ogisi narrates "the Origin and Development of Juju Music: 1900 – 1990", as an exposition that addresses the concept of Juju music holistically. In the introductory section, definite areas that Ogisi perused are the development of "Juju music from its inception to it decline, the influence of Western folk songs, European sea shanties, church hymnody, soldiers' songs, minstrelsy and Yoruba traditional music." Through the superlative investigations and profound submissions, Ogisi gave a clear view to all the salient areas of juju music. In his attempt to efficiently profound the historical perspective of Juju music in Nigeria, he gave an affirmative view that in the late 1940s, the genre was the most patronized among other popular music genres in Nigeria. However, he recalls the attention of Nigerian art music scholars on the need to project the silenced social significance of Juju music in Nigeria.

In cross-examining the origin of Juju music, Ogisi restated the socio-economic role of Lagos state to the development of Nigerian popular music.

This is due to British presence and commercial activities in Lagos; added to this is the arrival of 'returnees' that created a multi-ethnic and multinational composite, vibrant and receptive of divergent musical activities. Ogisi presented a comprehensive study on the birth of Juju music, 'as a musical genre that emanated from the activities of the drinking places' (Ogisi, 2006: 29). Ogisi captures some of the factors that are responsible for the dominance of Juju music as a brand of popular music in Nigeria to include, "the mass exodus of people from the eastern region, the high patronage of Juju music as a result of the economic impact of the oil boom in Nigeria, etc." Ogisi proposes that the emergence of Shina Peters in the 1980s, when Juju music was in decline, was his successful fusion of "up-tempo Juju with elements of Fuji and Afro-beat into a Christianized Afro-Juju" which became the tonic that revived Juju music back to prominence on Nigeria's popular music the scene.

Conclusion

There is no opposing the fact that the scholarly contributions of Arugha Aboyowa Ogisi has added to the human capital development that has brought an irrevocable and sustainable development to Nigerian art music. His copious studies in different areas of Nigerian popular music, has distinguished him as one of the leading erudite scholars of the genre. This study has adduced some of the excellent contributions of Ogisi through the abstractive review of three of his selected articles. The origin of concert music in Nigeria, 1850-1920, the origin and development of Juju music: 1990 and sourcing data in popular music research in Nigeria.

Ogisi's selfless and sacrificial service years that spans almost four decades has positively impacted on the scholarship and career of many mentees, supervisees, colleagues and academia, both locally and internationally. Finally, Ogisi's philosophy, sense of spirituality and mien is a paradigm that every scholar should replicate so as to create an enduring human sonic cusp humming from generation to generations.

References

Adeogun A. O. (2008). 'The Development of University Music Education in Nigeria'. Sage Open, 2018 - journals.sagepub.com An 1 –14 © The Author(s) 2018 DOI: 10.1177/2158244018774108

Agawu, F. (2008). 'Meki Nzewi and the discourse of African musicology: a 70th birthday appreciatio'.*Journal of the Musical Arts in Africa*.Vol. 5. Pp: 1–18 doi: 10.2989/JMAA.2008.5.1.1.784

Agu, D. C. (1984). 'Indigenous Choral Music Worship in African Christian Worship: An Analytical Study of the Youth Fellowship Songs in the Niger Diocese of Nigeria'. An Unpublished Doctoral Thesis, Queen's University, Belfast, UK.

Bode, O (2001). 'African Pianism as Intercultural Composition Framework: A Study of Piano Works of Akin Euba'. Vol. 32, No 2. *Resource in Africa Literatures.* https://www.jstor.org/stable/3820910 Retrieved on 19-08-2019.

Ndofirepi, A. P. and Ndofirepi, E. S. (2012). '(E)ducation or (e)ducation in Traditional African Societies? A Philosophical Insight Wits School of Education'. University of the Witwatersrand, Johannesburg, South Africa © Kamla-Raj 2012 Study Tribes Tribals, 10 (1): 13-28 (2012)

Ajirire, T., & Alabi, W. (1992). Three decades of Nigerian music: 1960-1990. Lagos Nigeria: *Limelight Showbiz.*

Bolaji, S. B. D. (2016). 'A Stylistic Analysis of Debo Akinwumi Compositional Techniques'. *Ikogho: A Multi-disciplinary Journal.* Vol. 14 (4) pg. 809-813 2016.

_____ (2019). 'The Creative Approach Towards African Identity: a Scholastic Discourse in Honour of Akin Euba'.*African Musicology Online.* Vol. 9, No. 2, pp. 26-41, 2019 ISSN: 1994-7712 (Online) | 26-41. Retrieved on December 19, 2019

Balogun O.A. (2008). 'The idea of an 'Educated Person' in contemporary African thought'.*The Journal of Pan African Studies,* 2 (3): 117-128.

Hamm, C.M (1989). *Philosophical Issues in Education: An Introduction.* London: The Falmer Press

Idolor, E. (Ed.). (2002). 'Music to the Contemporary African'. In E.G Idolor (Ed*.). Music in Africa: Facts and Illusions.* Pp: 1- 11. Ibadan: Stirling-Horden Publishers (Nig.) Ltd.

Idamoyibo. I. O. (2011), 'Meki Nzewi in the Industry of Manpower Development for African Musical Arts: Theory, Philosophy and Model,' in Y. S. Onyiuke, I.O Idamoyibo and D.C.C. Agu (Eds*.). Mekism and Knowledge Sharing of the Musical Arts of Africa: A book General Reading in Honour of Professor Meki Nzew.* Anambra, Nimo: Rex Charles and Patrick Ltd. Pp:54 - 62

Ogisi, A. A. (2008). 'The Origin of Concert Music in Nigeria, 1850 – 1920'. *EJOTMAS: Ekpoma Journal of Theatre and Media Arts.* Pp: 8- 18

_____ (2010). 'The Origin and Development of Juju Music: 1900- 1990'. *Ekpoma Journal of Theatre and Media Arts,*3 (1&2), 27-37.

_____ (2016). 'Sourcing Data in Popular Music Research in Nigeria'.*Ogirisi: A New Journal of African Studies,* Vol. 12

_____ (2008). 'The Evolution of Popular Music in the South-Western Nigeria', An Unpublished Doctoral Thesis, University of Ibadan.

_____ (2015). 'Optimizing Postgraduate Music Studies in Nigeria' In A.A Ogisi (Ed.). *Studies in Nigeria Music, Book 1: Music and Society in Nigeria.* Pp: 133 – 141. Lagos: Amfitop Book Company.

White, J. (2007). What Schools are for and why? London: Philosophy of Education Society of Great Britain.

Interviews

Abolagba J, A, (2019) Personal Communication. 23rd September, 2019

Igbi, M. (2019) Personal Communication. 22nd September, 2019.
Idolor G. E. (2019) Personal Communication. 17th September, 2019
Odogbor, P. O. (2019) Personal Communication. 22nd September, 2019
Ogisi, A. A. (2019) Personal Communication. 19th October 2019

SECTION II

Nigerian Musicology

5

Features of Orality in *Okpẹ Disco Popular Music of the Niger Delta Region, Nigeria*

Mus. Prof. Emurobome G. Idolor[*]

Introduction

Text constitutes a recognizable portion of *Okpẹ Disco* music. Details of what characterises its lyrics are yet to receive scholarly attention. As an oral art and a transient popular music genre which moves with the template of social change, its modification or extinction is expected and so a detailed documentary study of its practice is necessary. For this research, fifty *Okpẹ Disco* music texts were collected from ten sampled practitioners. These texts were subjected to critical analysis from which the use of humour, proverbs, parallelisms, repetitions and fables were identified. From the foregoing, it is recommended that the possibilities, treatment and presentational skills of these features should be improved upon by the practitioners in order to attract wider interests.

Contents in African music are designed to communicate issues about the society to audience or listeners. As a medium of documentation of events in the life of a people, its performances owe it a responsibility to replay societal issues through a platform that can best be understood by listeners; one of which is the vocal medium. The vocal medium is characterised with textual and structural features which create thematic developments in performance situations. Some of these features include sequences of thought, proverbs, fables, similes, wise sayings, borrowing of words/terms, exclamations, environmental features, and so on.

Ekwueme (2001:18) records that "the human voice is, at the moment, the only 'instrument' which can transmit intelligible language unequivocally to an audience. All other forms of 'meaning' ascribed to or ascertained from non-vocal music are subjective and vague, ambiguous and imprecise." Music

---

[*] Delta State University, Abraka, NIgeria

by the human voice uses text which, according to Bronislaw Malinowski in Okpewho (1990:1), "is extremely important, but without the context [of performance], it remains lifeless . . . The whole nature of the performance, the voice and the mimicry, the stimulus and the response of the audience mean as much to the natives as the text". The two positions stated above advocate the importance of texts in music.

Vocal delivery in music plays dominant essence in performance presentations. It is therefore, of great consideration to artistes, particularly of the African extraction, that contextualised music compositions to embody reasonable textual contents to qualify them for appreciation and wide patronage. With the understanding of internal competition amongst popular music artistes who scramble for recognition, patronage and career success within a given social space, extra efforts are therefore necessary to achieve perfect oration in public performances and disc recordings.

People in the Niger-Delta region of Nigeria have varieties of music for diverse socio-cultural activities where traditional popular music genre is used for entertainment interests. Popular music in most of all its varieties among the *Okpe*[1] people of the Niger Delta, is vocal in nature with visible features of oral elements. In its corpus of identity, music as a phenomenon in Okpe culture is highly text dependent and hence, there exist many vocal typologies and oral performances. The lyrics of the songs serve purposes such as education, praise to deities and personalities, documentation of events of the society, criticism of the social system, comparison of the past and the present, and counsel on profitable life endeavours. Textual compliance of *Okpe Disco* music in relation with this characteristic standard in African music is the concern of this paper.

Research Approach

The ethnographic research method using the modified version of Hood (1971) approach of Pre-field, Field and Post-field structure was adopted in this endeavour. With the assistance of key informants and research assistants on the field, the text of fifty *Okpe Disco* songs were collected, textually transcribed and analysed from which forty examples were used in this paper. Transcribed texts were transliterated in English language to indicate real contents and contextual usages. Further explanations/translations were made to provide literal meanings of transliterated lines.

Emergence of *Okpe Disco* as a Concept

Okpe Disco is a neo-traditional entertainment music genre used in multiple events/situations such as child naming, marriage, chieftaincy installation, achievement of feats and burial ceremonies. It is basically a vocal music genre performed in solo/chorus responsorial style in which the leader takes the solo while the remaining members of the group sing the chorus and play instrumental accompaniment (Idolor, 2014:16).

The text praises people of substance, expresses opinion of injustice on the less-privileged in the society; enacts the people's concepts of destiny vis a vis contemporary incidents; life and life-here-after; child upbringing; peaceful coexistence; benevolence and hard-work. The music is performed along with vigorous dance movements and loud volume of sound facilitated by electronic equipment like microphones, amplifiers, synthesisers and loud-speakers to reach listeners in crowded occasions.

Okpẹ Disco as a popular music genre was first played by Ọfọkpẹlẹ Ogorode[2] in 1977 as a personal kind of traditional music which was later popularised by over forty-seven artistes through their regular live performances and disc recordings" (Idolor, 2002:13). Commenting on the origin of the name *Okpẹ Disco,* Ọfọkpẹlẹ Ogorode states:

Initially, I thought of *Ikpokporo-Okpẹ* (modern *Okpẹ* traditional dance music) that has mass appeal. During my engagement performances in the late 1970s, it was usual to find a spot in the venue of the event called *Disco* where youths played and danced to varieties of English records. To distinguish between mine and theirs, the audience referred to the other as *Oyibo Disco* and mine as *Okpẹ Disco* - an appellation which I fancied, accepted, adopted and popularised (Ogorode, 1999).

From the foregoing, the term *Okpẹ Disco* was coined by the audience (society) and was adopted by Ọfọkpẹlẹ Ogorode and later by many other *Okpẹ Disco* artistes like Stephen Biokoro Ojabugbe, Emiko Okokoroko and Godwin Idọlọr[3]. The appellation *Disco,* electronic keyboard instrument, amplification system and contemporary textual themes, made the music neo-traditional and rebranded to contemporary taste of youths who patronised other Nigerian, African American and European entertainment music types then. In this connection, Omojola (2006:4) earlier observes that "Nigerian popular music derives from the understanding of the genre as a socio-artistic metaphor in which aesthetics, emotions and ideas are expressed as commentaries on the pattern and nature of human relationships in a particular social environment".

Structural Layout of Okpẹ Disco Music

Structurally, *Okpẹ Disco* comprises four main sections which are: *Ọtonrhọ* (Introduction), *Ekele* (Narrative), *Ikpokporo* (Instrumental) and *Irhirẹn* (Conclusion/end). See Fig. 1 below:
end). See Fig. 1 below:

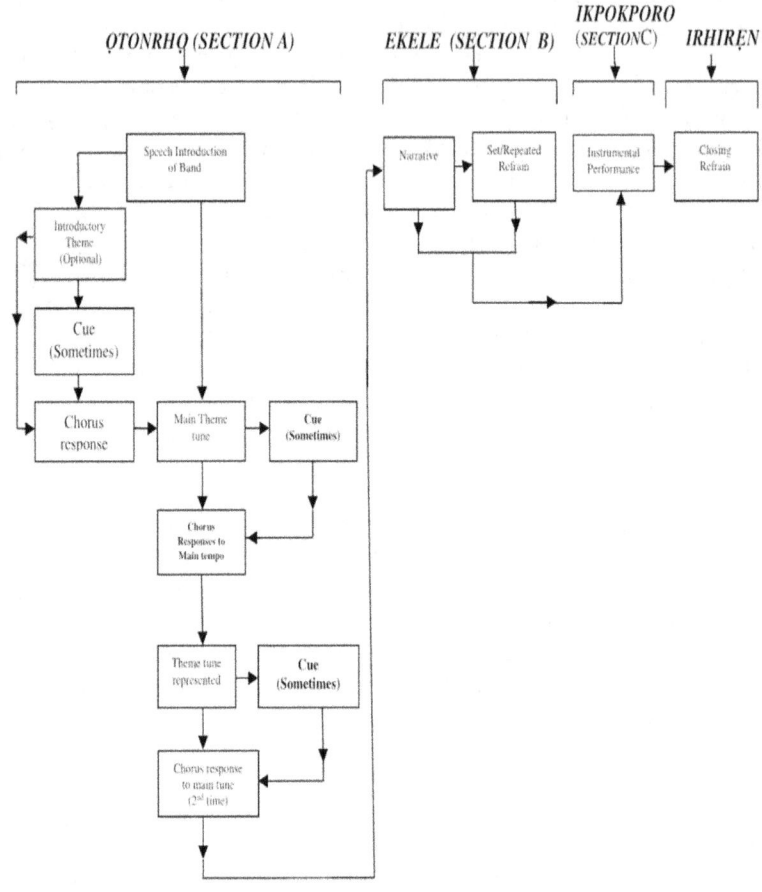

Fig. 1: Idolor's 2001 Model of Okpẹ Disco Oral Performance Structure.

In all the segments of the structure, vocal performance runs through either as singing or spoken words to communicate ideas and enhance collective participation of the musicians and audience.

Oral Features in *Okpẹ Disco* Popular Music

Okpẹ Disco is characterised by textual emphasis to educate, criticise, project the people's culture, exalt creditable gestures of individuals and above all, entertain. Thus, the music is assessed by the quality of ọhọ (wisdom) it contains. Analysts of *Okpẹ Disco* music would consider how accurate are the claims of the artistes on Okpẹ life, the humorous nature of the remarks, appropriate idiomatic expressions; and the level of balance between words of everyday life and metaphorical phrases. Consequently, these expectations are some of the factors that determine the degree of patronage and fame of the artistes.

To address topical issues in *Okpẹ Disco* songs, the traditional background of the genre and the world view of the indigenous audience for which it is performed are considered. This mandates the artistes to enact the past and present of the people's experiences in the oral delivery of the theme. Specifically also, is the regular feature of the people's habitat and experiences in the performance of the music. Earlier elsewhere in Idolor (1993) we observed the use of symbolism like the moon, tiger, lion, elephant, iron shakers, destiny, forests, history, occupation, etc., in *Ighophan-Okpẹ* songs. *Okpẹ Disco* songs reflect climatic conditions, vegetations, physical features, animals, birds, and life philosophies which are common experiences in the environment. For instance, Umẹayọvẹne Erhiẹmrọwaan (1999) used the following expression in his advice on Okpẹ unity:

Erhan re ekẹre, ọye ọlẹrhẹ emwerin sasa.

The closeness of trees to one another in the forest makes the monkey a smart animal.

This expression validates the fact that the people are found in rain forest vegetation with dense trees and animals such as monkeys which thrive in their springing acts due to the relative proximity of the trees to one another.

Stylistic Presentation of Language in *Okpẹ Disco* Music

Abimbola (1977:22) records that "*Ẹsẹ Ifa* is rich in language and stylistic features…The most characteristic features of [its performance] style include repetition, word-play, personification, lexical-matching, metaphor, parallelism, and onomatopoeia" while Akpabot (1998:75) upholds that a singer "can use metaphors, proverbs, archaic expressions, cryptic utterances, shorten or lengthen a vowel and criticise establishments". In like manner, *Okpẹ Disco* music is characterised with the following stylistic presentation in its oral performances:

Use of Humour (*Oboro ogbe echẹ*) in Textual Organisation

Entertainment, commercial and eulogistic nature of the music influences the mild and delightful choice of text for wide patronage and successful artistic career. Even when themes of criticism and ridicule are presented for the improvement of the society, the mode of textual and oral deliveries is sufficiently meek for listeners to absorb. For instance, instead of the artistes saying:

Uruemru ọrana obiobiomu.
That attitude is bad.
They rather say:

Uruemru ọrana ojemẹ tee.
I am not too pleased with such attitude.

Direct condemnation of actions and behaviours with hurtful satirisation of personalities is not common practice in the genre. Alternatively, a thought-out story-line (fable) or the use of imagery is employed to send messages across to listeners as the humorous performance style facilitates extensive patronages for their livelihood and career prospects. Besides this, an earlier awful experience of *Igoru* music practice from 1930-1960 where offended satirised parties harmfully attacked artistes was not a pleasant incidence to reiterate. *Okpẹ Disco* lyrics report/narrate societal activities and provide interpretation and possible implications for the people's wellbeing. In situations of ridiculous themes and unpleasant themes, it is common for artistes to dissociate themselves from the message either at the beginning of the presentation or somewhere suitable within the music performance with the use of the following statement:

Urhebro me havbọ.
I am just counselling.

Function of Textual Repetition (*Evbariẹn*) in *Okpẹ Disco*

This is the act of singing a phrase or a section in a piece of music more than once for clarity of presentation, emphasis of a fact or a stylistic option. In *Okpẹ Disco*, repetition of texts is either full or partial. Olatunji (1984: 17) states that "*full repetition* involves the repetition of a sentence structure as well as of all the lexical items occurring in it" as shown in the following example by Kharlil Edoja in his *Iroro* album:

Iroro, iroro, iroro, iroro, akpọna iroro;
Iroro, iroro, iroro, iroro, akpọna iroro.

Meaning:
   Diligence, diligence, diligence, diligence, life deserves wisdom;
   Diligence, diligence, diligence, diligence, life deserves wisdom.

Apart from *Full Repetitions* that occur in successions, varieties exist where a line or more intervene before another full repetition reoccurs as shown in the example below by Godwin Idọlọr:

Otu rẹ awariẹn ẹmron,
Are inẹ oma so nẹ ake wariẹn;
Otu rẹ awariẹn ẹmron,
Are inẹ oma so nẹ ake wariẹn.
Ọdafe wa mẹrẹn ran, ọvbọ karẹn ẹghwaa,
Ogbere wa mẹrẹn ran, ọvbọ karẹn ẹghwaa,
Otu rẹ awariẹn ẹmron,
Are inẹ oma so nẹ ake wariẹn.

Meaning:
   Those who bear false allegations,

Examine yourselves before making your allegations.
Those who bear false allegations,
Examine yourselves before making your allegations.
There is no family without a wealthy personality,
There is no family without a wretched personality;
Those who bear false allegations,
Examine yourselves before making your allegations.

In a *Partial Repetition*, "the sentence structure is repeated but not all the lexical items are included" (ibid, 19). Change of unrepeated words appears in any part of the sentence. The purpose of partial repetition is to emphasise an idea which, from the example above, the artiste's textural emphasis is on his determination to accept the challenge of *proffering a solution* to a nagging entertainment need be it music or dance. See the example below by Sylvester Ojoba:

Ijoro Okpẹ rẹ ọkaren ame na, me na chẹ oja ọna.
Igbegbe Okpẹ rẹ ọkaren ame na, me na chẹ oja ọna.
Meaning:
I will proffer solution to the inadequacy of Okpẹ music,
I will proffer solution to the inadequacy of Okpẹ dance.

In the above example, the whole sentence was repeated except *Music* which was replaced with *dance* in the second line.

Some words are repeated with a sentence structure for stylistic reasons most times to achieve the musical phrase or sentence that, without these repeated words, the statement is clear and complete. While this stylistic repetition emphasises the theme of the song, it also contributes to the full conclusion of the statements. In other instances, it helps to fill the rhythmic syllables required for a complete musical sentence. Repeated words in *Okpẹ Disco* appear as the first and last components of the sentence as show in the examples below by Godwin Idolor and Michael Enughwure respectively:

Ogbikun *ovbo gbẹ ere oma yee,* **ogbiku.**
A **tale-teller** does not relate his own issues, **a tale-teller.**
Or
Nyan worhe, *nẹ ọye aha hwẹ osa rimi anyanrhẹn,* **nyan worhe.**
Safe journey is the transport fare for my trip, **Safe journey.**

Another prominent form of repetition is the text designed as a set-response (refrain) normally sung by the chorus at regular intervals after the soloist. Most often, this set-response is the theme of the music and serves as the title of the album or track in recorded albums. See the example below by Stephen Biokoro in his album *Ẹghẹlẹ ifo*:

Soloist:	*Ẹghẹlẹ onyẹ akpọ oruẹ,*
Chorus:	**Ẹghẹlẹ ifo.**
Soloist:	*Wa mẹrẹn akpọ rẹ arhere,*
Chorus:	**Ẹghẹlẹ ifo.**

Soloist:	*Wu rhe ruẹ ọrẹ esiri,*
Chorus:	**Ẹghẹlẹ ifo.**
Soloist:	*Emru esiri ọye wa mẹrẹn,*
Chorus:	**Ẹghẹlẹ ifo.**
Soloist:	*Ẹghẹlẹ ovbo vrẹẹ*
Chorus:	**Ẹghẹlẹ ifo.**

Meaning:

Soloist:	Benevolence from somebody,
Chorus:	Benevolence is reciprocal.
Soloist:	In this life of ours,
Chorus:	Benevolence is reciprocal.
Soloist:	If you are charitable,
Chorus:	Benevolence is reciprocal.
Soloist;	You get good fortunes in return,
Chorus:	Benevolence is reciprocal.
Soloist:	Benevolence does not get lost,
Chorus:	Benevolence is reciprocal.

Stylistic Use of Proverbs (*Isẹ*) in Oral Performance

Proverbs are short, well-known sentences or phrases that state a general truth about life or give advice to the addressee. They are employed as techniques of speech variation, satirisation and for vivid and dramatic effect. In *Okpẹ Disco*, not only are proverbs used for the above stated purposes, a good handling of this speech technique endows artistes with high reputation and patronage. Often, songs are interspersed with spoken proverbs, and at other times a portion within the unfolding text of the narrative is devoted to series of related proverbs. See the example below by Paul Eyagha:

Oje gẹrhẹ ne erhie fughwẹẹ
It has not slanted, how much more to spill.

The above proverb may refer to a tin full of palm oil that can spill only if it slants. In this context of usage, the artiste informed his audience that though a bit of the performance has been watched, he is yet to start; much more will be presented. This statement stimulates high level expectation, activates more collective participation, energises and heightens the degree of the performance. The following are some proverbs various artistes use in their performances:

1. *Ọgọdọ rẹ ọvbẹrẹn, oma ye ogbe.*
A pit that caves in, refills itself.
2. *Amwan evba dẹ ogberhualẹ nẹ ojo rho boo.*
A town cannot buy a cock and fails to crow.
3. *Ame ọvbọ vuẹn ugẹẹn.*
Water does not fill a fish cage.
4. *Godogodo ọye amẹrẹn uloho.*
Iroko trees are few and far between.

5. *Kpẹ eni ọbẹẹn, sai kpariẹ tẹ oghwa ọye ẹmron na.*
To kill an elephant is not difficult; to carry it home is the problem.
6. *Avba hẹ ẹduhwẹdẹ gbe ikun akpọ hiẹẹn.*
It is impossible to exhaust one's biography in a day.

Application of Parallelism (*Udje eva*) in *Okpẹ Disco*:

These are structural similarities which appear in parallel sentences in *Okpẹ Disco*. According to Olatunji (1984:26); "the sentences express the central idea and complement each other ideationally... The relation between the lexical items in the sentences is equated in order to bring out the implication of comparison". See the examples below as sung by different artistes:

1a. *Uko wo ha vbavbọn rẹn ọreva,*
Ọye ana ha vbavbọn wẹn.
1b. *Obọ rẹ ariẹn rẹn ọmọero,*
Ọye ọmọero ọriẹn rẹn ọwan.
(By Umẹayọvẹne Erhiẹmrọwaan)

Meaning:
1a. The measure with which you gave,
is the measure with which you receive.
1b. The finger you point to the pupil of the eye,
The same finger the pupil of the eye points back to you.

2. *Ọmiọmọn ọye ovbiẹ agẹn,*
Ọdafe ọye ovbiẹ ovbiogbere
(By Benjamin Omirẹghwa)

Meaning:
2. The fertile parent gives birth to a barren,
The wealthy gives birth to a poor person.

3. *Ọke ohwahwa orho te, ohwahwa ọvbọ kpa;*
Ọke oso orho te, oso ọvbọ rhọ;
Ọke uvo orho te, uvo ovbo nyomẹ ọnẹye.
(By Jayife Onohwurighwe)

Meaning:
3. When it is harmattan season, there is cold;
When it is wet season, it rains;
When it is dry season, the sun shines its bit.

Use of Fables (*Ikun eramon*) in Communication

One other interesting feature in oral performances of *Okpẹ Disco* is the use of fables to teach moral etiquette. Not only does it illustrate, illuminate and present the theme in subtle mode to listeners, it also characterises the textual medium with indirect message to concerned individuals and leaves the interpretation and application for the audience. Fables in *Okpẹ Disco* are performed in *call and response* pattern where the cantor recites the story line and the chorus sings a regular *refrain* as response to the *call*. An excerpt of *Ęghęlę ọrhọ do phan* (When a favour is enormous) track by Sylvester Ojọba is given below as an example:

    Solo: *Ęghęlę ọrhọ do phan,nę oghini kpę ohworho.*
    Refrain: *Ukpe rę ęghęlę ono kpe mę, okpę ọre eru rięn.*
    Solo: *Are inę ughe, Okpę mę, are kerhọ!mie seme gbę ikun orhuę.*
    Refrain: *Ukpe rę ęghęlę ono kpe mę, okpę ọre eru rięn.*
    Solo: *Orhuę rę orię ibefi,ọrhọmeręn ugbo iroba rę ọtorhę.*
    Refrain: *Ukpe rę ęghęlę ono kpe mę, okpę ọre eru rięn.*
    Solo: *Obaro erharen na,ogbon ohrun rhọye.*
    Refrain: *Ukpe rę ęghęlę ono kpe mę, okpę ọre eru rięn.*
              etc, etc.

Meaning:
    Solo: When a favour is too enormous, it kills one.
    Refrain: Rather than my generosity to kill me, it should kill the recipient.
    Solo: Look! my Okpę people, listen! I want to tell the story of a hunter.
    Refrain: Rather than my generosity to kill me, it should kill the recipient.
    Solo: A hunter who went on hunting saw a burning rubber plantation.
    Refrain: Rather than my generosity to kill me, it should kill the recipient.
    Solo: In the fore of the fire was a wound boa.
    Refrain: Rather than my generosity to kill me, it should kill the recipient.
              etc, etc.

The full text of the above story enunciates what people do to their benefactors in return for their assistance. Listeners can best draw their conclusions from the narrative and interpretation of the fable. However, the refrain *"Rather than my generosity to kill me, it should kill the recipient"*, is a wish by the benefactor against evil activities of ingrates.

Digression (*Enudje*) as Textual Variety
It is a temporary wander from the main theme of the music to provide spice of variety, a relief from tragic scenes and to create suspense before its eventual return to the original theme. While this textual technique is common in *Okpę Disco* particularly in the unfolding of the narrative, it is by no means an extensive focus as it is short with infinitesimal emphasis. One of the forms of digression is praise speech for patrons, well-wishers and the

affluent in the society. For example, the following is a spoken text by Stephen Biokoro in his album *Are iromo* (With hold your actions):
Orhomu rẹn Okakuro Paulinus Omọkpokpọse Akpeki,
The Ugo of Okpẹ kingdom.
Userhumu ru wa yẹ ẹboijoro Okpẹ;
Obobaro wuna nyan.
Meaning:
May it be well with Chief Paulinus Omọkpokpọse Akpeki,
The Ugo of Okpẹ kingdom.
For your generosity to Okpẹ musicians;
You will always make progress.

Figures of speech such as proverbs and wise sayings are also inserted as digressions usually in spoken format to achieve any of the objectives stated earlier. Sylvester Ọjọba sang the following in his album *Akpo ahuaren* (Life in the past):
Avba mẹrẹn uphrophro onuko riaa;
Avba mẹrẹn edi uo kponroon;
Ọrẹ wu na ho riẹn, wu djeyi.
Meaning:
Nobody gets a piece of your plantain to eat;
Nobody gets some palm fruits from you;
In whose care will your old age be?

Plantain and palm fruits are staple food of the Okpẹ people which are common acts of generosity. In this context, these items represent all forms of benevolence. The above example is a wise saying that encourages generosity for what it earns individuals in the future. It also teaches foresightedness for old age, a stage in life that is relatively helpless and frequently dependent on people, sometimes who have been empowered to shoulder the responsibility. Since old age is a necessary stage in life circle, this digression admonishes individuals to plan for it during active years in life through benevolence to children, siblings, relations and neighbours.

Hyperboles (*Edje vrẹn ovban*) as Choice of Words in the Music

"This is a language technique deliberately and obviously exaggerated for effect. It makes an idea seem larger, better or worse than it really is (Idolor, 2001:322). See the following example in *Okpẹ Disco* as used in praise singing by Godwin Idolor in his *Madam Ofis Ọbọtojare Oriki* album:

1. *Ekpeti orimi inene,*
   Obẹ Inọnkon ọye onurhe

Meaning:
Mummy's casket
Was imported from abroad.

The above example was at the instance of Madam Ọfis Oriki's funeral who had a befitting burial from her children and relations. That the casket was beautiful and expensive, the artiste ascribed foreign manufacture and imported status to the casket.

Another example of a hyperbole is drawn from the stages of preparation for the building of the Ultra Modern *Okpẹ* Palace in Orerokpẹ which was completed in 1997. Senator Chief David Ọmueya Dafinonẹ played a notable role in the project. An *Okpẹ Disco* artiste, Sylvester Ojọba in his album *Aghwẹlẹ Orodje* (Orodje's Palace), described the building process as follows:

> *Ovẹrẹn (Senator Chief Dafinonẹ) riẹ Eko;*
> *Orho fonu riẹ inọkon.*
> *Iyibo re irhẹ iruo kparobọ,*
> *Asẹni aye vbẹ ọye.*
> *Ọnana rẹ miata na, unu mẹ ọye orho jiri.*
> *Rẹ atana, iyobo na erhene.*

Meaning:
He (Senator Chief Dafinonẹ) left for Lagos,
And phoned abroad that,
The most competent European builders,
Should be sent to him urgently.
It is rather more delayed in my speech;
      Speedily, the European builders arrived.

For the building of the palace, Senator Chief Dafinonẹ contacted the prestigious Italian construction company, G. Cappa Plc, for the project. It is a foreign firm that has been in Nigeria long before the plan for the project and not that it was speedily invited as stated by the artiste. Again the artiste stated that the time it took him to narrate this issue in the song was longer than the time of negotiation and the arrival of the company to start the project in Orerokpẹ which qualified it as a hyperbole.

Similes (*Edje họ họ emrun*) as Performance Style

Similes are comparisons of one thing with another and are commonly found in *Okpẹ Disco* texts. Their uses can be broadly divided into two groups: 1) Similes that modify adjectives as shown in the following example by Umẹayọvẹne Ẹrhiẹmrọwaan:

> *Ughwaro oruẹ ogbegbon,*
> **Ọhọhẹ isọn rẹ oso okpẹri;**
> *Ovbẹ ọrọ mẹriẹn rovbo dje erhẹrhen fughwẹẹ.*

Meaning:
The face of an evil-doer,
Is like an excreta;
No one sees it without spitting.

2). Similes that modify verbs as shown in the following example by Stephen Biokoro:
Omamẹ odẹ **ohwe ghwẹ igede.**
Meaning:
    A good name *sounds louder than the volume of a membrane drum*

Application of Metaphors (*Odjegba*) in the Lyrics

Metaphors describe objects, actions or situations imaginatively with words or phrases "that relate to man's physical environment as well as to man's encounter with various creatures (Nketia, 1974:200)" in order to show that they have the same qualities and to make the description more forceful. Idamoyibo (2006) upholds this position in his description of *Igoru* music of the Okpẹ which employs imagery to critique societal ills and expose deviant members of the society. *Okpẹ Disco* artistes also employ this language technique in their compositions. See the following example by Kharlin Ẹdoja in his album *Iroro* (wisdom):

Mẹmẹ Ikharlin, uloho mie ruẹ,
Bẹmẹdẹ, bẹmẹdẹ, ovbo vrẹ rhẹ etuu.
Meaning:
    I Kharlin, am an iroko tree,
    Forever and ever, cannot be subdued in a hip.

The above example of a metaphor shows that the artiste is destined for greatness and never can any obstacle retard or terminate his music career.

Use of Foreign/Borrowed Words in Textual Composition

Of all typologies of traditional music in Okpẹland, *Okpẹ Disco*, for its popular entertainment nature, is mostly known for the use of foreign words. Artistes use this technique in order to attract the interest of non-native speakers and widen the scope of popularity of the music. It also provides a mode of variety in the presentation of ideas, thereby avoiding monotony in thematic delivery. The most common source of foreign words in *Okpẹ Disco* is Pidgin English which is generally spoken and understood in the area. Below, is an example of this by Godwin Idọlọr in his album titled *Ogbikun* (Gossiper):

    Una wẹn dey make aproko dey follow town,
    Aproko no good o oo.
    You leave your own life,
    Na another person own you come dey judge;
    E no good – o!
    Meaning:
    You rumour mongers around town,
    You set aside your personal issues,
    And subject somebody's matters to gossip;
    It is not good!

Another source of borrowed words is pure English language which is Nigeria's *Lingua franca*. See the following example by Sylvester Ojoba in praise of Rev. Fulman Akpere, the Chairman of Okpẹ Local Government from 1999 to 2000.

Ohworho rẹ okpokpiruo,
Obọ ri jẹ ighwe,
Ọrhẹ ighwe na usun.
Akpere ọvọ ame irheri
Our God-sent chairman.

Meaning:
Anybody who attacks you,
The hand that opens a door
And the door itself move together.
Akpere, you are the only one we recognise;
Our God-sent chairman.

Sometimes, the English word is pronounced with *Okpẹ* intonation as shown in the following example by Ọmọghwigho Okpigbẹn:

Omizu rẹ okpokpẹ omizu,
Ejẹ orhon ọna!
Idraiva rẹ okpokpẹ idraiva,
Ejẹ orhon ọna!

Meaning:
A relation who attacks a relation,
Let him hear this!
A driver who attacks a fellow driver,
Let him hear this!

Words are also borrowed from other Nigerian languages for purposes of praise singing of non-*Okpẹ* speakers and as a style for wider dissemination of the music. Stephen Biokoro, in the following example, used Yoruba words as interpolations in his album, *Ọmọge,* when he cautioned men on promiscuity:

Oni jibiti, oniwayo;
Olo o fofo;
Ọmọge o, Ọmọge o,
You chop my money run away.

Meaning:
You are fraudulent and deceptive;
You are a gossiper;
Beautiful lady, Beautiful lady,
You enjoyed my money and ran away.

Lengthening of Syllables (*ukorẹ ẹmron ẹ lọ rọ*) in *Okpẹ Disco* Texts

Like everyday speech, *Okpẹ Disco* artistes sometimes lengthen the last syllable of the last word in a musical sentence mostly at points of pulse.

Sometimes the vowel which lengthens the last syllable is different in sound from the last letter of the original word. See the following example by Jayife Igele in his album titled *Me na chẹ oja ọna*(I will avenge this adversity):
Me na chẹ oja ọna- o - o - o
Okpẹ, are gba kerhọ, mẹ -o - o - o – o
Ijoro Okpẹ ọsama phia- o - o – o
In everyday speech, the above example would be as follows:
Me na chẹ oja ọna,
Okpẹ are gba kerhọ mẹ,
Ijoro Okpẹ ọsama phia.
The lengthening of the syllables does not utter the meaning of the word, rather it enables the textual line to balance-up with the musical phrase and provides a well-rounded poetic phrase that is acceptable in the society.

In the daily language of the people, the word *rẹ* is used only in apologetic, non-affirmative case, where the negative response is presented in a mild mode. For example, instead of:
1. *Obiomuu,* it is sung *Obiomurẹ*
2. *Oserhọọ* it is sung *Oserhọrẹ*

Meaning:
1. It is not bad.
2. It is not appropriate.

The word *rẹ* which has no precise meaning in the people's lexicon is often used by artistes as textual character of *Okpẹ Disco* music and the subtle purpose of commercial/entertainment language. Godwin Idọlọr has the following example in his album, *Ejimẹvbo Special* (1996).
Egodo orho din, are vba gbeyen rẹ;
Egodo orho gbe, are vbe hwerhie rẹ;
Ibiamon ohirin, are vba hwẹ osa oghwaa,
Orẹ ọtobọ mai damẹ na,
Osa ukpẹ ọrhọrhe, are vba hwaye rẹ.
Uruemru ọrana oserhọ rẹ,
Uruemru ọrana ọwiẹn rẹ.

Meaning:
When the compound grows with weeds, you do not clear them;
When the compound is dirty, you do not sweep;
When the month ends, you do not pay your rent;
The one I regret most,
When light bill comes, you do not pay.
These acts are not appropriate,
These acts are not mature.

Exclamations (*Ukperi*) in Textual Presentation
Exclamations in *Okpẹ Disco* are words uttered suddenly and loudly some of them have no specific textual meaning but are understood by members of

the ensemble and the audience in the performance context. They are designed to balance musical phrases or arouse interests where the need arises. Situations where some popular exclamations may have specific societal meanings, they are employed outside the usual context to stimulate serious and active presentation of *Okpẹ Disco* music performances. These exclamations include: *Akpọ, Nene, Ughe, Erhi, Dọ, Ominimini, Hwaya, Oma, E,* etc. The following is an example by (Ojọba 1997) in the track 'Ọmo ene whu riẹn' of his album titled *Be kind:*

    Nẹ ọmo ene whuriẹn, **akpọ***?*
    Nẹ ọmo ene whuriẹn, **wẹnẹ***?*
    Omizu mi vbori, ọyọ rhẹre mẹ rhẹ ada;
    Nẹ ọmo ene whuriẹn, **e***?*

Meaning:
    In whose care shall we die, *life?*
    In whose care shall we die, *wẹnẹ* (name of his band)*?*
    My close relation has publicly betrayed me;
    In whose care shall we die, *Yes* (oh)?

Elements of Elision (*Etinẹmron*) in *Okpẹ Disco* Sentences

Elision is the omission of a syllable or vowel as a convention of some languages. In the Okpẹ language for example, variations exist in versions of spoken and written presentations where the textual features in spoken variant are characterised with elision. Artistes perceive oral performances of *Okpẹ Disco* as platform for intra, inter and extra communications with performance group members, the audience and even supernatural beings and thus use the spoken variant for lucid understanding. In addition to effective communication, elision is appropriately underscored in oral performances to achieve highly prized oratory.

Features of *Okpẹ Disco* text are not different from usual speech in Okpẹ language which is characterised with frequent omission of one of any two border vowels belonging to two separate words. Most often, the last vowel of the first word is eliminated while the first vowel of the next word is retained. See the following example:

    Normal writing: *Siyẹ avbaye*
    Text for singing: *Siy' avbaye.*
Meaning:
    Sit there.

Michael Enughwure in his album *Atẹ Okpẹ gba,* sang the following text showing elision.
Written format: *Ẹghware Okpẹ rẹ ọgbare, egbobọ hiẹn Okpẹ nẹ iyibo adjẹ.*
Text for singing: *Ẹghware Okpẹ* **r' ọ***gbare, egbobọ hi'* **Okpẹ, n' iyib' a***djẹ*
    Meaning:
        In a gathering of Okpẹ people,

Instead of the Okpẹ language, they speak English.

Conclusion

Textual features are highly characteristic of African oral performance where its fundamental responsibility is to clearly communicate ideas of artistes who, sometimes, are the mouth piece of the masses. Purposeful choice of vocabulary for contextualised scenario is a core rationale for relevant textual features necessary for realistic performances in the people's culture.

Okpẹ Disco, a neo-traditional entertainment music genre in the Niger Delta region of Nigeria, is characterised with a fusion of indigenous and contemporary music idioms. Textual features such as parables, parallelisms, similes, borrowing of words, and elisions are prominent elements of its performance. Like everyday speech making, these textual features in the music, qualify the communication with aesthetic content that galvanise the theme of the music for comprehension. Its commercial essence through disc recordings and public performances, demands that *Okpẹ Disco* artistes be mature and effective in the art of language handling to guarantee good patronage and success in their music career.

Notes

1. Okpẹ, the sampled area for this research, is a territory, people and culture. Its territory which lies within latitude 05^0 33' 46" and 05^0 57' 41"north of the equator and within longitudes 05^0 30' 08" and 05^0 55' 05" east of the Greenwich Meridian (Fellow's map, 1928) is located in the Central Senatorial District of Delta state, Niger-Delta region, Nigeria. It has a landmass of 1,228.94 square kilometers, which comprises two hundred and four (204) towns and villages. Based on the official 2016 United Nations Population Census projection, Okpẹ has seven hundred thousand (700,000) people as at 2019 spread over Okpẹ, Sapẹlẹ, part of Uvwiẹ and part of Ethiope East local government areas of Delta state. This population is distributed within thirteen (13) traditional administrative districts with Orerokpẹ as the ancestral headquarters where an *Orodje* (Monarch) is the arrow head of routine administration of the entire kingdom (Idọlọr 2019:8).

2. Ọfọkpẹlẹ Samson Ogborode, (a.k.a. *Agboro*) born on the 5th February, 1948 in Ibada-Ẹlumẹ) is known as the first to practice *Okpẹ Disco* music in Okpẹland in 1977. In recent times, there are over forty-five of such ensembles in the area.

3. This artiste is different from the author of this article. References made in his regard are distinguished in his artistic contributions while those of the author are scholarly.

References

Abimbola, W. (1977). *Ifa Divination Poetry.* New York: NOK Publishers Ltd.

Akpabot, S. E. (1998). *Form, Function and Style in African Music.* Ibadan: Macmillan Nigeria Publishers Limited.

Ekwueme, L. E. (2001). 'Composing Contemporary African Choral Music: Problems and Prospects'. In Omibiyi-Obidike, M. A. (Ed.) *African Art Music in Nigeria: Fela Sowande Memorial.* Ibadan: Stirling-Horden Publishers (Nig.) Ltd. Pp. 16-57.

Hood, M. (1971). *The Ethnomusicologist.* New York: McGraw-Hill.

Idamoyibo, I. O. (2006). 'Igoru Music and its Historical Development in Okpẹ Culture.' *Awka Journal of Research in Music and the Arts (AJRMA).* Vol. 3, p. 114-131.

Idolor, E. (2019). *Ede Okpe: A Dictionary of Okpe Names with Pronunciation Guides and Concepts.* Ibadan: Kraft Books Limited.

Idolor, E. G. (2014). *The Traditions of Okpẹ Disco and the Challenges of Modernism.* Abraka: Delta State University Press.

Idolor, E. G. (2002). 'Okpẹ Disco: Its Emergence and Performance Practice'. *South African Journal of Musicology (SAMUS).* Vol. 22, Pp: 13-27.

Idolor, E. G. (2001). *Okpẹ Disco: A Neo-Traditional Nigerian Popular Music Genre.* An Unpublished Ph.D. Thesis, University of Ibadan, Nigeria.

Idolor, E. G. (1993). 'African Music as Culture Indicator – A Case Study of Okpẹ Traditional Songs'. *Journal of African Performing Arts.* Vol. 1, No. 1. Pp: 45-59.

Nketia, J. H. K. (1974). *The Music of Africa.* New York: W. W. Norton and Company, Inc.

Okpẹwho, I. (1990). 'The Study of Performance'. In Okpẹwho, I. (Ed.) *The Oral Performance in Africa.* Ibadan: Spectrum Books Limited. Pp: 1-20.

Olatunji, O. (1984): *Features of Yoruba Oral Poetry.* Ibadan: University Press Ltd.

Omojola, B. (2006). *Popular Music in Western Nigeria: Theme, Style and Patronage System.* Ibadan: Institut Français de Recherche en Afrique.

Interview

Ogorode, O. (1999). *The Emergence of Okpẹ Disco Music.* Oral Interview in Ibada-Elume.

Discography

Biokoro, S. (1994). 'Akpọ na ọdophan' track in *Ọmọge* album.

Biokoro, S. (1994). 'Ọmọge' track in *Ọmọge* album.

Biokoro, S. (1995). 'Omamẹ ọmọ' track in *Obedient Child* album.

Biokoro, S. (1995). 'Are iromo' track in *Obedient Child* album.

Biokoro, S. (1996). 'Late Godwin Jessa' track in *Greedy Man* album.

Biokoro, S. (1997). 'Atẹtẹ' track in *Atẹtẹ special* album.

Biokoro, S. (1998). 'Udogun' track in *Udogun* album.

Biokoro, S. (1999). 'Ọghwọrẹ oma' track in *Otega 2000* album.

Edoja, K. (1993). 'Iroro' track in *Iroro Special* album.
Edoja, K. (1993). 'Oma aye' track in *Iroro Special*.
Edoja, K. (1996). 'Owanrien emron' track in *Beware of bad talk* album.
Enughwure, M. (1994). 'Nyan wo rhe' track in *Ate Okpe gba special* album.
Enughwure, M. (1994). 'Ate Ykpu gba' track in *Ate Okpe gba special* album.
Erhiemrowaan, U. (1995). 'Evbe le omo adaa' track in *Ogho ifo* album.
Eyagha, P. (1994). 'Tru to God' track in *Gbale me special* album.
Eyagha, P. (1996). 'Onye akpo okpahen ufi' track in *For your mind na sugar factory* album.
Idolor, G. (1994). 'Ore omo orheri' track in *Ore omo orheri special* album.
Idolor, G. (1994). 'Ogbikun' track in *Ore omo orheri special* album.
Idolor, G. (1995) 'Eji me vbo' track in *Eji me vbo* album.
Idolor, G. (1995). 'Eji me te emaren' track in *Eji me vbo* album.
Idolor, G. (1995). 'Eji me te ede erhi' track in *Ominimini special* album.
Idolor, G. (1996) 'Tenant and Landlord' track in *Tenant and Landlord* album.
Idolor, G. (1998) 'Otu re awanrien emron' track in *Ono gi jiri* album.
Idolor, G. (1999). 'Ukore omo owhu' track in *Ene o wan rue* album.
Idolor, G. (1999). 'Ene owan rue' track in *Ene o wan rue* album.
Idolor, G. (1999). 'Meriaa meriaa' track in *Ene o wan rue* album.
Ojoba, S. (1993). *Gov. Felix Ibru* album.
Ojoba, S. (1997). 'Otu re erue odandan' track in *Be kind* album.
Ojoba, S. (1997). 'Henry Emajegbe' track in *Be kind* album.
Ojoba, S. (1997). 'Akpo ahuanren' track in *Be kind* album.
Ojoba, S. (1998). 'Me vbaire are' track in *Okpe special* album.
Ojoba, S. (1999). 'Oma akpo me' track in *The Indomitable Palace* album.
Okokoroko, E. (1987). 'Ebe Okpe' track in *Ebe Okpe* album.
Okokoroko, E. (1987). 'Ane me ojeri me' track in *Ebe Okpe* album.
Okokoroko, E. (1988). 'Ugo ofuanfon' track in *Ugo o fuanfon* album.
Okpigben, O. (2000). Akpo ogbe eva track in *Repentance* album.
Omireghwa, B. (1999). 'Orherhe' track in *Orherhe special* album.
Onohwurighwe, J. (1987). 'Me na che oja ona' track in *Me na che oja ona* album.
Onohwurighwe, J. (1987). 'Oke emrun ote' track in *Me na che oja ona* album.

Glossary

S/N	Word	Meaning
1.	Call and Response	Antiphonal singing of solo singer answered by a chorus.
2.	Cantor	Lead singer in a choral group.
3.	Chorus	A body of singers who sing the *response* to the cantor's *call*.
4.	*Efuen*	Cadence of finality.

5.	*Efuenhin*	Cadence of total finality.
6.	*Efueosedọn*	Cadence of non-finality.
7.	*Ehọ ekporo*	Music for spirit manifests.
8.	*Ekele*	Narration - a compositional technique in the second section (B) of *Okpẹ Disco* music performance structure.
9.	*Ighọphan*	Narrative and contemplative music genre of the Okpẹ people.
10.	*Igoru*	Narrative music genre that identifies bad behaviours and helps to correct same amongst individuals, group of individuals or communities.
11.	*Ijurhi*	Secular music drama that enacts aspects of Okpẹ culture.
12.	*Ikpeba/Ipayan*	Secular music genre originally performed by son-in-laws for entertainment in funeral ceremonies of their father/mother in-laws.
13.	*Ikpokporo*	Playing of musical instruments. It is the third section in *Okpẹ Disco* music performance structure.
14.	*Iphri*	Dirge.
15.	*Irhirẹn*	The end/conclusion of music.
16.	*Ọtonrhọ*	Beginning. It is the first section in *Okpẹ Disco* music performance structure.

6

Songs for Living
Interrogating the Complexion of Song-Texts and Healing in Nigeria

Prof. 'Femi Adedeji[*] & Prof. Charles Onomudo Aluede[*]

Introduction

This chapter interrogates music performance and healing in Nigeria. In pursuit of this objective, relevant literature was reviewed, while field investigation in South-Western and Mid-Western Nigeria was carried out. The Yoruba speaking people of South-Western and the Esan speaking people of Edo State in the Mid-Western region of Nigeria were investigated. In the course of the study, an interesting narrative evolved - it was discovered that music in Nigeria is beyond entertainment. Hence, from birth songs to dirges, satirical songs to those of allusion, the motive is whole and incorporates healing. The study draws inferences from Yoruba and Esan ethnic groups, which serve as relevant examples in this discourse. It is thus, concluded that for us to appreciate the healing effects of music, a retrospective look at music in the Nigerian traditional society is necessary because learning from the past is essential for laying a solid foundation for contemporary music healing practice.

In this work, the researchers have struggled with many thoughts on what is to be the working theme of this presentation. In trying to mull over such issue, topics like: "Through tension to repose: exploring the use of music in African traditional music healing" or "Let's song bathe ourselves in music, it heals" have come up at some points. In all these, much care was taken to avoid the term 'music therapy'. Music therapy as a generic term may not find a good place in African discourses. For example, music in traditional Africa is beyond entertainment and it is ritual/religious rites knitted. This provides

---

[*] Obafemi Awolowo University, Ile-Ife
[**] Ambrose Alli University, Ekpoma

the understanding for the reason why the different strands of African music perform healing functions.

In addition, Levitin's treatise (2014:56) maintained that by extension, humans who enjoyed singing, dancing, and marching together were drawn to it, attracted to it, and practiced it for thousands of hours were those who were the victors in any battles in which such drill conferred an advantage. The strong emotional, even neuro-chemical pleasure that resulted from synchronized movement may well have had a pre-historic antecedent. Our hunter-gatherer ancestors may have danced around the campfire before and after the hunt. By rehearsing their movement, they gained precision in their action and were thus more likely to succeed. And taking down a large swift mammal with handheld tools likely required the coordinated movement of many accomplices. Modern army drill is probably an extension of this prehistoric behaviour. Music traditionally has been characterized not only by sound but by *action,* and by *interaction* among makers of music-dance.

In another dimension, while sharing some thoughts with Pavlicevic, Meki Nzewi, (2001:1) maintains that: "Music in Africa is healing and what is music therapy other than some colonial import? Why is music therapy separate from music-making?" In the first case, to key into music therapy as it is presently is to accept its traditions of origin, scope of practice, training of practitioners and indeed the tenets of the practice of music therapy in the occidental world. We need to be reminded that in Nigeria and most other African states, there is belief in multiple variables in disease causation a mixture of environmental, cultural and clinical factors reacting simultaneously in an atomistic form. While further drawing our attention to the salient use of music in healing in Africa, Nzewi (2002:2) says that "preventive health includes scheduled and mandatory environmental cleaning avoidance rite to ward off evil forces (human and spirit mien), as well as constant musical arts theatre that coerces mass participation, annual group spirit purgation, music-drama (New year rites, compound hygiene etc.)".

As upheld by Aluede (2009; 2010), there is either no need for a new term to qualify one of the general attributes of African music or that there is a need to carve out a more realistic name for music healing and healing activities with music in Africa. The reasons for such opinions are not far from the fact that the concept, form and context of music healing in Africa need to be fully examined and distinguished. If we were to holistically examine African music performance in African context, we will, without doubt, see music in therapy and music as therapy. To most ethnomusicological scholars, music in therapy addresses the use of music and other associated rituals in bringing about healing while music as therapy is about the sole use of music to bring about total well-being of the individual. The need for an encapsulating nomenclature to envelope the connection between music and healing or simply put, music healing activities in countries of the orient and Africa has led to terms such as ethnomusic therapy and Medical Ethnomusicology. However, it is our belief that much could still be done in this direction. Rigorous thinking is most needed now because according to Culliford (2005:3), "Research and experience show that people have religious and spiritual resources to draw on when needed". Music to the African, is not only a social art, but a religious phenomenon. Contingent on this, therefore, to properly appreciate the functions and features of African music, a collaborative research is needed. The eclectic nature of music in Africa needs to be properly investigated because knowledge like weather condition does not obey national or territorial boundaries and so this issue should not be the concern of musicologists alone.

Disease in African Cosmology

In the opinion of Weil (1998:41), good health implies freedom from disease. Etymologically, it is a general view that disease means "lack of ease" (dis-ease). In African consciousness, disease and ill-health span beyond the *out-of-tune-ness* of the human body to environmental, spiritual cum cultural disconnect (Nzewi, 2002) Here, we will use two hypothetical examples in this segment as illustrations to enable us see how these variables relate with each other. In the Bible, we are told of the story of Moses and the bitter water of Marah river (Exodus 15:22-25), how the river whose water was not fit for drinking was made pure that the Israelites might have good and potable water to live on. Needless to stress that drinking from a polluted pool of water endangers one's health. Today, we hear of polluted fresh water and the resultant destruction of aqua culture in the Niger Delta region of Nigeria. Feeding on such polluted products certainly brings ill-health. In a more spiritual sense, a land could be polluted, if the age-old mores of a people are violated or trampled upon. The resultant effect of such egregious act is disease epidemic which could lead to death.

In Esan as well as in Yoruba cosmology, there are four kinds of disease causation and they are: Natural sickness, sickness caused by witches and wizards, sickness induced by the ancestors and sickness carried over from one's past life (Aluede, 2008). In the same direction, Adedeji (2008) while writing on the beliefs of Christ Apostolic Church, an indigenous Nigerian Pentecostal Church, asserted that 'traditionally, illness is seen in Christ Apostolic Church as being caused by evil spirits, enemies and sin'. It is thought that this issue does not require any further clarifications as Africans. However, in addition to the above, many Nigerian societies believe that poor sense of judgment such as not being in the right frame of mind when appraising issues and poor environmental health are all shades of illness. By environmental health we mean healthy surrounding. This includes safe water, food hygiene, vector control, good waste management, healthy housing among others. In foundation African music classes, students are taught the functions of music in Africa. When such a topic is taught, little or no reference is made to the core overall aim of music in Africa–healing. The silence on the healing potency of African music may be occasioned by the fact that it is expected of every African to know and have such information readily available and so it is superfluous to reemphasize the obvious. African indigenous knowledge systems are replete with communal living. As parts of the characteristic of African music, we often say that:

i. It is a communal property;
ii. There is no clear dichotomy between audience and performers;
iii. Hand clapping, foot stamping; chest drumming are parts of the instrumental resources that form the complete musical gamut during performances.

Be it a conscious or unconscious effort, this collective activity is result oriented and it is hinged on a strong scientific foundation. For example, Levitin (2014:51-52) observed, "In Africa, music is not an art form as much as it is a means of communication. Singing together releases oxytocin, a neurochemical now known to be involved in establishing bonds of trust between people." Levitin's position appears validate our indigenous practices. Here we find a comment which gives much credence to African musical practice which they themselves may consider mundane but has kept them going over centuries.

Analysis of some Healing Song Texts from Esan and Yoruba Cultures

Before going any further in this segment, we would like to define healing. In the view of Becerra (1997:5),

To heal (from *hal*, whole) is to make sound or whole whereas, Esoteric (from Greek *eso*, within Esoteriko) means "from within." Therefore, Esoteric healing may be defined as "to make sound from within," that is to restore health by means of sound or vibratory energy emanating from within the human being.

Music overtly has healing propensities and to the African that is much more music loving, it may function in many more ways than we cannot presently imagine. Human is always singing internally. At times, he/she sings out loudly but quickly looks at the faces of the people around then his/her impulse tells him/her to stop but to later do so in private. In private, most people sing endlessly but if beckoned on to repeat what they have just sung, they quite often feel hesitant. Not very many of us will immediately conjecture the reason for such hesitation. An intuitively prescribed music performed for a particular duration is likely to be abused should the singer honour such requests. In the Nigerian setting, everyone needs music healing.

Although in the time past, the profuse use of music in Africa has been derogatorily documented from the point of abuse, (abuse in the sense that most uninformed spectators feel that much of the Africans' time is spent on music making) it could probably be rediscovered that such notions were based on insufficient knowledge of the primacy of music. In Africa, music occupies eminent position in events from birth to death. In such events, music functions as a conduit for healing purposes alongside entertainment. In what follows, we present musical typologies of the Esan/Yoruba people as reference points to discuss six functions of music with their healing and they are women in labour songs » birth Songs » satirical songs » work songs and dirges. These song typologies have been chosen for logical sequence and their healing attributes. Below is a diagram indicating the song types to be addressed in this work. The Nigerian construct of music making is holistic-entertaining, educating, informing, reforming and healing.

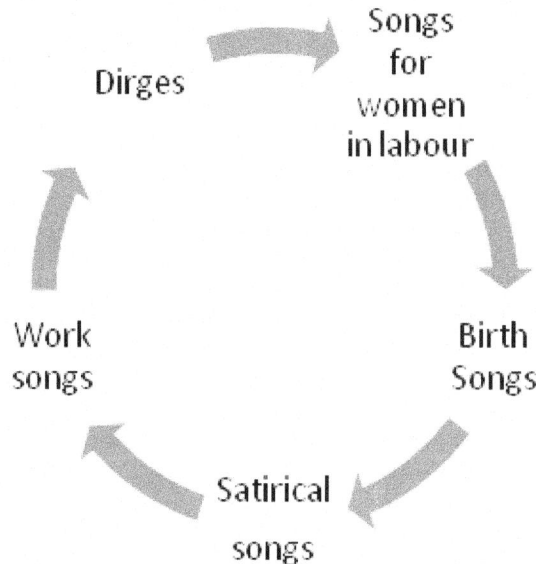

A Diagram of Five Song Types in Healing (Charles Aluede, 2019)

Women in Labour Songs

Moreno (1995) observes that music can and does have emotional and physiological impact on man outside the contexts of traditional cultures. To him, musical enculturation gives all forms of music a symbolic meaning to members of a particular society and culture. In the same vein, Ruzvidzo (1997) says music fulfils a medicinal function when through total involvement, the dance reaches its climax and patients find cure. Music is made to midwife women in labour to safe delivery. Giving an instance of music healing in Western Kenya, Mulindi-King (1990) talks of Kapanga – an institutionalized music that is usually performed for women during delivery. These women that are in labour are treated to a performance of special music by fruitful women in the community to help them reduce the traumatic experience associated with childbirth. Please note that the music is not performed for barren women. Similarly, in Iyayi society amongst the Esan in Edo State of Nigeria, women in labour are treated to songs whose texts extol the importance of children in a family or plead for safe delivery without complications. This practice also exists among the Yoruba of South-western Nigeria. Levitin (2006:223) observes that:

> Inside the womb, surrounded by amniotic fluid, the foetus hears sounds. It hears the heartbeat of its mother, at times speeding up, at other times slowing down. As the foetus hears music, as was recently discovered by Alexandra Lamont of Keele University in the United Kingdom, she found that, a year after they are born, children recognize and prefer music they were exposed to in the womb.

Below are two songs, one each from Esan and Yoruba which are performed for women in labour.

Text in Esan	Translation
Omo ai gbe mean	Oh child, do not kill me
Omo ai gba 'siendo	Alligator seeds, do not kill the Alligator fruit
Omo ai gba 'siendo	Alligator seeds, do not kill the Alligator fruit

This song is performed for women in labour by other women who have also gone through child bearing process. The song is simply performed in a call and response format and at some other times, the call could simply be in the form of just giving the cue which other singers follow. The text of the song says since the many seeds of the alligator pepper do not destroy the entire fruit and indeed its tree, the child in the womb should come out safely without killing its mother. Beyond the melody, the text of the song gives the woman in labour a kind of prophylactic treatment against fear of maternal mortality. In a similar vein, the Yoruba are very philosophical in their cultural expressions, generally. This norm is closely tied to their close relationship with the spiritual forces surrounding them vis-a-vis their engagement. These facts are revealed in all most Yoruba folk songs as would be demonstrated in the brief analysis below.

Yoruba	Translation
Motija 'we abiwere,	I have plucked the *abiwere* leaf,
k'e mi le bi were ooo.	for my child-delivery to be easy.
Gbedeniirokoko;	It is always easy for cocoyam;
aaro mi lorun o.	my delivery shall be easy.

The above song text, a quaternary structure, is a prayer for a woman that is preparing for child delivery among the Yoruba. It features incantation that makes the wishes of the singer efficacious. In Yoruba divination and healing systems, plant leaves are very significant, as it is believed that they possess supernatural powers. The diviners and midwives use them to effect healing, deliverance and to perform other supernatural feats. When someone plucks the right leaf, he/she has secured a supernatural power that is connected with the spirit world. The song text asserts that the singer has plucked the *abiwere* leaf, as a result of which her child delivery must be easy. The last two phrases constitute a metaphysical decree, a form of incantation: *Gbedeniirokoko, a aro mi lorun o.* (Itis always easy for cocoyam; my delivery shall be easy).

A woman in labour is encouraged to sing this song. Based on the easiness experienced by cocoyam, the song implies that the child delivery of the woman in labour must be made easy. The use of onomatopoeia is a common feature in Yoruba incantations. For instance, *bi were* in Yoruba language means deliver easily. *Ewe abiwere* therefore means the leaf that makes one to deliver easily. Hence, *Motija 'we abiwere* (I have plucked the *abiwere* leaf); *k'e mi le bi wereooo* (for my child-delivery to be easy).

Birth Songs

The news of childbirth gladdens the heart of every African and more gladdening is the news of safe delivery devoid of caesarean section or any form of complication. Delivery process and child bearing come with some attendant health challenges on the part of the birthing mother. Treating her to soothing music after delivery also aids in the recuperation process and the song below is an apt example of such birth songs in Esan. Between falling into labour and the news of safe delivery, we see a scenario of moving from instability to stability, pain bearing to relief acquisition-a movement from tension to repose. The song below is an example of birth song.

Text in Esan	Translation
Abiele so ma men bhe 'ho.	Isn't news of birth pleasant to the ears?
Abiele so ma men bhe 'ho.	'Isn't news of birth pleasant to the ears?

This is a short and simple song which asks if the news of safe delivery is not pleasant to the ears. It is in a call and refrain form and it announces the safe arrival of a new member of the family. No doubt, labour pains are often associated with child birth, but the joy of giving birth to a living child knows no bounds. In some cases, child delivery may come with some challenges such as episiotomy cut, bleeding, retained placenta which may prolong a woman's stay with midwives in the delivery room. Song bathing these newly delivered women to congratulatory songs which portray the importance of motherhood attenuates painful memories of labour ward experiences. In a similar vein, the Yoruba example of birth song says:

Yoruba	Translation
Iyaikoko o kuewu o.	Congratulations on your newly born baby.
Ewuinakiipaawodi.	An eagle does not die in a fire outbreak.
Ayo, o kuewu.	We rejoice, congratulations.

This song is of a ternary structure, both textually and melodically. It felicitates with the mother of a newly born baby. *Ikoko* means a newly born baby. Childbirth is believed to be accompanied with possible dangers from which the mother has been delivered, hence the greetings – *o kuewu* meaning thank God for your safety or survival. The second phrase is another form of incantation –*Ewuinakii pa awodi*(An eagle does not die in a fire outbreak). It is common among the Yoruba to reject evils or misfortunes. By such statements as this, a divine metaphysical law that no matter what happens, an eagle cannot die in a fire outbreak. By implication, the woman that gives birth survives such dangers because of the incantation. The third phrase is a recap of congratulatory greetings.

In the opinion of Tucek (2007:3),

> Music and artistic activities provide [the] disabled with such an opportunity and help motivate [them] to join artistic activities. There are families bringing up children with disabilities and those who have suffered psychological stresses and experiences, such as divorce, loss and other kinds of stress...Mothers who take care of disabled children spend most of their time at home looking after their children...Musical activities with their children are a good opportunity for them to strengthen their self-esteem. On the other hand, the disabled person who sings or plays music together with a member of his/her family or a close friend might feel not so lonely and secluded from the community.

In Africa, music is involved in varieties of contexts before, during and after a baby's delivery. Music making as a phenomenon has a wide remit of ministration in human life.

Satirical Songs

In Esan, certain songs are deliberately composed in a disrespectful manner and with wounding and mind piercing words. Such songs are performed for particular persons who go against the laws of the land. The overall motif of such compositions is to psychotherapeutically correct the offender. While talking of the enforcement of morality among the Ga-Adamgbe people of Ghana, Kudadjie (1998:170) opined that music is used as a weapon of public disgrace. He throws more light when he says:

A person can be publicly disgraced by publicly singing out his evil deeds (but without naming him) at community drumming during recreational drumming in the evenings or annual festivals on days specially set aside. On such occasions, names may be called or the group singing may go to the premises of the person being scandalized and sing to his hearing.

He stretches this thought further when he opined that to the uninformed spectator, this musical performance is meant to rubbish and malign the individuals in whose compounds the performance takes place, or whose names are used in the song texts. To such community people, it is one of their major mechanisms to cause tension and also institute repose. First, it draws everyone's attention to a certain irregular conduct. Secondly, it alerts every member of the community that this kind of musical concert could be held in their dishonour, should they transgress the laws of the land and thirdly it serves as a ritual/musical purgation and purification for the transgressors after which they are fully accepted back without any further future reference to their misdeeds. This scenario is replicated in Esan community where when a married woman is proved to have or have had carnal knowledge of another man is taken through a ritual/musical performance to retune her to the basic principles of neighbourliness and proper matrimonial leaving. In this retuning exercise, the song below is an example from the corpus of songs performed for the infidel to dance to. Please observe the texts of the song and the incivility involved in its craftsmanship.

Text in Esan	Translation
Ijonikirio 'lele	It is John who is now squeezing it for her
Orino 'rino	Squeezing, squeezing.
Ijonikirio 'lele	It is John who is now squeezing it for her
Orino 'rino	Squeezing, squeezing.

In Esan cosmology, a married woman is not expected to have sexual relationship with any other man. When once in a while a woman is convicted of this cultural misdemeanour, the woman is believed to have be squeezed and misused. It is believed that a husband will naturally treasure his wife and treat her tenderly during sexual relationship, but the intruder will invade her. This is what is technically portrayed in the song text. Living in fear for breaking the hedge is the precursor of this musico/healing ritual. The adulterer becomes agitated and full of anxiety. And at times could just start confessing her ill deeds. In an effort to heal her, the adulterer is taken round the village in a procession almost nude. In doing this, she will be purged of her impurities as she is once again tuned to community living. Once this is done, that anxiety, agitation and fear are arrested. In contemporary discourses, this type of healing is referred to as Anxiolytic music therapy.

Contrastingly, the Yoruba example portrays in clear terms the picture of a loafer and warns against laziness.

Text in Yoruba	Translation
O ji okoroko, oji okor'odo	A lazy person wakes up without any work
T'obaji a gbo'beka'na	He only wakes up to prepare food
T'obaje'ba tan a se'kunrondo	After eating, he loiters around with his filled stomach
Omoalaretiije'yinawo	A spoilt child who feeds on delicacies
O ji okoroko, oji okor'odo	Lazy person wakes up without any work.

The Yoruba have many satirical songs to condemn unwanted social behaviours. The songs are meant to ridicule the culprits in order that they might be ashamed of their bad behaviours. The song text above which falls within that category, 'abuses' a lazy, indolent person. The Yoruba generally detest and condemn laziness and indolence. The first line addresses a lazy person that refuses to embark on any work. The second and the third lines which state that 'He only wakes up to prepare food, and after eating, he loiters around with his filled stomach', show the activities of the lazy person. The fourth line describes the lazy drone as a spoilt child who likes to feed on delicacies, while the last line is a direct repetition of the first. Indirectly, with this satirical song and similar ones, the Yoruba confront and heal indolence and indiscipline as social diseases, while at the same time encourage hard work and diligence.

Work Songs

For a nursing mother to be fully involved in any serious work or economic activity, her child has to be comfortable first. This comfort may come from having the child bathed, well fed and put in a conducive place. Without these, a child's cry will disrupt the mother's chain of activities for any given day. Therefore, as precursor to work songs, mothers perform lullabies for their children. This performance has common targets and in strict sense, Levitin (2006:9), explains it all lucidly when he remarks "Mothers throughout the world, and as far back in time as we can imagine, have used soft music to soothe their babies to sleep, or to distract them from something that has made them cry". For example in many Nigerian ethnic groups, bathing, feeding and generally tending the baby is work for the nursing mother. Therefore, the lullaby may be playing two roles in this context, soothing the baby and enabling the mother to do more work before and after the baby sleeps. Where music is used on a restless baby as a calmative, a change from undesirable to desirable condition occurs and that's healing. There are core work songs in these two cultures from which we present two examples. We have decided to draw these lines of distinction because work songs are almost extinct and sometimes what appear to be lullabies are wrongly accepted as work songs. These song typologies are commonly seen together because of the theoretical background we have provided over mother and child relationship. These work songs are performed to ease the tension associated with tasks being done and this is what Mereni (2004) classifies as tensiolytic music therapy.

There are a few examples of work songs in Esan, this is understandably so because community work that will necessitate collective musical activities are dying away with great rapidity. On the field, we saw an apt song that stresses the need to read to avoid poverty-stricken life. In this culture, dropping out of school is a bad omen, which is synonymous with wretched life. Early in time, Mongo Beti (1957) in his novel, *Mission to Kala* had captured a scenario where Medza returns to his village in Southern Cameroons after failing his examinations at college to say that the task of reading was far more difficult than using a machete to work in a sugarcane plantation in the harmattan season. This common understanding rules the minds of everyone who dares to take to the art of scholarship. Difficult as it may be, it is more honourable than goofing around and loafing. This song serves as a constant reminder that no matter the difficulty in the task of studying, the pains should be borne in favour of a brighter tomorrow. The song serves to reduce the tension and encourage the individual to be focused so as to avoid being poor later in life. This is an example of a work song which serves to dilate one's capacity to accommodate stress and tension in the face of a tedious task.

Text in Esan	Translation
Me ho ni me tie 'be	I want to read
Me ho ni me tie 'be	I want to read
Me ho ni me tie 'be	I want to read
Ni mealoya so that	I will not suffer

In the Yoruba nation, a different picture emerges. Below is an example of Yoruba work song.

Text in Yoruba	Translation
E jekasise, iselaa se	Let us work, it is profitable to labour
Enibaja'le, s'oun lo b'omo je	Stealing is what is bad.

The indigenous method of getting works done faster and effectively is through corporate or cooperative approach known as *aaro*. It involves a group of people coming together to work in one another's farm in turn. Work songs among the Yoruba are of two categories. There are songs rendered while working on the farm, a building, hunting field, etc. The songs serve as stimulants and catalysts to make works done faster. Others generally encourage gainful employment and hard work. The above song text, a binary form, belongs to the first category and it calls people to work. It implies that no work is bad, but joblessness and stealing are detestable. From Yoruba philosophical point of view, idleness, poverty and stealing are social diseases. This song when rendered during group-farming exercises, boosts the morale of workers and positively transforms the lazy ones who indulge in antisocial activities.

The Healing Potentials of Dirges

Every mortal is a sojourner on earth. In most Nigerian cultures, the maxim 'this world is a market place' is a regular mantra on the lips. Although constant in Nigerian worldview are issues relating to death, no one appears to be ready to accept death whenever it comes. Yet it is commonly believed that no one comes to earth without departing. The sudden death of a family member throws the entire household and neighbours into complete disarray. To retune the shattered families, mechanisms are orchestrated to realign the wounded. Aluede (2019:5) reports such a mechanism in Esan when he opined that:

In times of bereavement, as soon as the departed is buried in the late afternoon, family members and friends gather in the deceased's home with simple musical instruments such as the bell, gourd rattle, samba, thumb piano etc to keep the night with immediate family of the departed. Prescribed dirges are performed for a circle of five days starting from every evening to midnight.

One of such songs often performed on such occasions is *Ole olerie*

Text in Esan	Translation
Ole olerie	He /She has said he is going
Ole olerie	He has said he is going
Ahi ragbon	No one comes to the earth
abharie e	Without departing

The Esan position is akin to that of the Yoruba. The beliefs of the Yoruba about life after death are somewhat peculiar. Possibilities include (1) a paradise-kind of heaven for the departed (2) severe punishment for the evil ones (3) reincarnation (4) participation in the affairs of the living even at death. The song text above, a quaternary structure, depicts belief in the paradise-kind of heaven. It affirms that the father that died has gone to heaven in a peaceful way. The same song is adapted for a mother at death by substituting the word for father with that of mother. The third phrase reveals the manner of death - the man died peacefully in the hands of his children. The last phrase is a direct repetition of the first phrase for emphasis.

Yoruba	Translation
Baba (Mama)awa lo, o r'orunidera	Our Father (Mother) has gone to heaven peacefully
Baba (Mama) awa lo o r'orunidera	Our Father has gone to heaven peacefully
Koku'ku moto, owoomo lo kusi	Not through motor accident, but in the hands of his child
Baba (Mama) awa lo o r'orunidera	Our Father (Mother) has gone to heaven peacefully.

No Nigerian culture talks of death, as the ultimate end of human life pleasantly or joyously. The severance of an old standing and cordial relationship in death is painful and therefore grief laden. The songs used during bereavement relief depression and emotional pains. It is this kind of soothing music performed on such occasions which Mereni (2004) describes as Psycholytic music therapy. This view is attested to when Tousley (2019:1) avers that:

When we are struggling with grief, music can lift us up, take us out of our current mood, and transport us into another time and place. When we cannot find the words, a particular song may express our thoughts and feelings even better than we are able to do. Whether with lyrics or without, music can be used as an escape or respite from our pain, or as a form of relaxation or meditation while we confront our sorrow. Music helps us to remember the one who died, and it can help to bring a sense of balance, peace and harmony into our lives, even if only for a moment.

From the above insight, the fact is corroborated that music heals deep emotional grief and pains; it cheers the bereaved and enhances ontological balance in the family.

Conclusion

In this work, the authors examined five events in human lives, especially in Africa, where music is a major phenomenon. From our background study, we explained that although music making may be seen as a means of entertainment, it is however focus-driven and highly functional. It is deep rooted in the understanding of providing healing at diverse dimensions and on different levels. By this, we mean that music making in Africa is not just a spectacle for spectators but a healing agent.

The paper has further reaffirmed why music making in Africa is for life's sake as against music for art sake as practised in Western cultures. From the two ethnic groups selected, it could be concluded that music is used as medicine and tool to stimulate, comfort, encourage, pray, invoke, provoke supernatural causations. These insights account for the reason African traditional music can never be fully understood without its functional and metaphysical dimensions.

References

Adedeji, 'Femi (2008). 'The Theology and Practice of Music Therapy in Nigerian Indigenous Churches: Christ Apostolic Church as a Case Study', *Asian Journal of Theology*. India. 22 (1). 142 – 154.

Aluede, C.O. (2009). 'Bibliographical Sources on Music Therapy in Nigeria'. *Voices: A World Forum for Music* 9 (3).

Aluede, C.O. & Eregare, E.A. (2009). 'Music Text and Therapy: The Potency of Selected Iyayi Songs of the Esan'. *AMA Journal of Theatre and Cultural Studies*, 4(1).83-96.

Aluede, C.O. (2009b). 'Towards the Technological Use of Music Therapy for Nation Building in Nigeria: Some Insights'. *AJAH African Journal of arts and Humanities.*

Aluede, C.O. (2010). 'Some Reflections on the Future of Music Therapy in Nigeria'. *Journal of Language, Technology & Entrepreneurship in Africa. A Cross Disciplinary Journal of United States International University, Kenya.* 2(1) 36-55.

Aluede, C.O. (2010). *Music as Therapy by Iyayi Society of Edo State, Nigeria.* Berlin Germany: Verlag Dr. Muller Publishers.

Aluede, C.O. (2019). 'Second Burial in Esan Weltanschauung Edo State of Nigeria: A Retrospective and Prospective Interrogation'. At a Seminar Organized by the Catholic Diocese of Uromi, Edo State on the 14th of August, 2019.

Becerra, J. (1997). Psychocentric Healing: Making Sound from Within, an Introductory Guide to A. A. B.-D. K.'s Exoteric Healingwww.ngsm.org html, Retrieved January 2, 2019.

Culliford, L. (2005). Healing from Within: Spirituality and Mental Health. Https//multifaiths.com, html, Retrieved May 1, 2019.

Iyeh, M.A. & Aluede, C.O. (2005). 'An Exploration of the Therapeutic Potency of Music and Dance in Ichu-Ulor Festival of Asaba People'. *Nigerian Musicological Journal"*1 (1) 124 –142.

Kudjadjie, J.N. (1998). 'How Morality was enforced in Ga-Adamgbe Society'. In Ade Adegbola (ed.) *Traditional Religion in West Africa.* Ibadan: Sefer Books Limited. 170-176.

Levitin, D. J. (2006). *This is your Brain on Music.* London: Penguin Books Ltd.

Levitin, D. J. (2014). *The World in Six Songs.* London: Aurun Press.

Mereni, A. E. (2004). *Music Therapy in Medical History.* Lagos: Apex Books Limited.

Mereni, A. E. (2007). *Music Therapy: Concept, Scope and Competence.* Lagos: Apex Books Limited

Mongo, B. (1958). *Mission to Kala.* London: Heinemann Books

Mulindi-King, L.C. (1990). 'Music Therapy'. *Lecture Presentation.* Kenyatta University, Nairobi Kenya.

Nzewi,M. (2002). 'Backcloth to Music and Healing in Traditional African Society'. *Voices: A World Forum for Music Therapy.* https//doi.org/ 10.15845/voices.v212.85 Re-trieved May 21, 2020.

Nzewi, M. (2006). 'African Music Creativity and Performance; The Science of The Sound'. *Voices: A World Forum for Music Therapy.*https//www. voices.no/mainissues/mi4006000199.html. Retrieved May 21, 2020.

Tousley, M. (2019). Grief Healing: Useful Information on Care Giving, Grief and Transition for anyone Coping with Loss. Retrieved November 6, 2019.

Tucek, G. (2007). 'Healing Yarns of Music Notes' (HYMN) 2006-2007 Years: Theoretical Background and Main Activities. Retrieved from *http://www.ethnomusik.com/* on August 15, 2019.

Pavlicevic, M. (2001). 'Music Therapy in South Africa Compromise As Synthesis?' *Voices: A World Forum for Music Therapy.* https//doi.org /10.15845.voices. v1i1.43. Retrieved April 3, 2018.

Ruzvidzo, R. (1997). 'Music Therapy in Zimbabwe Facing the Future'. *Conference Paper.* International Centre for African Music and Dance. University of Ghana.

7

The Role and Functions of Music *in Odun Isu/Ijesu* of Akokoland, Ondo State, Nigeria

- Ologundudu, Rotimi Peters[*]

Introduction

Akoko people in Yorubaland attach great importance to festivals, and one of such is *odun isu/ijesu* Yam festival. In celebrating this festival, deities are consulted before, during and after the festival using music as a vehicle. Music, as a medium for this phenomenon, is profusely utilized in the festival to invoke the gods. Hence, the Yam festival is intermingled with music to achieve its ultimate intent and purposes. The paper discusses the role and functions of music in the festival and its attractions for its compliments in the festival. An ethnographic research method using participant, non-participant observation and interview of selected practitioners were adopted and used to elucidate data in this work. The research concludes that the festival in Akokoland is all depended upon by the constant interchange of musical elements.

Akokoland is located in north-eastern part of the frontier zone of Yorubaland. The exact date of the founding of Akoko mini-states was not known in history, but oral sources and traditions suggested that it had grown to a moderately large size with enormous strength from about twelfth century when migration started at Ife in pre-colonial period (Oguntomisin, 2003:1). Thus, Akoko is a geographical expression of people with diverse cultures and it is a description of conglomeration of peoples who live in the region that shared boundaries with Kabba and Yagba (now in the present Kogi State to the north and north east), Owo in the south and Ekiti in the south west.

The Akoko region is sub-divided into five groups on the basis of dialectal spoken categories. The groups are classified below: The first group is the

---

[*] The Polytechnic, Ibadan

Owo-Akokos, which comprised Oka, Ikare, Akungba, Supare, Ifira, Ukpe (now Ipe) Ikpesi (now Ipesi), Oba, Afo, Ikun, Iboropa, Ugbe and Ora. These communities speak dialect of Yoruba phonology that is similar to that spoken in Owo and Ifon areas with negligible variations. It is important to point out that the dialect is generally mutually intelligible with the exception of Ipe. The second group is the Ekiti-Akokos, which comprised Ogbagi, Irun and Ese, etc. These communities speak the same Yoruba dialects as that spoken by the towns and villages of Ekiti. The third group is the Benin-Akokos. The communities are Arigidi, Erusu, Ojo, Oyin, Afin, Oge, Igasi, Aje, Uro and Oso. This group evidently has mixed origins of variations of Benin language. The fourth group is the Akoko-Bangerior Kukuruku. Benin is historically referred to a group that formed a clan comprising Kakumo-Ayanran, Aiyekoba group, Ise and Sosan, Isua, Epinmi, Auga, in addition to a number of satellite villages which all speak Benin dialects akin to those spoken in the Kukuruku/Afenmai area of Edo State. The fifth group is the Kabba-Akoko whose communities are Ikaram, Akunnu, Gedegede, Daja, Efifa and Eshuku (Beeley, (1934: 85-87), Adegbulu, (2004:186-187), Eweka, (1992: 183) *Akoko* literally means a *"Community"*. Despite differences in cultures, the people in Akoko land still retained Yoruba language as lingua franca. In the same vein, traditional festivals, such as *Ajagbo* in Ogbagi, Arigiya in Iyometa Ikare. Ere festival in Oge community, Okeagbe, odun ijesu (yam festival) were and still celebrated in these towns and villages which is a common festival to all communities in Akokoland.

The celebration of *Imana* and *Itegbe* social festivals are done in Akunnu and in Isua, also the celebration of *Ajagbo* was common to towns and villages like Irun, Ogbagi, Afa in Okeagbe, Afin and Ese, while ibegbe or Egbegun (age-grade celebration) and Imole (veneration of rivers) were common to all the people in Akoko. These festivals were always commemorated in between, August and March of every year and intermingled with accompanied music.

Theoretical Framework

This paper adopts the theory of Structural functionalism which sees the society as a complex system whose parts work together to promote solidarity and stability. Structural looks at how the society is structured while functionalism addresses society as a whole entity in terms of the function of its constituent elements, i.e. norm, customs, traditions and institutions. (Emile Durkheim: 1858-1917). While Talcott Parsons, was more realistic and emphatic in defining what he coined out as "structural functionalism" as a single word to connote a single meaning, he described it as a particular stage in the methodological development of society grows into a more fused and coherent entity. From the foregoing, it is evident that a study of music and it functions in *Odun Isu/Ijesu* (Yam Festival) of Akoko brings to the fore the structure of Akoko community and how music in the festival reflects the cultural norms in relation to its environmental and social structure. The emphasis on the role and functions of music within the creative and performance contexts of *Yam* festival, is necessary in order to bridge the gap created by the extensive linguistic work already done and thereby compliment the efforts of the early scholars on *Yam* festival of *Akokoland.*

Music in Nigerian Festivals

Akoko people have a deep heritage attachment with music in various facet of their life, owing to this, this paper seek to evaluate the role and functions of music in *Yam* festival in *Akoko* of Ondo State. Effect of music in this regard cannot be overstressed; this is owing to the fact that music plays an imperative role in the life of an average person in Akoko visa-vis the festivals. Iyeh and Aluede (2005:87) clearly concur that Africans are religious people who go everywhere with their religion, hence, they are always in touch with their gods and music is perceived to be linking function. Vidal (1979) also opined that: those functions of music are often multifarious and multi-tudinal when one looks at a single festival that is, the functions are very numerous and varied from one festival to another. Olusegun (2019) corroborated Vidal in this regard, he sees traditional music in Ekiti State (Yoruba) that: covers different facets of human endeavors. There are various types of traditional music that are specifically organized for ceremonies and festivals in the cultural life of the people. For example, *Ere*, *Ode*,*Osirigi*, *Egungu*n,*Ajagb*o, and *imole* to mention but a few, are festivals celebrated in Akokoland.

Festivals in the lives of Nigerians are unique occasions, not for cultural display alone but for recreation and talent hunt. What makes them unique is no more than their aesthetic qualities and music, the very cord that binds the people securely within the community. In festival and other celebrations, every indigene is actively involved both young, old, male and female. Women involvement in festival celebration is all inclusive except on some occasions where women are exclusively barred from participating as it is seen as taboo. For instance, while writing about the Sango festival in Yoruba land Omibiyi (2005:30-31) stated among other things the role of women in the worship of the deity through music;

> Among the various African peoples, women have been acknowledged as co-participants with men in festival musical performances. They join their male counterpart in choral singing and dancing performed by mixed audience of men and women when they are in procession either to or from the shrine at the onset of the celebration, as well as when they congregate at a particular venue such as village square, market, or at the house of the priest for the entertainment part of the celebration. Apart from playing this general role, they have specialized roles performed mainly by their gender.

According to Emeka:(1985:8) every festival brought out new discoveries both of materials and talents, and our music and musicians grew richer. The festival opened to us our indigenous musical life and enabled us participate in it. We discovered groups and people who then enjoyed wider recognition and patronage.

Okafor (2004) also opined that:

> Festivals in and to most Nigerians is the chain of activities, celebrations, ceremonies, foods, drinks and rituals, which mark the continuity of culture in an environment. These festivals occur at appointed times in the lunar calendar and mark the rhythm of life.
>
> Virtually, every one of them has its characteristic or associated music or dance, which can be found to occur along with other ubiquitous music and dances to give colour and tone to the festival. Within the context of the above, festival and music are indeed inseparable in discussing the subject of this paper since they are applicable to Nigeria traditional festival being celebrated in most parts of the country.

The opinion of various scholars as reiterated above and agreed to by the same, goes in line with the cultural practice of Akoko people in their festival and musical display. Omibiyi (as quoted above) in her opinion about Yorubas as well as other ethnic groups in Nigeria and in Africa in general has music as integral and functional part of their daily life. It permeates every level of traditional life be it social, religion, or ceremonial.

Nkwoka (2002) opines that there are certain tunes and musical instrument that belong solely to certain gods and their worshippers. In agreement with this statement, *Bata, Dundun, Sekere* and *Agogo* are the musical instruments associated with festivals in most part of Yoruba community and Akoko in particular.

Drewel (1954) explained that invocations, praises, poems, music and dance are all essential Yoruba ritual performance in which spiritual forces are actualized. Since festivals are held in honour of deified beings, usually there is ritual music designed mainly to summon and entice the gods to be present at the festivals. Writing in the same vein, Omojola (2010) also reiterated that the constant engagement between the elements of play and spirituality in Yoruba performance provides the setting for understanding the role of music as a mediator between temporal and spiritual domains of existence. Describing music of *Ulo* festival of Asaba, Uche (2005) divides music in festivals into two stages, the first part is a song – like incantations which come in form of prayers, requests, or appeal by the performers and are used to communicate to the gods who they believe manifests themselves through this music. The second and final stage of *Ulo* music performance is mainly social. These songs are meant to educate, correct and to expose the ills of the society, and this involves all members of the community and their invited guest. In Uchu – Ulor festival of Asaba, Iyeh and Aluede (2005) stated the importance of music as the principal point of the festival as the music was been played throughout as long as the festival lasted.

Okafor (2005) could not agree less again when he says that music and dance is a hallmark of every traditional festival, and every traditional festival is also a festival of traditional music and dance. Loko (2005) believes that music serves as a means of entertainment during the period of feasting and drinking that marks the climax of any festival. Music plays a vital part in the invocation of the divine being in festivals in Akoko land. At every facet of the festival in Akoko land music play a very vital roles both in the secret of the inner chamber where libation is poured, and also in the public appearances of the the festival.

Music in *Odun Isu*

Nkwoka (2002) captured the very scenario of *odun isu/ ijesu* when he asserted that:

> There are certain tunes and musical instruments that belong solely to certain gods and their worshipers The Yorubas are singing people, in their singing, which comprises of songs, lyrics, and minstrelsy, they tell stories of the past, the circumstances of the present and the hope and fear of the future. Their songs are embedded in their beliefs, and are employed in almost every sphere of their lives; this includes worship, naming ceremonies, wedding, funeral, wrestling, cultivating the farm, working, going to war, praising the rulers, rocking babies to sleep and in many other activities. Such songs are usually attended by drumming and dancing.

In this yam festival which is commemorative on every August, the date defers from community to community, depending on the dictate of the gods, starts with the men and women rising early in the morning and taking procession to the farm. Prayers are offered to the gods before the yam are dug out of the ground.

From the farm to the town centre where every sons and daughters gathered together to welcome the new yams, one could sense the frenzy of music in the atmosphere with drums and dances (fig.1). The King, chiefs, chief priest, and all miscellanies, welcoming the yam to the palace where libation is poured and prayer offered to the gods by the chief priest with incantation and music accompanied every process of the ceremony. It is worth to be noted here that one could hear the sound of music coming out of the houses dishing out sonorous melody from the aged women. At this juncture, every house in the neighbourhood is at the liberty to cook and eat the yam.

Fig.1 Chief Priest and elders welcoming the new yam with dance. (Photo: Author)

As soon as the priests are done with the ceremony in Kings' palace, the lead singer (male) raises the processional song to indicate the next destination, which is the the field. This is where the King hosts different age groups who perform to entertain the people, and the dignitaries who are in turn pay homage to the King. These simple lyrics are accompanied with instruments; drum and rattle gourd (fig. 2). The folks accompanied him with fantastic comic body movement, invigorating and melisma voices. Below are some of the various songs rendered during the festival:

Text	English meaning
1. *O- popoloro ire.* (Cantor)	- Straight ahead we are moving.
O- popoloro ire. (Chorus)	- Straight ahead we are moving.
O- popo Oba loromemu o (cantor)	- The ceremony is moving to the king's house.
O- popoloro ire. (Chorus)	- Straight ahead we are moving
O- popo Oba loromemu o (cantor)	- The ceremony is moving to the King's house.
O popoloro ire. (Cantor)	- Straight ahead we are moving
O- popoloro ire. (Chorus)	- Straight ahead we are moving

Song of Praise

These songs are rendered when the procession get to the field in front of the king house. It is to pay homage to the gods, thanking him for the past festivals and also imploring his guardians for the year as well.

Text	English meaning
2. *Baba omo,*	Father of children
Sogungun fomo o.	Prepare medicine for the children.
3. *Oni labiku o lo nileyi o*	Today, still birth will disappear from the land
Oni lolomo o jereomo won.	Today, parents will witness the joy of their Children
4. *Enisojuse'mu,*	He who makes eyes makes nose,
Orisa nimaa sin	It is god I will serve.
A dani bo tiri,	He who makes one as he chooses
Orisa nimaa sin.	It is god I will serve
Eni ran niwaye,	He who sent me here on earth,
Orisa ni maa sin.	It is god I will serve.
5. *Orisa gba mi,*	god accept me,
mi o leni kan,	I have nobody
yeye omo ni igbomo.	Mothers accept their children.
Orisa gba mi o ra mi,	God accept me wholly,
Orisa gbe mi leke.	God make me triumph.
Irukere ni igbomo Orunmila,	Horsewhip rescue god child,
Orisa gba mi o ra mi. Orisa	Accept me wholly.

Closing Songs

Parting songs are the ones rendered mostly in the night with the masquerades. It is believed that the masquerade*s (Egungun) are* sent by the ancestors to deliver goodwill to the people, this signifies the end of the festival and the return of the *(Egungun)* to the world beyond.

Text	English Meaning
8. *A simaa rira leeminrin,*	We shall meet again next season,
Odoodun laariyemeti.	Yemeti appears annually.
9. *Orisa jinginjingin,*	*Orisa* full of praises
Orisa mogbo oro kan /2x,	*Orisa* I heard something,
Won ni n wajoye ilesanmi.	That I should be contented at home.

Fig. 2: Musicians *playing during the festival. (Photo: Author)*

Musical instruments used during the festival. (Photo: author)

Role and functions of Music in *Odun Isu-Ijesu* of Akokoland   99

ONI LAA MOO SORO (Today is the Day of Celebration)

Idamoyibo (2005) described Igoru music as:

> A music that moves through a series of fourths and occasionally third and fifth and resolve on the consonance of a perfect fourth cadence, it retains a central tonality. While the upper melody may resolve from the submediant to the tonic, the lower pert may resolve from the submediant to the dominant at a lower octave.

As observed, the music of *Odun Isu* in this festival has almost the same similar pattern as described above. The rhythms are very complex one as most of the songs are rendered in fast tempo except some that are rendered in the king palace (Sacrifice house) to appease the gods.

The rattle and *dundun* keeps the tune and its function as the tine line, which the *agogo* (group) and hand clapping serves as rhythmic instrument. The rhythm pattern of the music is based on simple and compound metres. The rhythmic mode of the music includes the iambic meter where short note is followed by a longer note. An example is a quaver note followed by a crotched or minim note. The trochaic meter is where a longer note is followed by a shorter note and finally, the spondee meter, (note of equal value), example is quaver. Quaver, crotchet - crotchet and minim - minim. The *dundun* drum provides the lower note with steady bass rhythms of minim per beat.

The rhythms is accompanied with handclapping and *sekere* (gourd rattle) these rhythms made used of quaver extensively, semiquaver and crotchet in a very fast tempo and most time, the time signature revolves between *2/2, 2/4* and *4/4*. The songs rendered in kings' houses is rendered in *6/8* time signature.

Conclusion

In conclusion, the paper observed that music occupies an important position in the festival in that through music the folks always believe that their worship is acceptable and their prayers answered. Though *Yam* festival in Akokoland means the period of feasting and merry making, it also plays a very vital and important role in the life of the people and invocation of the divine being. It also suggests that music preserves and transmits the beliefs of traditions of the communities during festivals.

Music in this festival, as deduced, is that the festival is a social phenomenon, used to achieve social cohesion that results in deep sense of communion. This also enables members of the community to be both observers as well as mental participants of the event. In many instances, the function of music reinforces beliefs, customs, and values within a society, often within the context of rituals Mokwunyei (2005).

Although, the various towns that constitute Akoko land celebrate their annual festivals as dictated by ethnicity, kinship, language, and culture; they do so strictly as part of communal life. This speaks volumes for tourism and international opportunities. In addition, this festival provides relaxation of tensions and a feeling of well-being, satisfaction, and renewal of group mutual respects.

References

Adegbulu, F. (2004). *Akoko-Yoruba and Akoko-Edo: An Exploration of Relations between two Akoko Communities in the Pre-Colonial Era*. I n Faboyede,Olusola: *Akokoland before Colonial Rules: Earliest Times to 1900*. International Journals of Arts &Humanity, Bahir Dar-Ethiopia.

Akinjogbin, I. A. & Ayandele, E. A. (1980). 'Yorubaland up to 1800'. In Obaro, I. (Ed.), Groundwork of Nigerian History. Ibadan: Heinemann.

AAU: *African Studies Review*, Journal of the Department of History and International Studies, Adekunle Ajasin University, Akungba-Akoko, Nigeria, Vol. 3, no. 1, 186-187.

Akpabot, S.E. (1986) *Foundation of Nigerian Traditional Music*. Ibadan: Spectrum Books Ltd. Aluede C.O. (2008) *Music Therapy in Iyayi Song*. A PhD Thesis in the Institute of Africa Studies, University of Ibadan. Pp:164.

Awolalu, Omosade and Dopamu, P.A. (2005). *West African Traditional Religion*, Ibadan, Macmillan Co.

Bebey, F. (1999) *African Music: A People's Arts*. Chicago Review Press.

Beeley, J. H.(1934a). *Intelligence Report on the Akoko District*. N. A. I, C. S. O. 26, 29667, Vol.   II

Dopamu, A. P (2005). *West African Traditional Religion*, Ibadan: Macmillan Co

Drewal (1954). *Spiritual Significance of Music* www.xtrememusic.org

Eweka, E. B. (1992). *Evolution of Benin Chieftaincy Titles*. Benin: Benin University Press.

http://www.xtrememusic.org/Idamoyibo I.O.(2005) *Igoru Music in Okpeland: A Study of its Functions and Compositional Techniques* An Unpublished Dmus thesis; Department of Music,Faculty of Humanities, University of Pretoria.

Ikibe, S.O. (1998). *Ekuechi Festival in Ebiraland*. An Unpublished M.A Dissertation, University of Ibadan.

Iyeh, M. A. & Aluede, C.O. (2005). 'An Exploration of the Therapeutic Potency of Music and Dance in Uchu-Ulor Festival of the Asaba People'.*Journal of the Association of Nigerian Musicologists* Vol. 1. Pp: 86-96.

Mokwunyei, J.N. (2005). 'Continuity and Change in Nigeria Festivals: From Culturalto Modern'.*Journal of Association of Nigerian Musicologist*. Pp: 45-7.

Nketia, J. H. K. (1975). *The Music of Africa*. London: Victor Collanas Ltd.

Nkwoka, A.O. (2002). 'Music as Mode of Communication in Nigeria, in the Functional Role of Music in Egungun Festival- Otto Aworiland of Lagos'. *Journal of Association of Nigerian Musicologists* (2005) Vol. 1, Pp: 29-30

Okafor, R.C. (2004). *Music and national integration*. A paper presented at the Faculty of Arts, Delta State University

Olomu, J. (2005). 'Dance as Expression and Communication'.In Ugolo (Ed). *Perspectives in Nigerian Dance Studies.* Ibadan: Caltop Publications (Nigeria) Limited. Pp: 56-58.

Ologundudu R.P. (2014). *Music in Egungun Festival of Ikaram Community, Akoko land of Ondo State.* An unpublished M.A Dissertation, Delta State University, Abraka.

Ogen. (2007). *The Akoko- Ikale: A Revision of Colonial Historiography on the Construction of Ethnic Identity in Southern Yorubaland in History of Africa.* Vol. 34 Pp: 255-271.

Omibiyi- Obidike, M.A. (2005). 'Feminity in Traditional Festivals: The Place of Women in Sango Worship Performance'.*Journal of Association of Nigerian Musicologists.* Vol.1Pp: 29-30.

Omojola O. (2010). 'Rhythm of Gods: Music and Spirituality in Yoruba Culture'.*Journal of Pan African Studies.* Vol. 3, No 5.Pp 29-31.

Olusegun A. O (2019). *A Study of the Neo-traditional Music of Elemure Ogunyemi.* An Unpublished Ph.D Thesis, Delta State University, Abraka.

Oguntomisn, G.O. (2003*).* *Yoruba Townsin Perspective.* In Oguntomisin, G. O. (Ed.).*Yoruba Towns and Cities,*

Uche, M.A. (2005). 'Music in Ulo Festival of Asaba'.*Journal of Association of Nigerian Musicologists.* Vol. 1. Pp: 115-125.

Vidal, T (1997). *The Role and Function of Music at Yoruba Festival.* African Musicology: Current Trends.A Festschrift to J.H.K . Nketia

8

Philosophical Aspects of *Udje* Performance in Delta State
A Study of Chief James Edah Towel Musical Ensemble

Peace Onyenye[*]

Introduction

This chapter examines the philosophical aspects of *Udje* of Urhobo, Delta State, Nigeria. The music contains philosophy; its lyrics potently project the people's culture. Urhobo people in Delta State have the mastery for using of music to philosophize. The music has been reported from time immemorial; its practitioners exhibit skills and expressions that reflect the people's culture. Despite the aesthetic and philosophical values of *Udje* performance as art in expressing the culture of the Urhobo, the music has remained orally preserved. The paper discusses the philosophy of *Udje* using interview to collect primary data from select practitioner. The study utilizes textual analysis to interpret the generated data and found that *Udje* serves as a veritable means for philosophizing in Urhoboland. Philosophically, the music is laced with words of wisdom, proverbs and historical data which promote the people's culture. Therefore, it is recommended that musicological studies should take these attributes into cognizance with a view to achieving a holistic research.

Africans deploy their traditional music among other things to disseminate the philosophical thoughts of their cultural heritage. It is against this backdrop that African musicians are considered philosophers because their music is performed with a view to informing the audience on how to live a good life with the conscious effort while entertaining to make their audience know the meaning of life. African musicians are philosophers; they portray the attributes of philosophers by their musical performance as can be found in their lyrics. According to Hadot (1998), philosophers are persons

---

[*] College of Education, Agbor

that live according to a certain way of life, focusing on resolving existential questions about the human condition, and not someone who discourses upon theories or comments upon authors. Experts in African musicology such as Idolor (2005) and Idamoyibo (2006) indicate that traditional musicians are involved in philosophical discussion while they perform their music and the contents of their music reveals knowledge, values, reason, mindset and language which are characteristics of what a philosophical discussion is all about. African traditional music employs probing and questioning about fundamental problems in their society, through critical discussion, and rational argument which are systematically presented in their music. In addition the lyrics of traditional music potently project the wisdom of ancient times.

African philosophy concerns the way African people of the past and present make sense of their destiny and the world at which they have found themselves (Anyanwu and Ruch 1981). The conceptual clarification of Urhobo Musicians is referred to as "*Iburele*" which is translated to "Oracle" which means a person considered to be a source of wisdom. In Africa, an oracle is seen as someone who offers advice or a prophetical thought which comes directly from a divine source. The implication of oracle in traditional music is that indigenous musicians play the role of the custodian of the tradition of the communities. The oracle is often ambiguous, ascribed to a priest or priestess in a shrine as the representation of a god to an inquiry or the agency or medium of such responses. The philosophical implication of Chief James Edah Towel music ensemble of Otokutu is that they are endowed with so much spirituality as well as natural talents which give them the inclination to compose and perform music reflecting the philosophy of their culture.

The composition of *Udje* songs has been in existence before the onset of neo-African music and culture. This is in one way to promote contemporary traditions of the Africans. According to Mukhitdenova (2016), numerous traditional ensembles including *ABK, Urker, Nur-Mukasan, Muz-ART, Zhigitter, Konyr, Baiterek, ARS - Bakai, Zhalyn, Kaspyi, Arnau, SET, Orda, Udje* amongst others are appearing to complement the effort and taking the place of the uprising contemporary Americanized pop music. *Udje* music ensemble under the leadership of Chief James Edah Towel has played an important role in this art. Traditional ensemble like Udje have the characteristics of polyphonic style of music performance, harmonies made based on the European tonal-harmonic system, compositions accompanied by local instrumentation to meet the modern trends such as keyboard, guitar, and saxophone playing amongst others. Traditional musicians characteristically exhibit a unique traditional style, which displays cordial communication with the audience. The philosophical aspect of Chief James

Edah Towel has grown beyond the lyrical, ideological and patriotic music with global sense of musical enlightenment.

Theoretical Framework

The paper is hinged on the Flow Theory of Csikzentimihalyi and Harper (1990). In literal sense, the flow theory means the action or fact of moving along in a steady, continuous stream. The theory state that an altered state of consciousness in which the mind functions at its peak, at sometimes may seem distorted. However, a sense of happiness prevails. He further ascertains that in state of a conscious mind, the individual feels truly alive and fully attentive to what is being done. This state is distinguished from strained attention, in which the person forces himself to perform a task in which he has little or no interest. Kennedy (2017) defines Flow state theory as an "ultimate state of consciousness where one feels his performance as best" This theory is used to examine musical performance as an art that involves the flow action in state. Csikszentmihalyi, Abuhamdeh and Nakamura (2005) also describe the theory as 'an optimal experience that people report when they are completely involved in something to the point of forgetting time, fatigue and everything else but the activity itself' (p 600). Jackson, Thomas, Marsh, and Smethurst (2001) believe that experiencing this positive state while doing physical activity (e.g. dance, musical performance) can lead to better performance.

The relevance of the Flow theory to music practice was studied by Parncutt and Mcpherson (2002). They found that musicians, especially at improvisational level, experience a state of flow while playing their instrument and that performers in a flow state have a heightened quality of performance as opposed to when they are not in a flow state. A study by Orjan, Tores, Laszio and Fredrick (2010) report the study performed with professional classical pianists who played piano pieces several times to induce a flow state, a significant relationship was found between the flow state of the pianist and the pianist's heart rate, blood pressure, and major facial muscles. They discovered that as the pianist entered the new state, heart rate and blood pressure decreased and the major facial muscles relaxed. The finding of the study concludes that flow theory is a state of effortless attention and overall relaxation of the body, the performance of the pianist during the flow state improved.

The flow theory was adopted for this study because the *Udje* music in relation to the ensemble of Chief James Edah Towel in Otokutu requires a full state of consciousness to better the physical performance. Furthermore, the flow theory is suitable to explain African traditional music. African musicians who adopt flow state are found to sway expressively as they play in ways that seen clearly related to the music. According to den Brinker*et al.* (2011), postural sway reflects emotion, which is a major characteristic of

Udje musical performance. The theory also relates to the activity of the composers, the dancers and instrumentalist of the musical ensemble of the *Udje* musical tradition. Thus, it was adopted to study the philosophical aspects of Urhobo music in Delta State.

Philosophical Concept

Traditional music employs philosophical concepts to reveal the hidden meaning about life. Music composers of tradition derived most of the idea in their music from local and cultural sources. From a culture setting, they are able to perform the music by conceptualizing on those found ideas in their immediate environment. They rely on the environmental history prevalent in the community and instruct music on the basis of the near forgetting history and gives meaning to these ancient myth for the present generation to get a glimpse of the past. According to Landaver and Rowland's (2001), philosophical concept is a mental abstraction which allows generalization and the extension of knowledge from some known to unknown objects. The concept integrates two or more particulars into a common mental unit. This seems to describe what traditional musician are known for, as they attempt to evaluate and assess the prevailing concept in the past by analysing it in their musical performance by making the identified concept relevant to modern society. The implication from the above is that music is a vehicle for expressing philosophical ideas. Music being an organized sound, its texts or lyrics carries philosophical weight. This is because, music does not only wake emotions, it also provokes though based on the message or content conveyed to its audience. It touches on people's life experience. It expresses the deepest thoughts of life. Music is perhaps the art that presents the most philosophical puzzles. Music is performed with the intent that people will draw understanding on how to solve the puzzles of life created by diverse experience. Thus, different shades of meaning could be presented doing musical performance involving the display of artistic knowledge.

Traditional Music as an Art

Music is an art form whose medium is sound and silence in time. According to the United Nations Educational Scientific and Cultural Organization (2018), traditional music is a performing art. This is because the nature of traditional music aligns consistently with the features of the performing arts. The performing arts range from vocal and instrumental music, dance and theatre to pantomime, song verse and beyond. They include numerous cultural expressions that reflect human creativity that are also found in many other intangible cultural heritage domains. Traditional musical performances bear similarity with theatrical performances because they combine acting, singing, dance and music, dialogue and recitation. These art forms the peoples' perspective and they play crucial role in cultural performance than they are perceived as a mere performance. Professionals in the arts use their musical ensemble to create scene for sport, education and entertainment from a socio-culture context and also represent their cultural heritage before the outside world. The *Udje* musical performance, for instance, portrays the Urhobo cultural heritage. It acts as a testimony to the cultural values found among the Urhobo of Delta State.

Udje musical tradition, according to Ojaide (2001) is a unique type of Urhobo music which falls into the corpus of satire. The songs strongly attack what the traditional society regards as vices. Ojaide found that the *Udje* music constitutes an art form whose satiric poetry is highly imagistic and poignant. He revealed further that their collection, transcription, translation, study, and preservation are necessary, not only because of the poetic vitality of the genre but also because such collection will prove a valuable means of social ethnographic understanding of the Urhobo people who produce them. He believed that the songs are very relevant today, because of the philosophic aspect in the songs and they can serve as a lesson to today's journalists and publishers of tabloids as well as musicologist. In the *Udje* musical performance, excesses are checked. A distinction between the general good of the society whose ethos must be upheld and respected for the law abiding individual is maintained. Darah (2005) identified *Udje* musical ensemble to be performed by Udu, in Udu L.G.A. and Ughievwen in Ughelli South L.G.A. respectively. He was able to situate *Udje* musical tradition within the context of the Urhobo song-poetry. He study centred on the theoretical perspectives on the practice of satire in the *Udje* dance-songs. He considered the conceptual views of some *Udje* practitioners both as a literary art and medium for social reform without diving into the philosophical approach of the performances. *Udje* music has philosophical elements that are consciously or unconsciously performed by *Udje* practitioners.

Philosophical Aspects of *Udje* Musical Performance by Chief Edah Towel

Udje musical performances by Chief Edah Towel of Otokutu reveals some of the philosophical aspects of the *Udje* musical traditions of Urhobo in Delta State. The philosophy of African music according to Ozene-Okanfah (2007), is related to its roots in African thoughts and values even when its ideas are borrowed from elsewhere. In other words, the philosophical thoughts found in *Udje* musical tradition as performed by its practitioner can be explained and reconstructed for scholarship. The philosophy in most African music types including *Udje* of the Urhobo is probably to inculcate morals that have long been neglected. Some African scholars have agreed that Western aspects of philosophy and aesthetic education failed to reflect upon the human values of African. These include the studies of Casimir, Nwakego and Umezinwa (2015) and Onwuegbuna (2015). In the view of Onwuegbuna (2015), the omnipresence of music in the human society and its utilitarian stance in the human life necessitates their philosophical study. According to him, the functionality of music can be ascertained from a myriad of perspectives; it is the textual content and performance practices of folk songs that the general worldview of a people is exposed. By indication, *Udje* musical tradition will only be able to expose the Urhobo people's world view by examining the textual content in its musical performance. Thus, *Udje* musical tradition is based on Urhobo philosophy. Philosophy of the Urhobo as aligned with other ethnic groups states that a child lives up to the likeness or meaning of the name that she or he bears. This consciousness informs and guides most composers as well as practitioners of the *Udje* musical tradition, including Chief Edah Towel.

Chief James Edah Towel – *Udje* Music Composer and Practitioner

Chief James Edah Towel was born February 13th, 1962 into the family of Etaifo of Otokutu Town in Ughelli South Local Government Area, Delta State, Nigeria. He attended Okutu Primary School, Otokutu, between 1970 and 1976. He also attended the Post-Primary School at Otokutu Mixed Grammar School from 1980 to 1985. He started performing *Udje* music from 1972 till date. He started as a dancer in 1972. After five years, he then became the leader of *Udje* instrumentalist. As the leader of the ensemble, wherever the *Udje* group of Otokutu composers was composing he was always listening to them. It was from there that he got the talent of composition in *Udje* tradition.

Presently, he is a composer of *Udje* songs in Otokutu Community. He composed *Udje* songs for the Otokutu community at Christmas, Marriages, coronation and other events and ceremonies. He has composed about 40 *Udje* songs (Field interview section with Chief Edah Towel, 2019). Some of which are:
- *Osevwe ro kenaj*
- *Emuoma vwiouho,*
- *Urhuemu ro rovwe.*
- *Etairoro,*and
- *Ichurchi ro kena.*

Some of his philosophical songs are; *Osevwe ro kene, Otie dam re owata ko she.* He is married to Mrs. Bridget Onome Edah with seven children.

Edah Towel: *Udje* Songs
The Song Texts

S/N	The Song Texts	Meaning in English Language
1.	Oyeo Akpo Rhu Nu Phi Yo Reo	The world is not large
2.	Akpo Na Rhu Nu Ho Re Eye Re Royi Jo na Bo Bo Hwo	The world is opened, but to Live in it and succeed Becomes a problem.

Song Title: Akpo rhu nu phi yo
              1.   *Oyeo Akpo Rhu Nu Phi Yo Reo*
                      The world is no large
              2.   *Akpo Na Rhu Nu Ho Re*
                      Eye Re Royi
                      Jo na Bo Bo Hwo
                      The world is opened, but to
                      Live in it and succeed
                      Becomes a problem.
Translated: The world is not large
                      The world is opened
                      But to live in it and succeed
                      Becomes a problem.

The context in which the song was composed is in the setting of the performers experience about the difficulty associated with the physical life. He informed his audience that life offers equal opportunity to everyone. The indiscriminate nature of life makes everyone to make the choice about what he could secure from it. In other words no one is deprived in an open world, each person devices how to succeed it.

The song title – "*Akpo rhu nu phi yo*" – is philosophical because it is figuratively used to denote the moral lesson about the challenges that we encounter in the course of our existence in this physical world. From a literal translation "*Akpo*" is either life or world; "*Rhu nu phi yo*", meaning, mouth is opened. There is metaphoric attribution where the world is seen as an "open mouth". Its grammatical function suggests that there is opportunity for all and what you make out of it depends on you. "*Akpo*" is discussed as one of the philosophical concept in Urhobo mythology. According to Nabofa (2005), "*Akpo*" connotes the destiny of the individual – "*Ovue Akpo ro re*", meaning each person has his or her own *Akpo* or destiny and each lives in accordance with the way it has been predestined. In Urhobo mythology, the word *Akpo* is a prefix which represents different aspects of their lives. Ofuafo (2017) agreed with the fact that Akpo is a loaded term in Urhobo philosophical mythology. Thus, the implication of the song is that every man's destiny is in his or her hand. This life is an open contest; to live and succeed in it has always been a problem. However, those destined, '*Eye Re Royi*' will always be victorious.

Summary of the Song
The song attempts to counsel the general public to be conscious about life, *Akpo*, though it is opened or visible, what it contains is beyond what meets the eyes. Life –*Akpo* - is full of mysteries, it takes a diagnostic approach and proper planning to achieve ones destiny. The song advises every Urhobo child to take life serious. It reminds us that life is not a bed of roses. The song

draws attention to the fact that *Akpo* or life is not all pleasant, and that there are some bad parts too. According to Kuma (2013), life is not the bed of roses neither it is the bed of thorns. He found that a person himself or herself is responsible for making his or her life either the bed of roses or the bed of thorns. Thus, the sum total of the song is that success in every field of life never comes to you on its own. You have to strive hard to get to it. The philosophy about the song is that it teaches that happy and sad moments are the part of life. If sad moments are not faced, one can never realize the worth of the happy moments. Adversity is that great part of life which leads you towards the successful future. Hard times are like washing machines, they twist, turn and knock us around but in the end we come out cleaner, brighter and better than before. Thinker (2016) indicates that our lives are not an independent system. He found that it is interlinked and influenced by the lives of others, some heavily, some mildly. Hence the song is a philosophical puzzle about life, *Akpo*.

Song 2.   Title: ***Utien Mro Vwa Ta***

S/N	The Song Texts	Meaning in English Language
1.	*Utien Mro Vwa ta*	A Ripe Orange sees the Righteous
2.	*Ko che*	Then it falls

Contextually, *Udje* music is proverbial in nature following the textual analysis of the songs. *Udje* music of the ancient Urhobo mythology has long been proverb in the songs. According to Pa Secondi, one of the notable *Udje* practitioners in Otokutu, the traditional perspective of the songs is performed majorly by the *Udje* practitioners in several occasions. He noted that the Urhobo people cherish the righteous as an aspect of the cultural heritage. Base on mythological expression and interpretation, the righteous in the Urhobo communities are held in high esteem. He also noted that their good will toward others is honoured as the Orange Tree symbolizes which releases its ripe fruit to full at the appearance of the righteous as presented in song 2 above. The reward the righteous get was the ripe orange that falls at the time the righteous individual was passing through the orange tree. The meaning the song illustrates is that being righteous is an ideal life style and wroth emulating. Thus cultivating righteous attitude is rewarding and highly priced. The song provides advice in this direction.

The Philosophical Aspect of the Song, *Utien Mro Vwa Ta*
Most of the *Udje* music performed by Chief Edah Towel bears philosophical characteristics. His musical performance on '*Utien Mro Vwa Ta*' is philosophical. He re-enacted the proverb in the song. A proverb is a simple, concrete, traditional saying that expresses a truth based on common sense or experience. Proverbs are often metaphorical. The philosophy in the song is

shown in the figureof speech used by the composer. We understand a metaphor to mean a figure of speech in which a word or phrase is applied to an object or action to which it is not literally applicable. The song contains personification. *Utien* (Orange Tree) is seen in the song performing the duty of a person. That it could recognize and reward righteous performance by a human being to the point that its ripe fruit fell when it sees the righteous. This attribution of a personal nature or human characteristic to the Orange Tree is thought-provoking. It raises the question that, why would the ripe orange fall only when it sees the righteous? This is because the song as a proverb is used to convey wisdom, truth, a discovering of ideas, as well as life lessons. Proverbs are an integral part of African culture. Proverbs are used to illustrate ideas, reinforce augments and deliver message of inspiration, consolation, celebration and advice. The great Nigeria author Chinua Achebe in Things Fall Apart (1959) once wrote: "Proverbs are the palm oil with which words are eaten".

In philosophical terms, the proverbs mean that good things happen to good people. The ripe Orange is generally considered a good fruit because it contains sweet taste, it is nutritious and liked by majority of people. It is an excellent source of vitamin c. It is a very good source of dietary fiber. The good quality in an orange is attributed to the quality of a righteous person. Oranges are among the world's most popular fruits.

Consequently, the moral lesson from this proverbial song is that good people are highly respected. Similarly, they are the most qualified to occupy the position of leadership. This is in alignment with the Bible passage in Proverbs 29:2. "When the righteous are in authority the people rejoice: but when the wicked bears rule, the people mourn" (The New Community Bible, Catholic Edition). The text is similar to the song. The exercise of civil and religious rule by good governance and the exception of the laws in their hands are meant for the protection of good men and the punishment of evil men. The righteous in authority will encourage all that is good. The ripe orange could fall as it sees the righteous which implies the respect that society accord good civil authority as well as good community leaders. The righteous leaders are always welcomed, respected and they are able to win the support of the majority in society, especially during political event and other cultural event when respected leaders are given the honour that is duly reserved for them in such occasion.

Summary of the Song
The song stresses the need to be good particularly those charged with civil responsibility such as political leaders. Earning public trust and vote of confidence from the public is associated with a good name. Proverbs 22:1 states, "A good name is rather to be chosen than great riches, and loving favour rather than silver and gold" (The New Community Bible, Catholic Edition). The choice of public figure is influenced by the good qualities of

honesty, integrity, sacrifice, prudence and accountability and transparent found in them by the majority of the people in society. Like the ripe orange will not full unless it sees the righteous person so it is for men of good will. They will always find support from good people in society and this is linked to *Utien 'Mro Vwata Ko Che'*. The sympathy of the public often goes in the direction of the righteous. Therefore, we are to heed the Biblical injunction which states that we should do good to all men. The Bible in Galatians 6:10, states, "As we have therefore opportunity, let us do good unto all men. (The New Community Bible, Catholic Edition).

Conclusion

Udje musical tradition enables the general public to have idea about the philosophical worldview of the Urhobo people in Delta State. *Udje* music is performed on the basis of philosophical concept held in ancient times. Urhuobo Philosophy as contained in *Udje* musical tradition was exemplified in the *Udje* song performed by Chief Edah Towel of Otokutu Town. His *Udje* music contains numerous imageries which has assisted in the understanding of his music in modern time, because of the re-construction given to the song text for musicological discourse. Therefore, the paper concludes that *Udje* musical tradition is that type of genre that conveys philosophical thoughts about the Urhobo people in Delta State. Based on this conclusion, it is suggested among others that *Udje* musical tradition should be studied by both musicologists and ethnographers. This will enable the expressible, explicable, understand and taught nature of the philosophical idea found in music classes at all level of music scholarship.

References

Anyanwu, K.C. & Ruch, E.A. (1981) *African Philosophy: An Introduction.* Catholic Book Agency.

Casimir K. C. A., Nwakego, O. S., & Umezinwa, E. (2015). 'The Need for a Prorating Shift in Philosophy Music & African Studies: a Trilogical Identification of three conceptual Relevancies in State Tertiary Education'. *Open Journal of Political Science*, 5, 135 – 154.

Chinua Achebe (1959). *Things Fall Apart.* (1st Anchor book Ed.) New York: William Heinemann Ltd., p 179.

Csikszentimihalyi, M., Abuhamdeh, S., & Nakamuoa, J. (2005). Flow in A. J. Elliot & C. Dweck (Eds). *Handbook of Competences &Motivation*, 598 – 608, New York: Guilford.

Csikzentimihalyi, M. & Harper (1990). Flow: The Psychology of Optima Experience. Retrieved from: www.scholar.google.com, October 2, 2019

Darah, G. G. (2005). *Battle of songs: Udje Tradition of the Urhobo*. Retrieved from: https://www.amazon.com, October 2, 2019

den Brinker, B.P.L.M., Beek, P.J., Brand, A.N., Maarse, F.J., &Mulder, L.J.M. (Eds.) (1999). Cognitive Ergonomics, Clinical Assessment and Computer-

Assisted Learning. (Computers in Psychology; No. vol. 6). Lisse: Swets & Zeitlinger.

Hadot, P.M. (1998). The Inner Citadel: The Meditations of Marcus Aurelius. London: Harvard University Press. p 351

Idolor, G.E. (2005). 'Strategizing Globalization for Advancement of African Music Identity' *Abraka Humanities Review* 1(1), 81-85.

Jackson, S. A., Thomas, P. R., Marsh, H.W., &Smethurst, C. J. (2001). 'Relationship between Flow, Self-Concept, Psychological Skills, &Performance' *Journal of Applied Sport Psychology*, 13(2),129-153.

Jackson, S.A., Thomas, P.R., Marsh, H.W., & Smethrust, C.J. (2001). Relationship between Flow, Self-Concept, Psychological Skills, and Performance. *Journal of Applied Sport Psychology*, 13: 129-153.

Kennedy, A. (2017). Flow State: what it is & how to achieve it. Available at: https://www.huffingtonpostcomalayn-kennedy/

Kumar, S. (2013). Life is not bed of roses. Retrieved from: https://www.speakingtree.in, October 3, 2019

Landaver, J. & Rowlands, J. (2001). Importance of Philosophy. Available at: www.importanceofphilosophy,com, September 28, 2018.

MacDonald, R., Byrne, C., Varlton, L. (2006). Creativity & flow in musical composition: An empirical investigation. *Society for Education, Music & Psychology Research*. 34(3), 292-306.

Madimabe, G.M. (2014). The Study of Indigenous African Music &Lesson from Ordinary Language Philosophy.*Mediterranean Journal of Social Sciences*. 5(20), 2007 – 2014.

Mukhitdenova, B.M. (2016). Traditional Folk, Vocal and Professional Songs as the Basis for Development and Modernization of the New Forms of Kazakh Musical Stage. International Electronic Journal of Mathematics Education, 11(9): 3209-3219.

Nabofa, M. Y. (2005). 'Reincarnation: the Doctrine of Heredity &Hope in Urhobo Culture'. In *Student in Urhobo Culture*. Lagos: Intec, Printers Limited.

Ofuafo, P.U. (2017). 'Envisaging the Concept of Akpo in Urhobo Mythology in Visual Form. A Study of Bruce Onobrakpeya's Art'. *International Journal of Research in Arts and Social Sciences*. Vol. 9(2): 281-290.

Ojaide, T. (2001). *Poetry, Performance and Art: Udje Dance Songs of Urhobo People*. Internet:www.waado.org. Retrieved Wednesday November 18, 2016

Onwuegbuna, I. E. (2015). 'Philosophical Embodiments in Igbo music: An Analysis of Mike Ejeagha's 'Popular' Folk Songs Style'. *SAGE Open*, January-March, Pp: 1-7. DOI: 10.1177/215824401556966. Sgo,sagepub.com.

Orjan, D. M., Tores, T., Laszio, H., & Fredrick, U. (2010): The Psychophysiology of Flow during Piano Playing. *Emotion* 10(3), 301 – 311.

Ozene – Okanfah, M, (2007). In Search of an African Philosophy of Music. Available at: wikieducator.org, October 2, 2018.

Parcutt, R. & McPherson, G. E. (2002). *The Science & Psychology of Music performance: Creative strategies for Teaching & Learning Book.* Oxford: Oxford University Press.

The New Community Bible (1988). (Catholic Edition) Ibadan: St Paul Publications.

Thinker, V. M. (2016). Why is life not a Bed of Roses? Retrieved at: https://www.quora.com, October 3, 2019.

United Nations Educational Scientific & Culture Organization (UNESCO) (2018). Performing arts (Such as traditional music, dance & theater. Available at: https://ich.unesco.org

9

Textual Analysis of Owan Traditional and Religious Music as Educational Resources in Edo State, Nigeria

John Aideloje Abolagba, Ph.D[*]

Introduction

Music in traditional religious systems among the Owan people of Edo State is transmitted orally through the traditional educational system. But due to inadequate documentation as a result of insufficient literary work and researched materials available, the preservation of these musical genres is gradually becoming extinct. This chapter analyses some traditional and religious music for posterity purposes with great emphasis on their textual structure and meanings. The methods of data collection for this study are through documentary, interviews and participant observation methods. It is discovered that Owan people have many traditional and religious songs which are sung to school pupils towards improving morals and the standard of education in the land in so many dimensions. The paper recommends that these type of songs be taught to students, teachers and the community at large to aid learning. It also recommends that these songs be made into books as to be accessible to teachers and students alike. The paper concludes by scoring some songs for musicologists and music enthusiasts so as to be abreast with the Owan traditional and religious music.

Edo State is located in the South West region of Nigeria. It was carved out of the then Bendel State in 1991. The major ethnic groups are the Bini, Esan, Afemai, Akoko-Edo and Owan. Each of these ethnic groups shares identical historical origin and political institutions, with little cultural differences in certain regards. However, the name "Edo" refers to the common political structure, cultural similarities and the common historical origin which all the people share.

---

[*] University of Benin, Benin City, Nigeria

Owan people pride themselves as the custodians of culture and tradition and music is one of such veritable tools by which they preserve their culture. In spite of this assertion, very scanty scholarly attention has been given to the contributions of the various forms of music, particularly with reference to the standards of education. This study therefore, investigates the traditional and religious music genres of the Owan ethnic group of Edo State in order to highlight the socio-moral and the various traditional educational values inherent in them, which can be explored for the benefit of the people of Edo and Nigeria in general. Some selected songs from Owan ethnic groups, which serve as historical reconstruction enhance education and values of the Edo people. These songs are studied from critical and analytical point of view to uncover the various factors and philosophies of music education from the traditional, social and religious systems. They can help to instil values and moral standards on the Owan people, and as a result, be a model for other parts of Edo people in particular and Nigeria in general.

The Edo People and Demography

The entire Edo people have ancestral link to the old Bini kingdom (Benin City), which is now the capital of Edo State. The word Edo, according to Aluede and Braimah (2005), refers to all the ethnic groups who have this similar, historical and cultural origin as well as political origin. The Oba of Bini is the chief paramount ruler and the custodian of the tradition of the Bini who reside in today Edo State. The dialects of the other sub- groups vary from Bini language with their distance from Benin City. According to a statistics provided on the internet by Edo-Forum <(http://edoforum.se/community-activities), the Bini speaking people of Edo occupy seven out of the 18 Local Government Areas of the state. State viz: Oredo, Egor, Ikpoba-Okha, Orhionmwon, Ovia North – East, Ovia South – West and Uhunmwode Local Government Areas, constituting 57.54% while, others like Esan (17.14%) Afemai comprising of Etsako (12.19%), Owan (7.43%), and Akoko Edo (5.70%). The forum also noted that the Igala-speaking communities exist in Esan South East; Igbira related communities in Akoko and Afemai areas as well as the Urhobo, Izon, Itsekiri and Yoruba communities in Ovia North East and South West Local Government Areas, especially in the borderlands. The above demography probably explains a lot of things as to why there seem to be much concentration on the Bini culture and tradition. Again, much attention is drawn on Benin City as the commercial nerve centre and the seat of political power of the Edo.

The Owan people embrace both traditional and foreign religions. There are so many churches for the Christians from different denominational backgrounds. There are as well so many Muslims of different theological persuasions with mosques all over the major towns and villages across the length and breadth of Edo State.

Esu and Junaid (2011:535) noted that the ancient Bini Kingdom dates back to 900 AD and that historical evidence lends credence to the fact that the Oba of Bini used to send his sons to different parts of the then Bini Kingdom as governors of vassals to establish and consolidate his imperial authority in these areas. This explains the cultural similarities of these people with the core Bini ethnic stock. Again, the statistics provided by Edo Forum corroborated that:

> The colourful traditional festivals in the state manifest its rich cultural heritage. Critical among these are the *Igue* and *Ihi Ebo* festivals. With an estimated population of 3,218, 332 made up of 1,640,461 males and 1, 577, 871 females and a growth rate of 2.7% per annum (NPC, 2006), as well as a total landmass of 19,187 square kilometres, the state has a population density of about 168 persons per square kilometres. (Edo-Forum Activities (http://edoforum.se/community-activities)

The *Igue festival* is one major popular traditional festival in Edo land which incorporates the use of music. To the Binis and the Edos in general, music plays significant roles in different activities of the people.

Music and Traditional Education System

Esu and Junaid (2011:536) have defined traditional education as the process by which every society attempts to preserve and upgrade the accumulated knowledge, skills and attitudes in cultural setting and heritage to foster continuously the wellbeing of mankind. Certain musical skills have continued to be preserved as part of the traditional religious system among the Edo people, with each ethnic groping preserving its musical culture as part of the traditional political system. During festivals, social, cultural and religious gatherings, the kings and their chiefs are custodians of the traditions ensure that the cultures of the people are upheld. Though the incursions of Christianity and other Western religions is fast penetrating the traditional institutions, there are certain parts of the culture of the people that are being preserved and music has continued to play dominant roles in this regard.

The traditional political structure of all the ethnic groups among the Edo people has continued to be a factor for the continuity and change in the religious system of the people. Thus, the relevance of the traditional education system cannot be overstated. These social, political and religious institutions have kept the continuation of some festivals and it is in some of such institutions that cultural heritages are preserved and transferred from one generation to another. Esu and Junaid (2011) posted that:

Education has been a means of transmitting one's culture from one generation to another. It is the process of bringing about a relatively permanent change in human behaviour. As the oldest industry, it is the main instrument used by the society to preserve, maintain and upgrade its social equilibrium. A society's future depends largely on the quality of its citizen's education (p.537)

Map of Edo State

Among the Edo people, musical activities are associated with satirical connotations and socio-cultural backgrounds which have continued till the modern times in socio-cultural contexts such as burial rites, marriage ceremonies, naming ceremonies, puberty rites and festivals. The pattern of call and response singing and deft chorographical dance steps seen in all the areas of Edo usually characterize the responses of people during social and cultural activities. These practices have continued over the years, because the music is part and parcel of the culture of the people. Most traditional songs are accompanied by heavy beats which the dance step in tune with the songs. Praise singing is common among musicians and the involvement of youths in the performance of these songs and dances ensures continuity in the heritage of the people.

In Owan culture, the transmission of Musical knowledge is usually informal. This corroborates Fayemi and Adeyelure (2009:49)who posited that:

> Education in traditional Yoruba culture was not a formal system as is the case with the modern Western one. Rather, it was informal and functional, with the aim of producing honest, respectable, skilled and socially responsible manpower that would conform to the social order of the day and contribute to its development. The people were guided in skill acquisition of varying types in accordance with what a particular community required and the natural environment in which the community lived. (p.49)

Educational system (through religious or traditional music) has the capacity to inculcate values and skills as required to transform the entire community. According to the Encyclopaedia of Educational Research (1969;1123), religious education is defined as "those enterprises designed to induct each new generation into the attitudes, beliefs and practices of a particular religion, thereby perpetuating the religion and at the same time providing for the individual unifying the centre of his life". Music education that is delivered through the religious beliefs of any religion has the capacity to effect the entire life of an individual or a community.

Music has a lot to do with religious practices in Nigeria. There is virtually no religion that does not make use of music. There is no doubt that the influence Christianity in music education in Nigeria has been tremendously predominant, yet this is not the write off the influence of the social, cultural, geographical and the traditional educational systems of each community in shaping their musical and religious values. Writing about music education in Nigeria, Emielu (2011:353) observed that:

> While we must acknowledge the Christian roots of music education in Nigeria through the arrival of various Christian missions with their penchant for hymn singing, there is the need to change this perception in contemporary times. Music is a human behaviour in particular cultural and geographical context, not necessarily as a product of religion.

Music and religion complement each other positively and when it is built into the educational system of the people, it becomes a major factor for rapid growth. It is this factor that has contributed to the rise of Western music in

Nigeria, for when Christianity was introduced, music education through mission schools was prominent. Therefore, as Emielu (2011:354) opined, the delivery system of music education in Africa must strive to reflect the diverse socio-religious configuration and economic needs of the people. He reiterated the need to do this to include the introduction of popular music into the music curriculum because of its socio/non-religious nature, its contemporary relevance as commercial viability.

The Place of Music Education in Sustainable National Development in Edo State, Nigeria

A nation cannot be developed if there is no unity amongst its people. Music is a magnetic agent that draws people together, creates room for the sense of brotherhood and instils the sense of belonging and collective responsibility. This research sees music education as a subject that fosters national development. National policy on education in Nigeria and in particular in Edo state sees music education as the acquisition of appropriate skills, abilities and competence, both mental and physical, for a citizen to live and contribute to the development of his society. Music education is a concern that all societies share since music is central to the cultural life, and monitors the mental advancement of a society from generation to generation. Idolor (2007:17) stated that:

> Music is a phenomenon which accomplishes purposes in the lives of individuals or groups of individuals. Africa has had remarkable pressures from foreign administrative invasions, social interactions, mass media, new curricular in formal education, alien religions, new job opportunities, and emerging technologies leading to some changes in the lives of individuals and indeed the entire society.

Also, Okafor (2005:45) opined that music education is designed to equip the individual not only to earn a living but also for life itself, through the encouragement of socially desirable knowledge, attitudes and skills. All these and more is what this research seeks to address.

Music Education towards National Development among Edo Youths

Education is about preparing the young for a changing world and is an attempt to bring about change in people. That is the intention of education, and any custodial or curatorial activity has to serve that end. A fundamental aim of music education is to develop what popper calls "imaginative criticism", which is, he says the only way in which we can transcend our local and cultural environments. Since music education has to function within cultural orbits, we therefore tend to look for psychological universal procedures and criteria that enable us keep a steady focus on what we are doing, no matter what the musical style or what its origins might be.

Nevertheless, from an educational perspective the perceived cultural origins of music are very influential. Music is particularly subject to instant prejudice and more sustained value judgments, and I wish to distinguish between these. An example of prejudice would be instantly turning off a radio channel which happens to have been selected by mistake. We are looking for something else. Valuing, on the other hand suggests coming to a judgment about music having direct knowledge and experience of it. We may even feel able to make judgments about music which we happen to find not especially amenable at a particular time but can still say of it that it is a fine piece or good performance.

When we engage with and respond to music we are extending our ways of making and taking the world through symbolic discourse drawing on deep psychological wells of a universal play impulse. Music shares these fundamental processes of mind with other arts and indeed with other symbolic forms, including science and philosophy. The unique qualities of music lie in its intensity of sensorial impression, its expressive vividness and imagery and the coherence and concentration of its structure. Music expands our universe of thought and feeling; it takes us 'out of ourselves". No cohesive community gets by without music, Edo State is a case study in this regards.

Owan Songs and improving standard of Education in Edo State

1. Vava Ivbo gha nikere

OWAN

Va va ivbo ghan ni kekere

Re o hi ebe we (2x)

We we kha kie gbe gbomo

Ve himi akhue.

ENGLISH TRANSLATION

You little children, focus on your education and you will be a good leader in the future.

Little children like to play a lot when in the mist of others in the school,and as such, this song is composed to be sung when it is noticed that pulpils are playing too much to the neglect of their studies and this song is sang to stop their habit of playing, sothat they can concentrate on their studies.

2. Gbogbele gbo gbe le

Gbogbele, gbogbele

Gbogbele, gbogbele

Ibi Jesu gbogbele

Regho da' mieho' o

Jesu

Be ready, be ready children of God be ready money cannot buy you faith' o children of God be ready.

This is a moral song which urges people to seek things of God and not material things which will eventually passaway.

3. Akava

Akava

Isuku la jo mo

Oja leke, aimiunu re odion

Ena so je vbe moi agba o.

(chorus)

English (Way-ward child)

A child was sent to school and because of poverty, withdrew and went into fishing, this made her the laughing stock of the village.

4. Ebe lo o mo le

Ebe lo homo le	English
Ebe lo homo le, yoi khi	The best book to read is the Bible if you
Brabu Ebe lo homo le,	read it everyday it will help you on your
yoi khi babu ukha koro,	way. The best book to read is the Bible.
ede de, ero kpa iwe we obo	
ebe lo homo le, yoi khi Babu	

Far as long as a child can read, he/she is also admonished to read and study the bible as it contains a lot of moral teachings that will help the child grow up well without blemish. The song is usually sang when a child is going off track and he/she needs to retrace steps, hence this song helps to remodel the life of the child

5. Ekhe oda eyon gbe gbe

Ekhe Oda e yon gbe gbe

Ekhe oda eyon gbe gbe

iwo w ova yi isuku,

ekhe oda eyon gbe gbe

iwowo va oyi koleji

va va, ore gbe hunu

I wow o va ye vasiti

Va va re ghe lunu

English

Drunkards, your age mates are in school,

drunkards,

your age-makes are sending their children to

college: you disgraceful people,

your mates are in the university,

you disgraceful people.

This song has to do with school agemates following bad gangs to drinking bars thereby abandoning schooling because of this bad behaviour which has caused disgrace to them as well as their family members. Meanwhile their mates who do not follow their bad examples are doing well in colleges and universities. This is a moral call to our children to be of good behaviour, it they must excel in life, through the singing of this song.

6. Ya mu le

Ya mu le mu le erio da mi suku

Ya mule mu le erio da mi suku (2x)

Mule mu le, oh

Mule mu le oh, oh

Mule mu le, erio da mi suku

English

I am running a race to get my education (2x)

running a race, running a race,

running a race, to get my education.

The pursuit of a sound and qualitative education can be likened to a race, running a race is like having a target to pursue e.g, education. Someone that is pursuing education needs to be focused to achieve his goal. Hence, this song is meant to ginger our youths to be focused aand to pursue their educational career deligently.

7. Baki chio lo rukpa na

Ba ki chio lo rukpa na

Ba ki chio lo rukpa na

Ukha re'O,

Ukha re. u re no mon

English

What is the name of this light (Education)

you will eat and leave enough for your children

The pursuit of education is likened to light that brightens the place. Education pursuit will not make a recipient to lack or suffre in life, as a result, he will acquire wealth and have surplies to leave for his children.

8. Ohonmon, Ohonmon gbe

Ohonmon, ohonmon gbe

Okhi ne me

Ohonmon, ohonmon gbe

E ghe ni re mi suku

Okhi re me

English

Good, better, best I shall never rest until my education is achieved I shall never rest.

A song composed to ginger(motivate) our youths to attain the zenith of education in whatever field of study they are in. the acquisition of education is best when you have attained its peak(never give up).

9. Ebe me ri isuku

Ebe me ri isuku

Ebe me ri isuku (2x)

Da e de li kio mie be me

Da e de likio miebe vbe o

I kha me ebe me a

English

My books are at school when will I behold my books (2x) so that I will not forget my studies.

In the early days, pupils leave their books in school for safety, even during holidays. When pupils are tired staying at home for the holidays, songs of this kind is sung to remind them that they will soon be going back to school to continue their studies. This song in a way which also inspires those contemplating of not returning to school after the holidays to think twice and remember that they have a mission which has not been accomplished.

10. Ha FueGhe A

Do not waste your time
Time does not wait for anyone
It is when one is breathing he is able to work
Once our eyes are close (in death)
The strength for work leaves

This song discourages drop out of pupils from school to do petty jobs like fishingWhich can not generate enough money for the Child up keep in the future and as such bacameA laughing stock by those who went to scholand are able to provide for their livelihood. In essence education is the key to success in life.

Ha fueghe a
Procastination and time wasting is dangerous for one to be successful in life. Whatever one is doing, it should be pursued deligently as time waits for no one. The composer believes that you can achieve success now than to procastinate. No one knows tomorrow, tomorrow may be too late.

Conclusion

From the songs analysed in this chapter, it is glaring that music and religion have been the vehicle by which the Owan people inculcate moral education on the young ones. It was discovered that both were very effective in character moulding of the young ones as well as adults. Traditional music and religion are inseparable form of education among the people of Edo state. Traditional religious music among Owan people thus serve as education medium as well as inculcation of moral values on the citizenry. This people of Edo state continue to cherish and hold very dearly the importance of religious music in the upbringing of the young ones. Furthermore, it was discovered that the absence of religious music in the life of present day generation has had negative influence on the way they think and in their behaviour both at home and in the school environment. Arising from this, it is recommended that music educators and composers should always develop apt texts laced with themes bothering on godliness, neighbourliness and brotherhood in their works. This no doubt will engender patriotism and promotion of acceptable societal norms.

References

Abolagba, John .A. (2010). 'The Place of Music Education in Nation Building: Nigeria in Focus'. Unpublished Ph.D Seminar Paper Presented in the Department of Music, Delta State University, Abraka. Nigeria.

Aluede C.O and Braimah Abu A. (2005). 'Edo Folk Songs as Sources of Historical Reconstruction'. *Studies in Tribes and Tribals*. 3 (2): 123-128:

Aluede C .O and Eragare E. (2006). 'Dance without Music: An Academic Fable and Practical Fallacy in Nigeria'. *Anthropology* 8(2): 93-97

Edo Forum Activities, http://edoforum.se/community-activities/ (accessed on 14/05/2013)

Emielu, Austin (2011). 'Some issues in formal music education in Nigeria: A Case Study of Kwara State'. *British Journal of Music Education*: Cambridge University Press. 2011 28:3, 353–370

Encyclopedia of Educational Research, 4th Edition, 1969.p.1123

Egharevba, J.U. 1968. *A Short History of Benin*. Ibadan: Ibadan University Press.

Esu A. and Junaid A. (2011). 'Educational Development: Traditional and Contemporary'. http://www.onlinenigeria.com/education/?blurb=536accessedon 14/05/2013)

Idolor, G.F. (2007). 'Music to the Contemporary African', *Journal of Social Sciences*. Vol.14 No.1 Pp:13-18.

Okafor, R.C. (2005), *Music in Nigeria Society*, Enugu: New Generation Books.

10

Ogotun-Ekiti Bata Music: A Documentation of a Royal Music Ensemble

Osunniyi, Joseph Akin[1]

Introduction

Traditional music has been defined by scholars of different leanings in different epochs. For example, Merriam (1964), observes that traditional music is a cultural indicator, which contributes to the continuity and stability of societal mores. Ofosu (2001), defines it as music which is obscure and of indeterminate antiquity and has been passed into general currency and acceptance. By implication, the origin in terms of composer or creator is unknown. Similarly, Echezona (2004), describes traditional music as music of the indigenous or ethnic people which has been practiced for long, and passed from one generation to the other through the process of oral transmission.

The concept of oral transmission forms the core of indigenous theory; for any item to qualify as indigenous music, it must have been in oral circulation passing from individuals without aid of any written text. Indigenous music could be vocal or instrumental, among the Yoruba of Western Nigeria, the vocal music are: *Ijala, Ekun-Iyawo, Ewi, Rara* and *Iyere* to mention but a few. Also, in the instrumental sections, are *Dundun, Adamo, Apiri, Ogbene* and *Bata* music among others.

Brief History of Ogotun-Ekiti

Ogotun Ekiti was founded by Ojorube, one of the grand children of Oduduwa, like Oranmiyan he too was a warrior. Ojorube grew up a brave and fearless warrior. He was loved by his father. Primeval oral source had it that, there was a particular room in the palace of Oduduwa where beaded crowns were kept and princes were barred from entering. It was at this particular place that Ojorube loved to play, because of the fondness the king had for him; he had to prepare a charm for his little Prince to avert the wrath

---

[1] College of Education, Ikere-Ekiti

of the 'gods' who watched over these crowns. It is a taboo for any king or prince in Yoruba land to see the inner parts of a beaded crown except Ojorube who founded Ogotun (Ogunniyi, 2012).

Ojorube was to defend Ile-Ife against any war that came from the right side of Ile-ife. He became the commander of the right hand part of the war zone hence the name "*Olori ogun otun*". It was *Olori ogun Otun* that was changed to '*Ologotun*'. When Ojorube was departing from Ile-Ife with his retinue, the oracle was consulted and the oracle instructed them to charm a big cow, and they should follow the cow until it would be too tired to move. The carried out the instruction and the cow stopped at the present site of Ogotun-Ekiti.

Statement of Research Problem

There is a lacuna in early publications on Bata music of the Yoruba people in Western Region of Nigeria, especially with reference to Bata music of Ogotun Ekiti by notable scholars such as Akpabot, Vidal, Omobiyi-Obidike, Ajewole and Okunade. In all these works Ogotun Ekiti Bata music has not been mentioned, though forms and styles of Bata music are discussed extensively in foundation of Nigeria Traditional Music by Akpabot (1982). In his contributions in "Oriki": praise chants of the Yoruba, Vidal (2012) analyzes to details, the poetic meter of Bata songs Omobiyi-Obidike gives the sociological use of Bata Music, in Nigeria Musical Instruments Omobiyi-Obidike (2007). Ajewole (2010 discusses the construction of conventional Bata drums while Okunade (2011) deals with Performance Techniques of Bata drums in Ubiquitous Music among the Yoruba people. Despite the in-depth research carried out by these scholars on the Bata music, there is a palpable omission of Ogotun Ekiti Bata music in the research of these musicologists, though the music is said to have existed since 200BC. The construction, cultural and musical values have not been investigated. Although Bata in Ogotun Ekiti and the conventional Bata bear the same moniker they differ in all such area: construction, functions and sociological use. "The importance of any music can be ascertained from its socio-cultural roles and the scholarly attention that it receives", Agata (2011). Despite the widely accepted social significance of Bata music in Ogotun Ekiti, it is yet to receive commensurate scholarly attention. Therefore, the above identified gap needs to be abridged. This study would therefore remove the veil of attendant obstructions earlier identified above, and address the construction, functions, sociological use and lastly engage in documentation of Ogotun Ekiti Bata music.

Ogotun-Ekiti Bata music is relatively unknown to the outside world; this theory will help in bringing to fore, the usefulness, functions and functionalities' of the music to other cultures and also to compose some of the songs to art compositions which will be useful for educational purposes thus help in presentation and propagation of Ogotun-Ekiti Bata music.

The Ensemble Repertoire of Bata Music of Ogotun-Ekiti
The Instrumentation of Bata of Ogotun-Ekiti
The ensemble of *Bata* of Ogotun Ekiti comprises three pieces, i.e. The *Iya ilu*, *Gangan-un* (Talking drum) and Opon which is *Gudugudu*.

Iya Ilu
The Bata here is referred to as *Iya ilu*, the master drum, it is made from the vine of genius *lageneria* (gourd).

Two gourds are used, the first one is cut at both ends while the second is cut only at the head while they are still fresh to avoid cracks when dried. The contents in the gourds are removed, and placed under the sun. After drying the two gourds are mounted on one another. The upper one's face is covered with the membrane of animal fastened together and pulled over them in a transversal way so that they are obliged to adhere to the body and so increase the tension while the lower gourds serves as resonator. In between the two gourds is a rag or foam to act as cushion, so that the gourds do not crack when beaten.

The foetus of a sheep is preferable when fashioning the membrane because of the fragility of the gourds that need to be covered by a soft skin. The foetus of a sheep is believed to be soft, tough and last longer (Adegbite (1989). Cob of corn (the hard core to which individual kernels of corn are attached) is used to remove the hair from the leather rather than blade which could damage the lather. This drum is mono-membranophonic, covered at one end.

Performing Technique
It is hung vertically in the front and it is being beaten with bare two hands, it is a soft spoken instrument. It could be tuned in two ways, if the sound is high more than expected, the skin straps could be relaxed; and if it is too low the required water is sprinkle on the face, rub it and put it under the sun. Like Bata of Oyo Alaafin, it regulates the music and dictates the tempo in which other instruments move.

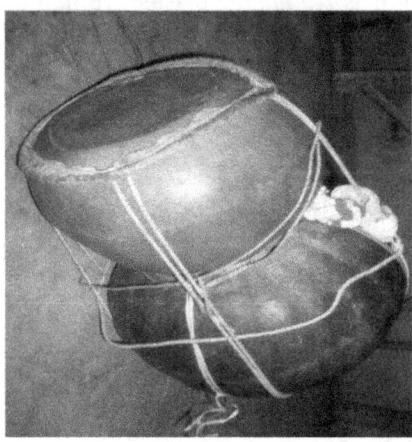

Gangan-un
Gangan-un is a small member of Dundun family, it is made out of a hollowed out piece of log covered with membrane at both ends. It is about 16cm wide and 35cm. Idamoyibo (2009). The Hourglass tension (Talking drum) is the best known of Nigeria talking drum Olaniyan (1999). It is double-headed, leather straps connect the binding cords at each drum head. Pressure on the leather straps increase on the leather with a curved stick called 'kongo'. The stick is about 36cm long and is made from *Omo* tree.

PerformanceTechnique: The drum is usually slung on the shoulder and supported by the arm. The drumstick is held with the right hand while the drummer manipulates the throngs with his left hand. Gangan-un in the ensemble plays an ostinato rhythm accompany the Iya ilu.

The Third Drum is *Opon* or *Gudugudu*
Gudugudu (*Opon*) is not a tension drum. It is a single headed membrane drum. It is the smallest in this ensemble. This drum is also carved from *Omo* tree and the face covered by ram or goat skin. It is shaped like a bow. The

membrane is held in position by five small planks on which the leather straps made of ram skin are fastened.

Performance Technique: Gudugudu is played with a two twisted leather throngs made from ram skin. Gudugudu is the only member of this ensemble that is dual toned because of ida substance that is pasted on the surface of the membrane. This black substance makes tone variation possible when played. The drum is hung around the neck region while the drum itself is sustained by the abdomen. The rope that is used to suspend it is tied to the drum.

Tuning Techniques of *Bata* Drums of Ogotun Ekiti

In *Iya ilu* Bata of Ogotun, the tuning is done by tightening or loosening the skin strap threading the upper and the lower gourd together, water is splashed on the surface rubbing the membrane, with palm to relax the tension. In the case of the Gangan-un, i.e. the talking drum, the skin strap around it is tightened when the sound is too low or loosened when the sound is too high. Opon is quiet different, the pegs around the edge are knocked on the head to increase its tension.

Ritual Dimension/Purpose of *Bata* of Ogotun-Ekiti

Being a royal music, the ensemble is kept always in the king's palace and it is highly venerated. Before the commencement of performance, it is customary for the leader of the ensemble to pour libation and eulogise the spirit of the ancestors particularly those of departed *Obas* of Ogotun Ekiti so as to have an itch free performance.

The ensemble is performed during the coronation of an Oba, chieftaincy ceremonies and lastly when an *Oba* dies in Ogotun, the remains is not conventionally buried, but cut into many pieces and with the aid of Bata drum at midnight the pieces are thrown to all nooks and crannies of Ogotun, It is believed that the *Oba* is used as a sacrifice to appease the spirit of the fore-fathers so as to allow peace to reign in the land (Oral Interview by Chief Oni Oke the 'Apena of Ogboni' Ogotun Ekiti). Before this day, announcements must have gone round the town that people should not come out or put on any light in the night. This sacrifice is performed by the Ogbonis, i.e. a powerful secret cult in Ogotun Ekiti. Only the heart organ of the king is preserved for the next *Oba* to eat. Prior to installation, the new *Oba* eats the preserved portion of the late kings, he will be asked a question three times 'what did you eat?' he would answer ('I ate an *Oba*', *mo jo'ba)* and from then on he becomes the king of Ogotun. Today, at Ogotun Ekiti, no burial ground of any *Oba* can be sighted anywhere, it is a taboo for any woman to go near where Bata drum is hung in the Oba's palace not to talk of being played.

Rhythmic Pattern

Bata of Ogotun Ekiti has only one rhythmic patterns.

Illustration 2: Musical Expert Indicating Ogotun Ekiti rhythm pattern Bata Music of Ogotun Ekiti Songs

Song 1:
Oloye Mon Joye

Illustration 8: Musical for *Oloye mon joye* (Ogotun Ekiti).
Translation
The chieftaincy title owner has gotten it

Song 2:
Eruku Ku Le Le

Illustration 9: Musical expert for *Eruku ku le le oni oye* (Ogotun-Ekiti).
Translation:
Dust everywhere
Today is festival day.

Song 3:

Illustration 10: Musical Expert for *Oloye moijo* (Ogotun-Ekiti)
Translation
The chief is dancing,
father is dancing good

Functional Roles of Bata Music in the Social and Cultural life of Ogotun Ekiti people

Oloye Moijo

Arr.By Osunniyi

In Ogotun Ekiti, there is only one Bata ensemble in the town and always in the king palace, Ogotun Ekiti Bata is confined to *obas'* installation ceremony, chieftaincy ceremony and announcement of demise of the Oba. The Ogotun Ekiti Bata is destroyed at the final burial ceremony of *Oba ologotun,*

Symbolic Role: The Bata drums of Ogotun Ekiti community signifies royal symbol and unity among the people.

Historical Affirmation Role: People of Ogotun Ekiti community are always looking forward to the performance of this ensemble, because during the performance historical facts about the lineage of the obaship are always rolled out through the songs, chants and musical displays.

Communicative Roles: In Ogotun Ekiti, Bata music is used as signal and announcement of the demise of the *obas*, whenever the *Ogotun* of Ogotun Ekiti join their ancestors, Bata music is used to announce to the people of the community.

Why Ogotun-Ekiti Bata Music has not been explored enough
Sacredness of the Drum
The origin of Ogotun-Ekiti Bata music is hinged on oral tradition and this is in tandem with Yoruba cosmology in Ifa chapter 'Obara-Osa' Olawumi (2018). Performance on the drum outside this instruction is considered an abomination, since Bata music has remained unchanged since time immemorial.

Climate Change
Nigeria is endowed with many varieties of musical instruments as a result of differences in vegetation, climate, occupation and culture as observes by Agatha (2011). Unfortunately because of the climate change due to

insaneness burning of the bush, the activities of the saw millers which has affected the Ozone layers has reduced these vegetation's into almost becoming deserts. Some of the trees used to produce these musical instruments like *omo* trees are becoming so scarce. The gourds which were found every nook and cranny of the villages are no longer their, this is posing a big treat to the production of these local musical instruments. This has great negative impact on the production of Ogotun Ekiti Bata drum.

Restriction to the King's Palace
Ogotun-Ekiti Bata Ensemble is confined to the Oba's palace and so it is performed whenever there is an occasion for it, it is a taboo for the instrument to be taken out of the King palace for any reason.

Performance Technique:-The performance of the drum is restricted to only Omo-Owa family, i.e. the royal family and only the aged are allowed to beat the drum. Any ensemble that is not open to the youth will one day fissile away. As Yoruba adage, *Oro ti won ko ba ti mu omode lo, rira lo n ra* (any festival that is void of the youth will die a natural death.

Construction of the Drums
The bata drum is constructed only when there is a new Oba to be installed and only the old man that are constructing this drum. If this trend is not checked, the drum might expunge from the society.

Rhythmic Structure
Unlike other musical ensemble like *dundun* and Oyo-Alaafin Bata music, Ogotun-Ekiti has only one rhythmic structure, this rhythmic structure is so slow, when it is performed because it lacks innovations and variations, within a short period, the music becomes boring.

Notation
The use of Western notational system is still a barrier; the notation only represents the sound duration and not the actual sound. For example, when the drum is tapped at the edge by only the fourth finger, the sound is usually different from when the whole five fingers are used. When the palm is sharpened like a cup the sound will be different the whole fingers are stretched. The ensemble is not used in the social engagement circle or in the school, or in the theatre.

Exponent of Bata
Unlike some other Traditional musical Ensembles like Asiko, Apiri, Apala, Waka which have been popularize by such Exponents as Comfort Omoge (Asiko), Alhaja Adepeji (Apiri), Ayinla Omowura (Apala) and Alake Alariigbo (Waka), Ogotun- Ekiti Bata has not gotten any exponent to transform the music, hence it remains unknown.

Surrogatory Power
Yoruba people cherish a musical instrument that can imitate their voices, like *dundun*, g*udugudu* and *ekutu*. Unlike all these instruments, *Bata* drum of Ogotun Ekiti does not possess the ability to imitate voice, it can only give a rhythmic beats. This has not attracted any exponent to spring up.

No External Influence
It has not been affected by any external influence being church, mosque, or schools. If Bata drum has been affected by external forces many people would have been using it as a personal Band like Asiko music by Comfort Omoge.

Conclusion
Bata music of Ogotun-Ekiti, is a royal music, the materials for construction is found locally and it is very easy and cheap to construct. Despite this fact, that there has been change in the cultures of the African people, especially the people of Ogotun-Ekiti, due to urbanization industrialization and civilization, Bata music still remains undiluted and untapped. This trend if not checked could send the music into oblivion.

Therefore, to avert these problems, the people of Ogotun-Ekiti need to be educated on the usefulness of Bata music to the unity, upliftment of the cultural heritage of the people and the replica of the drum should be constructed (this does not need any ritual before)

References
Adegbite, A.O (1989). 'Symbolism in traditional Yoruba music practice'. *Ijotee*. pg 1
Agatha, I. (2011). Nigerian Musical Instruments. *Journal of Music and Aesthetics* (JOMA) Volume 1 Number 2. Pp: 74.
Agawu, K. (2003). *Representing African Music: Postcolonial Notes, Queries and Positions*. New York: Routledge. Pp: 23
Agu, D.C.C. (2003). *Music in Nigeria Cultures: Nigeria People and Culture*. Enugu: John Jacob's classic publisher. Pp: 60
Ajewole, J. O. (2010). *Foundation of Instrument Vocal Ensemble Music*. Mercy-ken Services ltd. Ibadan. Pp: 60.
_____ (2007). Social Organization and Musical Style in the Court Music of the Alaafin of Oyo. *An Unpublished Ph.D Thesis, Obafemi Awolowo University, Ile Ife*.
Akpabot, S. E. (1982). *Form, Function and Style in African Music*. Ibadan: Macmillan. Pp: 12
_____(1986). *Foundation of Nigerian Traditional Music*.Ibadan: Spectrum Books, Limited. Pp: 29.
Babalola, S.A. (1976). *The Content and Form of Yoruba Ijala*. Ibadan: University Press Pp: 45

Euba, Akin. (1980). *The Dundun Tradition.* Bayreuth: Bayreuth University.
Ofosu, J. O. (2001). Krimono Music: A Christian of Native Air Genre of Urhobo of Delta state of Nigeria. *Unpublished PhD thesis of University of Ibadan.*
Federal Government of Nigeria (1991). National Population Commission (NPC). Abuja: Federal Government Printer.
Fiagbedzi, N. (1989). Towards a Philosophy of Theory in Ethnomusicology Research in Djedje, J.C. (Ed), *African Studies Centre University of California.*Pp: 45-58.
Layiwola, D, (2000). Introduction. *Rethinking African Arts and Culture,* Series 4. Pp: l-14.
Manson, J. (1992). *Orin Orisa: song for selected heads.* Brooklyn, New York, Yoruba Theology Archministry. Pp: 42.
Marriam, A.P. (1964). *The Anthropology of Music.* U.S.A. North Western University Press.pg 15.
Nettles, B. & Gral, R. (1970). *The Chord Scales Theory & Jazz Harmony.* Rottenburg: Advance Music.
Nketia, K. (1974). *The Music of Africa.* W.W Norton and company.
Nzewi et al, (2007). *Musical Sense and Meaning, An Indigenous African Perception ed Saskia Stehouwer, Rosenberg Publishers,* Bloemgracht. Print
Nzewi, M. (2001). *Musical Practice and Creativity.* Bayreuth Hermany: INACeWA-Hans, University of Bayreuth.
Nnamani, S.N (2007). 'Problem and Prospect of Using field trips in the Teaching of Music in Nigeria schools'. *Awka Journal of Research in Music and the Arts* (AJRMA). Pp: 121-128.
Ogunniyi, A.O (1979). *History of Ekiti.* Ibadan: Caxton Press.
Ogunniyi, M (2012). *Natable Indigene of Ekiti State.* Ado-Ekiti: Laayegbo Communication.
Okafor, R. C. (1994). *Nigerian Organology and Classification of African Musical Instruments. Nigeria People and Culture.* Enugu G.S. Unit ESUTH.
Okunade, A. A. (2011). 'Ubiquitous Music among the Yoruba People'. *Journal of Music and Aesthetics (JOMA).* Vol. 1, No. 2. Pp: 74.
_____ (2010). *Comparative Study of Court Music in Egbaland. Abeokuta, Ogun State Nigeria.* Ibadan: An Unpublished Ph.D Thesis, University of Ibadan.
Olaniyan, O. (1999). *Ethnomusicology and an Approach to its Research.* InD. Layiwola (Ed). A Handbook of Methodology in African Studies. Ibadan: John Archers Publisher Ltd. Pp: 71 – 74.
Omibiyi-Obidike. (2007). Nigerian in the Context of the International Musical World: Problems and Prospects. *An Inaugural Lecture,* Ibadan: University of Ibadan.
Vidal, O. A, (2012). *Essays on Yoruba Musicology: Theory and Practice.* Femi Adedeji (Ed.). Ile-Ife: Obafemi Awolowo University for IWEF African Music Publishers.
_____ (2012). *Selected Topics on Nigeria Music.* University Press, Ile-Ife Nigeria. Femi Adedeji (Ed). Obafemi Awolowo.

_____ The Poetic Forms of Yoruba Songs, *Nigeria Music Review* (2012). No 5 1-17.

Reconstructing *Opre* Indigenous Knowledge for Musicological Studies

Margaret Akpevweoghene Efurhievwe, Ph.D[*]

Introduction

Urhobo indigenous music especially the *Opre* is an expression of the comic experience in the environment, and often performed in Delta State, Nigeria. It uses other literal expressions such as proverbs and idioms to convey the belief systems and worldview of the people. It entertains, informs, educates and creates awareness of the surrounding. However, *Opre* has not received significant scholarly attention; this in part could be responsible for the steady decline of this genre. The study utilized phenomenological approach for data collection. Information were collected through personal conversation (oral interview) and review of related literature. The study shows that *Opre* communicates knowledge and meaningful ideas. The educative knowledge can be elicited for musicological studies through knowledge extraction, transmission and textual interpretation of the selected songs. It is within this cusp that the chapter calls for reawakening of musical genre. It is thus concluded that the knowledge inherent in *Opre* is a resourceful material for musicological research, teaching, learning, and as such should be documented. It also recommends that musicologists should strive to integrate the inherent knowledge systems of *Opre* in contemporary music education.

Indigenous knowledge systems make up community development processes. They pertain to spheres like agriculture, food preservation, animal husbandry, ethno-medicine, which are often expressed in form of songs, story-telling, folklore, rituals among others. Indigenous knowledge of any society is a corporate communal experience acquired by an individual from its local environment and which is peculiar to the society in which he resides. Ibagare (2016) defined indigenous knowledge as a means by which traditional music is practice using the experience in the environments which

---

[*] Delta State University Abraka, Nigeria

are presented in form of comic, satirical, proverbial, idiomatic, simile and metaphorical expression. He expressed further that:

> Knowledge connotes a kind of acquaintance with something... knowledge is gathered ostensibly to ease human existence...and such knowledge includes the skills, experiences and beliefs which the people have adopted to sustain their living. It therefore constitutes the basis of the people's indigenous knowledge system (p. 116)

Urhobo indigenous musical knowledge discloses unique characteristics and ethical values. Some of the knowledge contain moral lessons and others contain the events within the society. According to Ayanwu (2016), "the bulk of indigenous knowledge, undocumented as it is, resides with our old men and women who most times die with their knowledge, leaving the living worse off". In fact, many Urhobo musical knowledge are gradually disappearing due to an intrusion of European influence. The embedded knowledge of Urhobo indigenous music has unique experiences which help to facilitates communication and decision making. It also helps to dictate how they make sense of the world around them. Researching on the relevance of the Urhobo indigenous music therefore became paramount so that the indigenous knowledge of the "Opre" music will not be at risk of becoming completely extinct in the face of rapid cultural changes and natural environment on a global scale. The collected traditional songs are analyzed, interpreted and transcribed with the text written in poetic form, both in Urhobo and English language to enable readers understand the indigenous knowledge contained in them.

A Brief Background of the Urhobo of Delta State

Urhobo is one of the linguistic entities occupying a geo-political area, the largest group in this region (Ofosu, 2001). Urhobo is one of the thirty-six (36) ethnic groups of the Federal Republic of Nigeria, citizenship of the southern Nigeria, closely connected to the North Western Niger Delta (Ekeh, 2005). Urhobo people speaks Urhobo language, they are located within latitude $5^0 40$ and 6^0 25 East in the central region of Delta State. They have neigbourhoods, the Isoko to the South-East, the Itsekiri to the West, the Benin to the North, Ijaw to the South and Ukwuanni to the North-East. The Urhobo have an estimated population of over two million according to 2006 census in Nigeria (Wikipedia, 2019). Idamoyibo (2012) also notes that:

> It was on October 1, 1938 that the name 'Sobo' or 'Subou' was officially changed to Urhobo as the appropriate and desired collective name for the socio-cultural ethnic units which used to be independent of one another due to their separate settlements in their present territories (p.112)

He also writes that Urhobo are the fifth largest ethnic group in Nigeria and the largest in Delta State. Urhobo migrated from a village known as 'Udo', Benin-City in Edo State in the fifteenth century due to harsh rules of Ogiso dynasty, the '*Oba*' of Benin (Ofosu, 2001). Although, the Urhobo were named after a famous man who settled in Benin known as 'Sobo', which today called Urhobo, they founded a kingdom with separate governmental organization and leaders. Today, Urhobo people are grouped politically as administrative division in Delta State of Nigeria. They have about nineteen chalets, nine local government areas and twenty-four clans. Urhobo as a community is rich in terms of cultural and natural resources.

Approaches to the Study

The study employed phenomenological approach for the purpose of data collection. This approach enable the researcher to obtain basic knowledge and detail of how 'Opre' music was practised from time immemorial, preserved by the custodians and the performers of the music genre. The relevance of this method was explained by Adogbo and Ojo (2008). According to them, "the method attempts to explicate the inner experience of the people." Therefore, the phenomenological method enabled the researcher to explain the observation drawn from the participants of the *Opre* music. This method was adopted for this study because it guided the collection of data as well as analysis of generated data.

The Urhobo people like many other African societies are known for music-making. Music is performed s a culture to conceptualize their belief systems and values that reflect their human and communal experiences. The study utilized information derived from personal discussion trough oral interviews, they study also employed secondary sources. The use of audio tape recorder was adopted in gathering information and collection of songs from the field. However, two songs were collected, interpreted and transcribed as an example in this study. The songs collected were used as an inclination in this paper due to intrigued indigenous knowledge essence it has imparted to members of the community. Thus, seeing how it could be reconstructed for musicological study.

Transformation Theory

The study adopted the transformation theory. Transformative theory according to Daszka and Scheinberg (2005) is the creation and change of a whole new form, function or structure". According to them, transformation is a change of mind set based on learning a system of profound knowledge and taking action based on leading with knowledge and coverage. Mezirow (2000) cited in Burns (2001) connect transformation theory to learning process. According to her, "we make meaning from learning process", which indicates the assumption of transformation theory. She states that, "transformative learning involves participation in constructive discuss to use the experience of others to assess reason justifying this assumption and making an action decision based on the resulting insight". Burns seems to justify the use of transformation theory in the assessment or reconstruction of knowledge. This is because the three elements of transformation theory such as participation, experience and insight are involved in the gathering of data from indigenous people particularly as it relates to traditional music. To transform has to do with the creation of something. Adedeji (2010) states that transformative musicology is the musicology that aims at the transformation of our environment and world at large. He explained further that, it encompasses all musical activities that focus on transformative purposes, a product of intellectual musicology and serves as a vehicle of transformative processes needed in society. This theoretical framework found in transformation theory is relevant to the knowledge reconstruction of indigenous music such as that of *Opre* genre. If transformation has to do with the creation of something new and ability to predict from the past and a profound knowledge system which determine action then, the theory aligned with the concept of knowledge reconstruction of *Opre* of the Urhobo for musicological studies.

Concept of Indigenous Music Knowledge Reconstruction

The fast pace of change that brought about by the new discoveries and innovations in science and technology and in social and cultural issues necessitates the need, ways and means for knowledge reconstruction and skills development. That is, there are ongoing reconstruction of knowledge, reconstruction of Urhobo indigenous knowledge, therefore, cannot be an exception. Knowledge reconstruction according to Banks (2002) refers to "the process which relates to the extent to which teachers helps students to understand, investigate and determine how the implicit cultural assumptions, frames of references, perspectives and biases within a discipline influences the way in which knowledge is constructed within it." This concept indicates that music as a discipline is the responsibilities of a teachers to understand how the models or curricula can be understood when exposed to the method of inquiry. By implication, indigenous knowledge using *Opre* music genre can become a source of gathering information about Urhobo culture.

Marie Battise in Idamoyibo (2011) states that;

> Indigenous knowledge comprises the complex set of technologies developed and sustained by indigenous civilizations and transmitted via the oral and symbolic structures of indigenous languages to the next generation through modelling, practice and simulation rather than through written documents (p.114).

In Urhobo culture as it was in many other African societies, no event happened that was not associated with music. Indigenous music is music created and performed for socio-cultural activities, although, such knowledge must have been developed and make suitable, shared to impact both the old and young members of the local environment or community overtime at different stages in different occasion.

Knowledge reconstruction helps knowledge transfer. It is until knowledge is reconstructed that it can be transferred. By definition, knowledge transfer is a process by which knowledge, ideas and experiences move from the source to their recipient. The 'Opre' indigenous music is the source of knowledge transferred to upcoming generations. This knowledge transfer is possible through documentation of the songs, which involved their organizational practice, believe system, attitudes and norms.

Hitzler (2005), regards knowledge as the reconstruction of meaning as most general epistemological goal of interpreting sociology. This refers to the fact that indigenous knowledge could be understood by wider society when the hidden knowledge in cultural activities such as the songs in different communities are extracted for modern scholarship. This concept underscores that reconstruction is the practice or process of re-enacting an incident for the purpose of investigating the specific fact and circumstances surrounding it. This description of the concept favourably applies to musicological studies whose activities relates with the practice of recreating musical ideas from local practitioners.

Similarly, knowledge reconstruction as viewed by Hitzler (2005) corresponds with knowledge translation proposed by Groeneboer and Whitney (2009). According to the duo, knowledge reconstruction implies the "creation of knowledge typically using the paradigm of the community in which the knowledge builder is situated." The idea proposed in this contextual framework indicates that, existing knowledge in a community provides resources for knowledge reconstruction.

Groeneboer and Whitney (2009) provided an overview of the usefulness of knowledge reconstruction to modern scholarship. According to them, knowledge recreation become useful when it flows from its construction in one context to its use in another context. This flow is made possible through knowledge exchange, transfer, translation, reconstruction, dissemination, mobilization and knowledge utilization. Consequently, approaches for knowledge reconstruction is found in the model proposed by Groeneboer and Whitney. The model suggests that indigenous music of the Urhobo people when researched upon, can be used for music curriculum implementation. With this, music students will have access to information on the origin, the historical context, the medium of expression which is the language of the music. They will as well have access to the content of the music which is the message it convey and usability of the knowledge gain for musicological studies.

Olorunsogo (2008) suggested that 'Nigerian traditional ensemble performances such as dances, group singing, instrumentation, etc., can serve as resources for teaching-learning in the classroom situation". There is the need therefore to emphasize the use of *Opre* indigenous songs in order to inculcate knowledge of right values among the educational system in the state. According to Idamoyibo (2012), "every occasion for musical performance is thus an occasion for learning new knowledge ... providing a new knowledge in a new context of performance". The writer therefore advocates that, '*Opre*' indigenous songs should be reviewed, recorded, analysed, interpreted in a simple language and compiled as books, compact disks, tapes for musicological studies in contemporary educational system. According to Idamoyibo, "this will enhance general human development in terms of personality improvement and the general growth and development of the society."

Extraction Approach for Knowledge Reconstruction
Knowledge extraction is the creation of knowledge from structure and instructive sources. The resulting knowledge need to be in a machine readable and machine interpretable format and must represent knowledge in a manner that facilitates information. In practical terms, devices such as compact disk, cassette, tapes use in capturing sound are relevant devices for knowledge extraction. Stored information in the devices enable the extractor to use the information for reconstruction and make the extracted knowledge explicit for users. Since indigenous music of any given society serves as a pivot in shaping music scene in Nigeria, in order to attract the younger generation interest in cultural music, the knowledge and socio-cultural value can be extracted and reconstructed to make indigenous music meaningful and desirable.

Interpretation Approach
The second stage of the model of the knowledge reconstruction applicable to observable data is to subject the generated data to interpretation. This is done to provide phenomenological meaning to the practice that was observed. Interpretation is the action of explaining the meaning of something. Using this approach, the *Opre* can be reconstructed in a language that will convey its meaning for modern readership. The reconstruction gives it a better understanding of the component parts found in the practice. For example, satirical language, idiomatic language and the proverbial are often used with shades of meaning during the *Opre* performance. When reconstructed, it will become meaningful and enable the modern listener to acquire the knowledge that was hidden.

The assumption portrayed by this approach is that, not until the observed experiences are interpreted, the knowledge will remain vague in the mind of hearer. Local musicians of the *Opre* genre specialized in the use of language that is not made plain to the audience. This approach is an aspect of the knowledge system in Urhobo community. *Opre* has been performed for many years by conveying message to society using proverbial sayings. The importance of interpretation of language found in music as a means of reconstruction of knowledge is to enhance understanding. When people are made to understand the knowledge contained in *Opre*, they can easily make up their mind to show interest in it.

According to Shedreff (2001) "context shape our perception and interpretation of meaning." The indication of this assertion points to the fact that interpretation of data is relevant to gaining knowledge of the experience contextually derived either by participation or by observation. He suggested that when interpreting data, we use explicit means such as text, visuals and experience. On the other hand, he suggested that hidden context employed gesture, clues and hunches to unveil their meaning. Another form of the process involves presentation of the idea to be interpreted to form and shape the information. He argued that, "when we tie streams of information together and add complexity, we form knowledge."

Opre in Context

Opre is one of the foremost musical genres in Urhoboland. Ovwigho (2018) opines that the music is one of the oldest genres among the indigenous music in Urhoboland, and is created for relaxation and socio-cultural activities. The origin of *Opre* appears not too clear but it evolved before other genre such as Udje music in 1920 (Eni quoting Ofosu, 2001); Ikenike, Ovenren and Gbogoniyan flourished precisely between 1930s and 1950s (Oghi, 2014). Opre music is a true representative of the Urhobo ingenuity, many villages and towns such as Oviorie, Eku, Abraka, have performed *Opre* music under various groups like Arigo, Ododo, Evuarere, Igbeneke, Idarighofua, amongst others (Efurhievwe, 2018).

Opre genre whose songs are valuable has gone into extinction; people no longer perform nor rehearse the songs as part of communal activities. According to interview with Adarighofua (2018), *Opre* existed through oral tradition. This is because the practitioners in the past were not conscious about western influence neither were their performers influenced by academic pursuit. As a result, the custodians were unable to account and documents the *Opre* music knowledge for scholarship.

The *Opre* genre has metamorphosed into *Opiri*, however, the songs are no longer considered so important because of western influences. Although, the tragedy of the impending dematerialization of the knowledge and practice of *Opre* musical genre is likely most obvious among the practitioners who have developed the genre as a source of livelihood instead of communal activities. However, it will be detrimental when the skills, knowledge, artefacts as well as the song essence are lost. There is the need for its revival. The study calls for ways of preserving or documenting the knowledge gained through extraction, interpretation and translation for musicological studies.

Opre Performance

Opre is performed as an ensemble, usually community base. It involves performance carried out during the evening hours as a means of relaxation and entertainment. Knowledge contained in the *Opre* focuses on the historical, socio-cultural, biographical experiences of the past, present and the future of the region. The *Opre* performance consists of eight to fourteen members. The members are assigned different musical role according to their musical skills. The leader of the *Opre* ensemble is the chief vocalist, the composer of the songs, he/she trained others how to sing the composed song which takes place during the rehearsal sessions.

Other members of the group include the assistant leader (also known as organizer) whose roles is to control, organize the dance aspect of performance and direct the dance steps to follow the rhythm of the instrumentation. The instrumentalist play the instrument to guide the dancers step while the dancers specifically compliments the job of the instrumentalist by responding to the rhythm in a grand style. The *Opre* performance has diverse paraphernalia, notable costume in the paraphernalia includes body appendages known as *Ewian* (rattles), small clapper-less bell (*igege*), head-ties and wrappers tied around the waist and legs. In addition, the body costume also consists of sleeveless white blouse for female dancers while singlets and wrapper for male dancers.

Opre ensemble is performed by both men and women, old and young who are energetic young and old males and females. The performance is accompanied with one short cylindrical drum called *Ukiri* placed on the drummer's armpit, one '*Sekere*' known as 'Akise' played by the lead singer. The *Akise* helps facilitate the rhythmic movement of the body as well as the upward and downward throwing of the hands which is the main step of *Opre*. As the dance progresses, the dancers perform demonstratively by clapping their hands with simultaneous tapping of the feet on the ground. The beats of the song are structured to synchronize with the upward and downward movement of the hand, to give a rhythmic emphasis.

The opening begins with the lead singer and the group who salutes and honoured the elders in the community in a walking pace movement while the instrumentalist follow suit. The group members move round until they get to the proper point of the performance where they could face the spectators. *Opre* is a free medley dance in which the drummers play romantically while the dancers dance in different directions to attract admiration and reward. At times, their hands are stretched to the spectators and their eyes widely focused on the audience on an important person in the audience as an invitation to join in the dance.

Opre is a free dance where every dancer displays his/her individual talent or dexterity for cohesion between his/her movement and instrumentalist. When the movement gets to a climax, the drummer calls their attention using the *Ukiri* drum code to communicate the dancer retiring them to their normal position. As soon as they are re-assembled, the music suddenly drops to a slow tempo and the group gracefully moves out of the stage in an atmosphere of prolonged enthusiastic applause.

Opre Musical Instruments

African musical instruments are categorized into four by Sachs (1956). Out of the four, only two categories (the membranophones and idiophones) feature in 'Opre' music. The *Ukiri* is a short single drum, a membranophone instrument made of wood and membrane (animal skin) stretched on the wood and fastened together to enhance sound production. Attached to the drum is a rope wore on the drummers' neck to enable him/her suspend the drum from the ground and placed it on the armpit for easy manipulation. The rope enables the drummer stand firmly as he/she manipulates the drum with stick. When playing the drum, the drummer has the ability of improvising some specific or different kinds of expression depending on how the chief vocalist directs the song. *Ukiri* serves as a communicative instrument in the dance performance. The sound of the drum serves as an embellishment to the music and helps in alternating the beats or style of the rhythmic pattern during performance. The *Ukiri* drum plays a prominent role, that is, the basic rhythm that maintains the time line of the music. The drum texture adds flavour together with other instruments produces different kinds of percussive rhythm that excite the dancers.

The other instrument found in *Opre* musical performance is the *Agogo* (bell) – it is a struck idiophonic instrument made of metal. It plays the time-line in the *Opre* musical ensemble. *Akise* (maracas) – it is a shaken idiophone made of indigenous calabash in a cup-like shape surrounded by a chain of beads. It plays very short and tight rhythm that heighten the density of the music. It provides a twittering sound when rhythmically shaken thus, it embellishes the *Opre* musical ensemble and creates excitement for both the dancers and the spectators. It also plays a progressive rhythmic pattern in the ensemble. The rhythmic style of the African music is also emphasized in *Opre*. This is because the role played by the collective rhythmic sound produced by these instruments provides the aesthetic value of the *Opre* instrumentation and heightened the level at which the *Opre* music could entertain.

Lyrics in *Opre*

The poetry translation approach is adopted in the translation of selected *Opre* music as a means of the reconstruction of it for musicological studies. Lyrics found in the indigenous music is identified with what Idamoyibo

(2012) referred to as inspirational given to the chief vocalist through his dreams, revelations and deep reasoning. Having captured the songs by inspiration introduces it to members of his group through rote learning. Since the preservative means of the music is through word of mouth, reconstructing them by expanding on the meanings using modern language and scholastic approach make the indigenous music usable for musicological studies. The role of musicologists to lyrics interpretation is seen in the fact that, through the lyrics, the songs become lively, interesting and understandable. Below is one of the songs found in the study area that project proverbial lyrics as well as idiomatic expression produced by Okpa Aribo titled "Ona Ugbeya bẹvwẹ" meaning, this method of friendship am fed up. The song is rendered as follows:

'Ona Ugbeya bẹvwẹ'

Urhobo Language	English Translation
Ona Ugbeya bẹvwẹ nene	This method of friendship is difficult mother
Ona Ugbeya bẹvwẹ	This method of friendship is difficult
Ona Ugbeya bẹvwẹ baba	This method of friendship is difficult father
Ona Ugbeya bẹvwẹ	This method of friendship is difficult
Afioto v'Orere	Rabbit and African squirrel
Aye hwivi k'ugbeya	Two of them are friends
Orere yaso – rẹ	Squirrel does not walk at night
Afioto y'uvo – o	Rabbit does not walk in the day
Mav' ohwohwo ru mro 'ohwo	How do they see each other
Ona Ugbeya bẹvwẹ	This method of friendship is difficult

'Ona Ugbeya'

Reconstructing *Opre* Indigenous Knowledge for Musicological Studies

Indigenous music is conveyed through imagery as shown in the lyrics where friends whose relationship are not straight forward are metaphorically described by two animals that could not meet at a given point because they had different world views. One of the animals walked in the night while the other in the day, so, they could not meet at a point. The song teaches a lesson that people should beware of friends who are not straightforward in their dealings and should be avoided. The understanding of the lyric shows that songs can be used in a coded manner to provide piece of advice and counsel for the benefit of society. The application of the lyric to musicology is that, music students who have heard the song previously who are not attaching meaning to it seeing the translation can gain understanding. The lyric will enable them to take precaution and carefully choose the type of friends to keep even while in school.

Another song found in the area that is metaphorical in expression produced by Johnson Aja, an exponent of *Opre* is titled "ko'bie", meaning becomes clouding. See the following example:

Ko biẹ

Urhobo Language	English Translation
Ko'biẹ	Become clouding
Ko'biẹ	Become clouding
Osio da mro' rokehwe	When rain sees who he will shower on
Ko'biẹ	It becomes clouding

'Ko bie'

The understanding drawn on the lyric depict that; it is the person you can defeat that you challenge to a fight. The lyric of the song conveys the idea that people who are defenceless in society are those attacked, makes them vulnerable to oppression. Without this translation of the lyric, majority of the people in the society may not have gained the knowledge contained in the song. Wisdom are found in the lyric; it teaches the society the need to have respect for the vulnerable rather than to oppress them. Musicologists are able to use this approach in conveying hidden truth without necessarily drawing much attention to them. This way of conveying meaning through songs is suitable way for training the up-coming musicians, especially Opre musicians of the Urhobo community.

Conclusion

The chapter concludes that musicological studies could be enhanced through knowledge reconstruction of indigenous music. *Opre* which develops as indigenous music in Urhobo community in Delta State has existed orally for many years. Knowledge inherent in this genre is suitable for musicological study when its reconstruction is approached through modern scholarship of extraction and interpretation of the songs. *Opre* performance has a structure that is relevant for musicological study because, it gives a framework on how to organize *Opre* musical performance for scholarly study. Its reconstruction provided the detail of its organization, performance, aesthetic value documented to assist musicological study. The context in which *Opre* music is performed consists of an ensemble which makes it a community base music performance. It represents or provide a medium of relaxation for agrarian settlement and also a medium of socialization, indoctrination and cultural transmission for the young generation.

Recommendations

1. Musicologists should reconstruct *Opre* music by extracting the traditional techniques found in the practice. This will enable them develop strategies for introducing the practice for musicological studies.

2. Musicologists should provide textual interpretation of the lyrics found in the Urhobo traditional music. Such interpretation will provide a clearer and better understanding of the *Opre* genre for musicological studies

3. Musicologist should collaborate with the local musicians of the *Opre*'. This will provide a ground for gaining first-hand information of the practice for reconstruction.

4. Musicologist should engage the practitioners of *Opre* in an interactive session to encourage rehearsal schedule with the younger ones. This will enable researcher carryout participatory observation on the *Opre* music genre for data collection used for knowledge reconstruction for musicological study before it is obliterated.

References

Adarighofua, (2017). *Personal Communication at Abraka, Delta State.* 25th January, 2018

Adedeji, F. (2010). 'Transformative Musicology: Recontextualizing Art Music Composition for Societal Transformation in Nigeria'. *Revista Electronica de Musicologia,* 14, 24

Adogbo, M. P. and Ojo, C. E. (2008). *Research Methods in the Humanities.* Lagos: Malthouse Press Ltd.

Anyanwu, A. (2016). 'Nollywood and the Preservation of Indigenous Knowledge Systems: A Study of Selected Movies'. *Journal of Faculty of Arts,* 7(1), 154-162.

Banks, J. A. (2002). *An Introduction to Multicultural Education.* Michigan: Allyn and Bacon

Burns, R. W. (2001). *Core Concept of Transformation Theory Notes.* Retreived on 20th October, 2016 from www.rebeccawestburn.com

Daszka, M. and Sheinberg, S. (2005). *Theory of Transformation.* Retreived 20th October, 2016 from www.mdaszko.com

Efurhievwe, O. (2018). *Personal Communication at Oviorie. Agbon clan of Urhobo,* Delta State, 17 May, 2018.

Ekeh, P. (2005). *Studies in Urhobo Culture.* Buffalo: Urhobo Historical Society, 2

Groeneboer, C. & Whitney, M. (2009). 'An Overview of Knowledge Translation'. *Encyclopedia of Information Science and Technology.* 2nd Edition, Pp: 7

Hitzler, R. (2005). 'The Reconstruction of Meaning. Notes on German Interpretative Sociology'. *Qualitative Social Research,* 6(3)

Ibagere, E. (2016). 'Developing Indigenous Knowledge Systems in Nigeria through the Mass Media'. *Journal of Faculty of Arts,* 7(1), 115-124.

Idamoyibo, I. O. (2012). 'Musical Arts Composition and Performance – Composition as Indigenous Knowledge System in Okpe Cultures: The Poetic Essence'. *Sun Yat-Sen Journal of Humanities,* 33, 111-132.

ldamoyibo, O. (2011). 'Socio-cultural Orientation and Image Transformation of Nigeria and its Citizens through Music: the Issues of Re-branding'. *Nsukka Journal of Musical Arts Research,* 1, 96-110

Longman (1995). *Longman Dictionary of Contemporary English,* England: Pearson Publishing Ltd, 480

Maziar, P. (2011). *Different Approaches in Translating Lyrics.* An article Submitted for the Fulfilment of Requirements of Translation Quality Assessment Course, AllamehTabatabai University.

Mezirow, J. (2000). Learning to Think Like an Adult: Core Concepts of Transformation Theory. In: J. Mezirow (Ed) and Associates, *Learning As Transformation,* Pp: 3-34. San Francisco: Jossey-Bass

Ofosu, J. O. (2001). Kirimomo music: A Christian Native Air Genre of the Urhobo, Delta State of Nigeria. *An Unpublished Ph.D Thesis, University Ibadan*

Oghi, F. E. (2014). The Ikenike, Ovenren and Ogbongoniyan Dance of Ughievwe of Western Delta, Nigeria: A historical interrogation. *IJHSSE,* 1(9), 93-99.

Olorunsogo, A. O. I. (2008). Traditional music as Resource Avenue for Music Education in Nigeria: *JANIM,* 77-88

Peterkin, C. (2016). *Musicology: a World of Possibilities.* Retrieved 20th October, 2016 from www.majoringinmusic.com

Sachs, C. (1986). Classification of African Musical Instruments. *Anthony Bains & Klans Wachmann. Galpin Society Journal,* 14, 3-29.

Shedreff, N. (2001). *An Overview of Understanding.* In Richard, S. W. information Indianapolis: Que

Wikipedia (2019). *People, People.* Retrieved: 19th February, 2019 from www.en.wikipedia.org

Interview

Ovwigho, E. (2018). Personal communication at Eku, Delta State, 19 August, 2018.

SECTION III

Popular Music and Music Education

Applied Theory of Nigerian Highlife

Sunday Ofuani, Ph.D[*]

Introduction

One of the major problems that hinder optimum inclusion of popular music in Nigerian music education curricula is the lack of theoretical contents in genres such as highlife. In this chapter, the musical contents and quality of highlife music are theoretically provided. The study is basically practical and qualitative in conception. This is to enable readers appreciate and have knowledge of the theoretical contents of highlife music. Since the theory is applied and qualitative in essence, it will guide readers towards appreciating, understanding and acquiring fundamental skills in highlife music making.

Highlife is the most successful nationalistic popular music in West Africa. Although the music is recreational in essence, it is highly aesthetical in the creative hands of professional highlife musicians. Depending on the aspect that is more prominent in a piece, highlife could prevail as vocal music with instrumental accompaniment or instrumental music with vocal accompaniment. Textual subjects discussed in highlife music are comparable to those of folk music. There are therefore philosophical themes of social issues, insult, moral, dirge, love, motivation and praises of a celebrity, personage, wealthy or aristocrats. It is sung in various indigenous languages, however, instances of English and Pidgin English highlife lyrics abound.

Highlife is essentially ethnical in style, language and instrumental combinations. As a popular music genre, it is thus characterised by ethno-nationalism. In Nigeria, for example, ethnical highlife types such as Igbo highlife, Yoruba highlife, Edo highlife exist. In fact, the list goes on to include those of the diverse ethnic nationalities in Nigeria. Nationwide, all ethnic groups essentially create and exert their musical identity of place through highlife. The genre is, therefore, rooted in a people's musical tradition. Although highlife bands are owned by individual musicians, it could be regarded as a new form of folk music. The ethnic implication and varieties in

---

[*] Delta State University, Abraka, Nigeria

highlife have helped to expound and disguise the original features of the genre that, sometimes, its traits become obscured and a different name given to the genre. Thus, we may start to think of some Nigerian hip-hop music as obscured or offshoots of highlife. Its practitioners have successfully fused the instrumental, idiomatic and stylistic materials of Western and indigenous music. This endows it with exotic sonic impetus and places it as a new popular music genre.

The origin of highlife has been a subject of much discussion that provides contradictory views. Consequently, several assumptions and conclusions have been advanced. Smith (1962:11) informs: "The *Daily Graphic* in Accra [Ghana] ran a contest on the subject in 1960. Widely speculative answers were received which placed the origin of highlife as Sierra Leonean and Nigerian. Most Ghanaian musicologists, however, agree that the *Konkomba* band was a forerunner of highlife music." Vidal (2012) traces the origin to Ghana. According to him, "The Post-Second World War bands [in Nigeria] adopted the emerging popular genre known as highlife which visiting Ghanaian artists have transplanted into Nigeria." The historic analysis in Omojola (1995:21-28) seems to point to Ghana as origin of highlife music. Even, the *Delta Heritage Magazine* (n.d: 21) traces its origin to Ghana.

In recent times, the need to statutorily situate pop music genre in Nigerian music education curricula remains a recurring issue. While the proposal is considered ideal and needful, we cannot deny the importance of stylistic and idiomatic theories that musically describe and define some indigenous pop music types, such as highlife. Without theoretical contents of the music, its pedagogy becomes a mere oral tradition – a basic problem that hinders civilisation of sub Saharan African indigenous arts.

The problem of lack of theoretical contents of indigenous pop music in Africa, which affects its classroom pedagogy, has been well identified and discussed in Emielu (2013). While previous studies of highlife music have been on its historic perspectives (see: Sprigge,1961; Omojola, 1995:21-28; Vidal, 2012: 20-22), its textual contents, philosophies and themes (see: Vidal, 2012:20-26; Van der Geest, 1980; Van der Geest, & Asante-Darko,1982), and qualitative surveys of its primary traits (Sprigge,1961; Smith, 1962), this study provides applied/creative theory of highlife music. This is achieved by way of general analytical theory of fundamental features in typical highlife music. Significantly, this study provides basic highlife music theory (of applied essence) with which development of its pedagogical curriculum and teaching of the music in classroom contexts become a scholarly reality.

Rhythm

Although African rhythm is generally explored in highlife, one can perceptively differentiate Akan (Ghana), Igbo, Yoruba, Edo (Nigeria) highlife through their peculiar rhythmic and melorythmic nuances. Of course, we have the slow and fast highlife. However, they both operate within the same rhythmic parameters. The fast or slow attribute is merely occasioned by metric-time and tempo factors. Rhythm in highlife music is essentially African oriented. Metrically, it is either in duple time (2/4, 6/8) or quadruple time (4/4, 12/8). Sometimes, in a single piece, alternate combination of the both is encountered. Most frequently, common quadruple time (4/4) is largely favoured. The slow and fast triplets abound in highlife rhythmic nuances.

Familiar phrasing-referent-rhythm patterns of traditional African music are generally adopted. Some of the most commonly used among them are:

Fig 1: Some of the most commonly used "phrasing-referent-rhythm" patterns

Phrasing-referent-rhythm pattern functions in highlife as: prompter of the rhythmic orientation, pilot of the rhythmic tempi, rhythmic signature/identity, reference for organisational correction and rhythmic aesthetics.

The vigorous-piecing tone quality of small-metal-bell and woodblock permits them as most favourable instruments in projecting the phrasing-referent-rhythm pattern in highlife. They both have loud-firm volume that endows them in galvanising and piloting the rhythmic and structural affairs of the entire ensemble. One of the two instruments is often used to play the phrasing-referent-rhythm pattern. Sometimes the two are used simultaneously.

Once the small-metal-bell or woodblock plays a familiar phrasing-referent-rhythm pattern, other instrumentalists in the ensemble are psychologically placed in the mood of highlife orientation rhythm. From the phrasing-referent-rhythm pattern every other instrument starts to queue in and in a moment the rhythmic organisation is fully established. Though the phrasing-referent-rhythm pattern seems submerged when the ensemble is dense in texture and volume, its role continues to pilot the music.

The phrasing-referent-rhythm pattern is played in strict perpetual *ostinato*. If the player falters at any point, the entire ensemble automatically displaces/dangles. But if any other instrument falters, it seeks for correction and reunion by tracing its line with reference to the phrasing-referent-rhythm pattern.

The tempo and rhythmic structure of highlife sometimes modulates to hot/fast tempo/rhythm towards ending of a piece. This characteristic change of tempo/rhythm is often initiated through fastening the established phrasing-referent-rhythm pattern or changing to a new faster pattern.

Highlife musicians solely depend on the phrasing-referent-rhythm pattern to pilot the rhythmic structures and tempi of the music. Sometimes the instrumentalist and singers have mastered their lines that they can pilot their individual rhythmic and structural obligations without needing the phrasing-referent-rhythm pattern. Yet, we find that phrasing-referent-rhythm pattern abstractly sounds in the musicians' mind-ears when the supposed phrasing-referent-rhythm pattern is not sonically heard from any instrument. The roles of phrasing-referent-rhythm pattern operate in sonic and psychological realms. If these roles are by any reason transferred or simulated by another instrument in the ensemble, the same function is always maintained.

Generally, notable rhythmic roles in highlife are: phrasing-referent-rhythm, background *ostinato* rhythms, foreground rhythm, rhythm for organisational pulse/balance and fill-in rhythms. These rhythmic roles are assigned to various instruments in the band. The realised rhythmic roles conglomerate to endow highlife music with dense and polyrhythmic texture. Generally, recurring pulses in the rhythmic roles may include all or some of these rhythmic patterns: divisive, additive, triplet, duplet, displaced, as well as *hemiola* and *hocket* techniques.

Harmony

In highlife bands, the harmonies give the songs tonal pedestal as well as outlining the tonal levels and progressions of the sung music. It sometimes functions as articulation signal to the singers. Aside from the rhythmic and linguistic facets, harmony in highlife bears and portrays some levels of ethnic sonic inflection and identity. Although similar chord idioms are generally used in highlife music of various ethnic backgrounds, one can perceptively differentiate Akan, Igbo, Yoruba, Edo highlife through their peculiar harmonic nuances.

Harmony in highlife music is undoubtedly western in idiom, but it is creatively and stylistically permutated to sound African in conception and perception. It is essentially characterised with simple harmony. Primary chords I, IV and V are therefore harmonic basis of typical highlife music. Alternatively, each of the primary chords is sometimes substituted with its relative secondary chord vi, ii and vii°/iii respectively. The substitution technique is basically employed for harmonic variety, otherwise highlife music is usually accomplished with the essential chords I, IV and V. Chord I or its substitute (chord vi), can either progress to chord IV or V. Chord IV or its substitute (chord ii), can move to chord I or V. And, chord V or its substitutes (chord vii°/iii), can progress to chord I or IV. We can therefore infer that harmony in highlife music is largely triangular in chord idiom, chord progression and chord substitution. The diagram (Fig. 2) elucidates the essential chords, their substitution and, their progressions in highlife music:

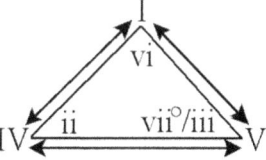

Fig. 2: Essential chords, their substitution and, their progressions in highlife music. (By the author)

Harmonic-rhythm in highlife music is essentially two or four beats prior to chord change. In time 4/4, for example, a chord may harmonically occupy a minim beat (two-beats) or a semibreve beat (four-beats). Shorter beat of harmonic-rhythm (one-beat) or longer beat of harmonic-rhythm (six-beats and above) is however, scarcely employed. Within a harmonic-rhythm beats, inversion(s) of a prevailing chord is used to enhance harmonic variety.

Chromatic note, such as 'minor-seventh' of tonic chord (I^7) is usually unmistakable in a highlife song that permits for chord I-IV progression. Although "diminished seventh chord" ($^o7$) built on a raised-tonic note is rarely used, it is usually employed in highlife piece that allows for chord ii. While "major minor-seventh chord" (Mm7) built on the tonic chord (I^7) progresses to the subdominant chord, "diminished seventh chord" built on a raised-tonic note is followed by a supertonic chord.

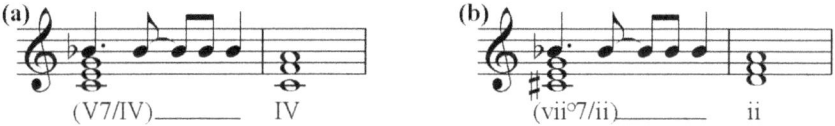

Fig. 3: Seventh chords: (a) Tonic minor-seventh; (b) Diminished seventh, built on a raised-tonic

These chromatic seventh chords and their respective progression evince that the resolution chords IV and ii (in Fig. 3) are often transitionally tonicized in highlife harmony. Observe, in each case (Figs. 3a & b) the minor-seventh in the chords is rhythmically emphasized in preparation of the transitionally tonicized chords. Chords IV and ii are adjacent chords because chord ii substitutes chord IV and either of them is transitionally tonicized as secondary tonic in highlife music. All these harmonic idioms, substitutions, progressions, chromatics and transitional tonicizations are though western in contents, but in essence, they are reconceptualised and contextualised to reflect the sonic matrix and rhythmic nuance in a specific cultural background of a highlife band.

Orchestration

As mentioned earlier in this chapter, highlife could prevail as vocal music with instrumental accompaniment or instrumental music with vocal accompaniment. The theory and craft of highlife orchestration is therefore unavoidable. Music instruments prominently used in highlife bands are of two cultural backgrounds – combination of some European and some African music instruments. The European instruments include: trumpets/cornets, trombones, a drum set, electric treble guitars and an electric bass guitar. While the last two musical instruments are necessarily amplified, depending on space/audience the music is expected to cover as well as taste and available resources, the first three musical instruments may be played unamplified. The saxophones are occasionally used.

The synthesiser keyboard is a late addition to highlife band instruments and is often optional – hence it is neither prominent nor statutory instrument of highlife music. Because synthesiser keyboard is endowed with tone simulations of virtually all instruments, it is used to play multiple roles of the trumpets/cornets, trombone, electric treble guitars, even the electric bass guitar, by using the 'split' technology. The multiple tones and 'split' endowments of the synthesiser keyboard exceptionally make it very useful, especially where manpower for other instruments is unavailable.

Notable African instruments in highlife bands are mainly percussive or melorhythmic in timbre. These include the small-metal-bell, woodblock, maracas, and conga. Beyond these instruments, highlife bands from various cultures exert instrumental identity of ethnicity by integration of selected music instruments of their respective cultures. For example, while the slit-drum is sometimes included in Igbo highlife bands, the hourglass (talking) drums are usually incorporated in those of Yoruba background.

The trumpets/cornets swell the highlife band in tone. In harmony, they play fragments of tones/melodies that combine to form block chords. Such fragmented block-chords are sometimes used to mark/punctuate the sung melodic motifs and phrases, thereby prompting the singers' melodic creativity. The trumpets/cornets and trombones are exceptionally vigorous, necessarily noisy and enhancing the highlife band with more lively timbre. Sometimes, a trumpeter extemporizes while others emphasize the harmonic progressions of the music. The trumpeter(s) could put its/their mute device for exotic sound effects[1]. The trombone sonority gives the brass instruments more harmonic depth and balance in highlife band that, in a band where the trumpets and trombones feature, full block harmonies are heard from the brass section.

---

[1]Trumpet mute is often used in Chief Osita Osadebe's highlife music. Listen to the track: "Nwannem Ebezina" or "Jesus Onye Ndu".Catch the music at: https://mdundo.com/a/182990

The tones of small-metal-bell and woodblock are essentially melorhythmic, vigorous and piercing. Hence, the small-metal-bell or woodblock plays a phrasing-referent-rhythm pattern that was discussed under 'rhythm'. There are rare and isolated cases where small-metal-bell or woodblock swiftly undertakes improvisation or extraneous melorhythmic task but it immediately returns to its role of 'phrasing-referent-rhythm'. The maracas are essentially percussive. They play twittering background rhythms that brighten the music.

The conga is a melorhythmic instrument. A two-in-one set or three-in-one set is often used in highlife bands. Whichever, the conga is endowed with well-tuned sounds – high, mid and low, which usually follow the tuning standard of the specific culture of a prevailing highlife band. Conga is used to play a set of *ostinato* melorhythmic pattern. But at appropriate point in the music, the conga departs from its statutory pattern to melorhythmically 'talk' in extemporisation realms. Sometimes, some instruments or the entire band silences for the conga to 'talk' and appeal the emotions of listeners who often get overwhelmed by its melorhythmic intricacy. Whenever all the instruments resume in full, the conga falls back to its statutory melorhythmic pattern.

The drum set, maintains the metrical pulse and balances of the music metrically. Three parts of the drum set are significantly important in highlife music. These include the high-hat, snare-drum and bass-drum (kick). Although the cymbals and tom-toms are used to achieve musical fill-in, emphasis and performance climax, highlife bands may play without them. Like maracas, the high-hat bestows the music with twittering background rhythms that brighten the music. While the sharp-jingling rhythm of the snare-drum complements the high-hat rhythms, the bass-drum marks the beat and endows the music with balanced and firm rhythms.

Electric guitars are very significant instruments of highlife band. The treble guitars essentially play melorhythmic and harmonic roles in the music. In a typical highlife band, the treble guitars are by musical role divided into two sections. The rhythm-guitar(s) plays stable (*ostinato*) sequences of a melo-rhythmic pattern or chordal (harmonic) progressions, upon which the lead-guitar introduces songs, plays interludes and extemporises. Sometimes, the lead guitar falls back to the central melo-rhythmic pattern or harmonic progressions of the rhythm-guitars. The treble guitars (especially the leading-guitar) may switch-on their mute, tremolo or *wah* effect for exotic sound.[2] The guitars are also sources of harmony in highlife bands. Collectively, they play wide range of the discussed chords, though with contrasting non-chord notes incorporated. Meanwhile, the bass guitar endows the music with depth

---

[2] The mute, tremolo and *wah* effects are often used in Chief Osita Osadebe's highlife music. Listen to the track: "Jesus Onye Ndu".Catch the music at: https://mdundo.com/a/182990

and firm sound which balances, galvanizes and illuminates the entire band. Stylistically, bass-guitar in highlife music is simply melo-rhythmic replication of African drumming techniques of big membrane-drums. As bass part of the harmony, the bass-guitar somewhat plays *ostinato* sequences of pitches within the chord progressions of a prevailing music. The *ostinato* sequences of the bass-guitar are sometimes slightly varied in pitch and/or rhythm. Octave alternation, broken and arpeggio styles are some of its significant melodic outline features, which conglomerate with other tonal-sounds from the entire band to form the desired chord idioms, invasions and progressions. Generally, sometimes, (especially during interludes) the instruments may play a couple of call and response patterns, wherein one instrument calls while others answer. This furnishes the music with dialogic and dramatic connotations.

Notwithstanding ethnical instrumental additions in highlife music, the notable instruments used in the band are divided into three sections. They are: (a) the brasses – trumpets/cornets and trombones (b) the percussions/melo-rhythmic – drum set; selected indigenous instruments – small-metal-bell, woodblock, maracas and conga (c) the electric guitars – treble guitars (lead and rhythm) and bass guitar. The gamut of notable highlife instruments is shown in Fig. 4 below:

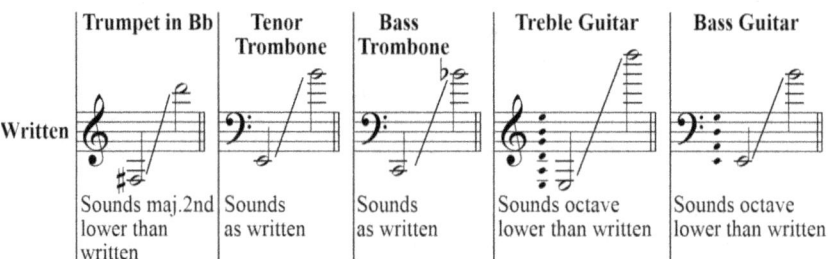

Fig. 4: The gamut of notable highlife instruments

Trumpet in B^b is F#3-D6 in written. It sounds major 2nd lower than the written. Tenor and bass trombones are E2-B5 and C2-B^{b}5 respectively. They sound exactly as written. In written, the common six-string electric treble guitar and four-string electric bass guitar are E3-D7 and E2-B5 respectively. They sound octave lower than the written gamut. In Fig 4, the open strings for tuning the guitars are shown with small-black-head note. Let us elucidate all these with analytical transcription of a dense section in "Ọsọndi" by Chief Osita Osadebe.[3] Catch the music at: https://mdundo.com/a/182990.

---

[3]Chief Osita Osadebe (March 1936–May 11, 2007) was an Igbo Nigerian highlife musician from Atani. His career spanned over 40 years, and he is one of the best-known Igbo highlife musicians. I decided to use his music as a representative, given his years of experience, consistency in style, creative maturity, restrain of emotion, and high creative/aesthetic quality of his music.

Fig. 5: Analytical transcription of a dense section in "Ọsọndi" by Chief Osita Osadebe

Qualitative Analysis of *Osondi*: Boxed regions in the transcribed music indicate the statutory role/pattern of each instrument/voice, which they usually fall back to after extemporisation or variations. Tonally, the harmonic-idioms, harmonic-progressions and harmonic-rhythms of the music include: a bar of chord I, followed by a bar of chord V. The harmonic-rhythm and progression are recycled throughout the music. The Solo Trumpet only featured at the climax point, which was reached at the ending of the music. It extemporised series of exciting call phrases that were all answered by the Backup-Chorus Singers amidst the background instrumental music. The dramatic calls of Solo Trumpet extemporisation and the resultant responses heightened the ending of the music and creating sonic impression of festivity. However, the Chorus Trumpets only featured at the opening/introduction section as response to instrumental calls.

Although the Conga played multiple brilliant extemporisations, it retreated to its statutory melo-rhythmic pattern in the boxed region. Woodblock strictly maintained the established phrasing-referent-rhythm pattern throughout the music. Although the Drum Set maintained the established pattern, rhythms of the bass-drum, hi-hat and snare-drum were severally varied. For example, sometimes, the bass-drum alternated the pattern in the boxed-region with this rhythmic pattern:

The Lead Guitar severally played magnificent and extensive extemporisations, but always retreated to the melo-rhythmic pattern in the boxed region, which further enriched the music with more dense chordal harmony. The Rhythm Guitar unmistakably maintained its melo-rhythmic pattern in the boxed region. Stability of the player from beginning to the end of the music is commendable. Save for the climax point where the Bass Guitar slightly varied its line, throughout the music, it strictly maintained the melo-rhythmic pattern in the boxed region.

The hub of the piece is on the Lead Singer who sang several varied tuneful phrases that were answered by the Backup-Chorus Singers. The Lead Singer used recitative singing style to rap long textual prose. He also used spoken rhetoric dialogue and spoken adages that are relevant to the textual theme. On the other hand, the three parts Backup-Chorus Singers dialogically responded to the Lead Singer's calls in homophonic harmony impetus. The Backup-Chorus Singers devotedly maintained the central textual theme (ọ*so'ndi, owe'ndi*) which was sung with the musical phrase in the boxed region.

Some of the highlife music elements and theories that we established in this study are apt in the analysed representative music. African rhythmic patterns and organisational structure dominate the piece. For example, "call and response" structural pattern remains dominant both in the instrumental and vocal sections. The text is entirely philosophical and advisory too.

Melody and Vocalism Techniques

Highlife songs are simple folk-like melodies. They are essentially simulation or quasi coinage of indigenous melodies. The song is not always sung to the end of a piece uninterrupted. It is sometimes abridged or interrupted by some melodic phrases and emphatic statements from Backup Chorus Singers and/or instrumental motific punctuations. Although, highlife songs linguistically match in some cases, linguistically mismatched tunes are characteristic in the music.

Highlife singers utilise various African vocalism techniques to initiate sonic expression, aesthetics, picture/imagery and dialogue in their songs. They creatively harness African vocalism styles through simulation of any fancied vocal effect, quality, idiom and ornamentation that are notable in the cultural musical norms of a specific highlife band. Vocalism techniques such as deep-throat-voice, coarse-voice, sobbing-voice, whispering-voice, groaning-voice, speech-voice, recitative, ululation, laughing, glissando/gliding, yodelling, humming, heaving, shouts and, nasal voice etc. are appropriately interwoven in the sung music to paint sonic picture of their vocalised narratives. Spoken or recitative (*parlando*) style is sometimes used to poetically and swiftly enact series of words or statements, especially where a long narrative is involved. In this case, a Backup-Chorus sings *ostinato* fragment that becomes pedestal for the Lead Singer to sing in poetic speech-rhythm using spoken or recitative (*parlando*) style. The chief objective of harnessing African vocalism elements and creative styles is to create the music in semblance of folk music without necessarily proliferating, arranging or transcribing folk music.

Song performance in highlife is essentially dialogic and dramatic in its structural pattern. For example, the Lead Singer sings a phrase/statement while the Backup Chorus answer alternately – 'call and response' structure. Other times, the Lead Singer sings a section, as the Backup Chorus refrains – 'call and chorus refrain' structure. The Lead Singer may choose to solo the song while the Backup Chorus repeats it – 'solo and chorus refrain' structure. Sometimes the Backup Chorus initiates a thematic *ostinato* fragment on which the Lead Singer does a spoken or sung solo – 'chorus-*ostinato* and solo' structure. There are rare cases where the Lead Singer solos with juxtapositions of fragmented statements (spoken or sung) by Backup Chorus singer(s). In most cases, all of the structural patterns are creatively integrated in a song performance – this is known as a 'mixed structural pattern' (Agu, 1999). He gives detailed illustrations of all the structural patterns.

Lyrical Techniques

Highlife Lead Singers are usually prodigious oral prose creators. They are philosophical and literary beings. Their ideologies in song lyrics seem to mean that they have fundamental knowledge of practical solutions to the social, political, economic, cultural, religious and psychological problems in human existence. The subjects and themes in their songs appeal to all of the above existential facets. Hence, highlife lyrics are reflection on and of the society.

To initiate oral-literature impetus, indigenous literary devices in form of adage, pun, figures of speech, imagery and oral-narrative (tale) are synthesized in their lyrics. Entire story or multiple statements could be summarised in an adage. Figures of speech devices not only endow a statement with literary aesthetics, they also help to engrave and cast a picture of the lyrical messages in the minds of listeners. And, oral-narrative technique helps to illustrate the lyrics with practical scenarios of life events for listeners to reflect on. Highlife singers usually adopt mythical tales, real life story singing, commentaries on social issue, satires or social documentaries as basis of their lyrics. For life security purpose, highlife singers use allusive technique in lyrics that affect a dreadful political body, politician or aristocrat etc.

Another notable lyrical device in highlife music is the use of non-lexical syllables (otherwise referred as 'nonsense syllables'). They use it to imbue the lyrics with exotic sonics, poetic imageries and allusions. For example, in praise songs, someone's greatness could be onomatopoeically sung using a non-lexical syllables pattern, for instance, *"o gi di ga da", "o ti ti gbo ti gbo"* etc. Generally, the purpose for adoption of the indigenous literary techniques is lyrical negotiation towards representation of folk oral-literature elements for lyrical aesthetics and effective/artistic message delivery.

Conclusion

This chapter has attempted to provide a theory of highlife, through the use of analytical and qualitative methods. This research presents a theoretical basis for highlife to be taught in classroom contexts. Within this study, the identified ethnic and idiosyncratic diversities notwithstanding, African music idioms and creative norms are bases for highlife music. Even though some European instruments are used in the music, they are always deployed as African instruments. Even the European harmonic idioms (that characterise the music) are crafted to sound African.

References

Agu, D.C.C. (1999). *Forms and Analysis of African Music.* Enugu: New Generation Books.

Emielu, A.M. (2013). 'From the Classroom to Stage: Developing an African Popular Music Pedagogy'. *EJOTMAS: Ekpoma Journal of Theatre and Media Arts.* 4(1-2).

Omojola, B. (1995). *Nigerian Art Music.* Ibadan: Institut Francais de Recherhe en Afrique.

Smith, E.M. (1962). Popular Music in West Africa. *African Music,* Vol. 3(1), 11-17.

Sprigge, R. (1961). 'The Ghanaian Highlife: Notation and Sources'. *Music in Ghana.* 2, 70-94.

The Delta State Government, (maiden edition). A Search in the Labyrinth. *Delta Heritage* (maiden edition), 21&32.

Van der Geest, S. (1980). 'The Image of Death in Akan Highlife Songs of Ghana'. *Research in African Literatures* 11(2), 145-73.

Van der Geest, S. & Asante-Darko, N.K. (1982). 'The Political Meaning of Highlife Songs in Ghana'. *African Studies Review.* 25(1).

Vidal, A.O. (2012). 'Nationalism or Ethnonalism? A Historical Musicological Perspective through the Musical Experience'. In Adedeji, F. (Ed.) *Selected Topics on Nigerian Music.* 12-33. Ile-Ife: Obafemi Awolowo University Press.

Teach Children the Music They Enjoy: *Incorporating Community Music into Basic Schools' Music Programmes*

Yemi Andrew Akperi, Ph.D[*]

Introduction

Children are born with musical intelligences; except handicapped, every child is capable of performing musical tasks as well as they would perform numeracy, language and physical responsibilities. The theory of multiple intelligences proposes that, "musical intelligence is innate in all humans" (Reimer, 2003:220). The ability to perform childhood tasks enables children to adjust and have senses of belonging as members of homes, peer groups, and communities. As they learn to speak, they hum; imitating the sounds they hear and as they grow older, they sing and mimic the sounds they enjoy in their immediate environment. These may be sounds produced by parents, siblings, birds, radios, televisions, phones and later by peer groups. These sound media form the informal music curriculum of children.

Schools are designed to develop/refine the home/community acquired skills and knowledge. However, in most African countries, pupils are introduced to foreign/western music principles that disconnect them from the music prevalent in their immediate environments. This anomaly, forks the child's perception of music, leading to a loss of interest in the music of his/her early childhood or both.

While most African children find it difficult to imbibe the new music precepts taught in school, utmost numbers of children in the West, improve on their community acquired skills in school. For instance children, who learn at home to play the violin as infants, hone their skills in school, because they meet the violin learnt at home, in the music class. The disjoint in curricula between the music of the African child's community where he/she has competence and the school, transform most African children into musical neophytes in school. Many hitherto music enthusiasts become

---

[*] Baptist Seminary, Benin City, Nigeria

frustrated, when encountered by Western music and staff notation. They become disinterested not because they do not love music, but because of the emphasis on Western music, while community music is excluded.

Purpose and Methodology

This chapter examines the musical interest of Nigerian children, whilst presenting some of the major music repertory of the twenty first century widespread in Nigeria, especially amongst children in basic schools, which includes popular, religious and indigenous music. This paper equally explains what community is and the enjoyment, generally derived from music, including the media employed for music propagation, as well as the state of music programmes in Nigeria's basic schools.

The study adopts a mixed methodology (quantitative/qualitative); the quantitative aspect enlists two hundred students in four schools in Warri and Benin-city, they were asked to list in order of importance, five songs/ music, which they enjoy. The study, due to lack of logistics is limited to merely two hundred students which is a random representation of hundreds of thousands students that constitute the basic school system in the two cities.

Conversely, qualitative methodology based on an interpretative phenomenological analysis (IPA) is employed to discern the interest of five students in music and their reason for been disinterested in other forms of music, than their choices. It examines the genres of music that gives the research population the most satisfaction and why. Phenomenological studies "explicates the meaning, structure and essence of the lived experiences of a person or a group of people, around a specific phenomenon" (Simon, 2011:1). IPA studies are useful in recording the unpretentious experiences of participants.

Current State of Basic Schools' Music Programmes

In previously perceived Western territories, there are gradual assimilation and inclusion of music from non-western climes into the music classroom. For instance, "Current music education curricula across Canada designate Western classical music as the music most worthy of study through emphasis on elements of music that are decidedly Western. Despite the way the curriculum is constructed many music *teachers strive to create diverse* programs for their students" (Hess, 2019). Canada, hosts a large population of Asian and African immigrants and Western music is alien to most of them, necessitating teachers to deliberately accommodate students' interest in the music of their home countries (i.e. Indian and African music) into the classroom. These are subtle attempts by teachers to satisfy pupil's musical interest. Immigrants in the United States of America (USA), advocated for desegregation, which "resulted in a gradual inclusion of musics from a variety of cultures in the school music curriculum, and the shift from a

Western music perspective to a multicultural perspective in music education." (Volk 1998: xi)

Conversely, in Africa, Chadwick (2012:430) describes Botswana's basic school music programme as "technical, meaning that it is concerned with factual information delivered through teacher-centred pedagogy and assessed by student reproduction of information through written testing." The programme is largely theoretical, musical performances are rare and are mostly accentuated by foreign music examples, unfamiliar to most African students.

Music programmes in Nigeria's basic (primary, Junior Secondary and Senior Secondary) schools, remain fortuitous. It is rare to find schools that regularly prepare music students for the West African Examination Council (WAEC) or General Certificate Examinations (GCE) examinations. Majority of music students enter Nigeria's tertiary institutions through other means, such as remedial programmes. Few students obtain the WAEC/GCE ordinary level credit in music, which is the prerequisite for admission into the universities.

Despite a dearth in qualified students, candidate's prowess in African traditional or popular music are not allocated credits or considered for admission into tertiary schools. Anya-Njoku, affirms that Music is the least patronized school subject in WAEC, NECO and Joint Admission Matriculation Board (JAMB) examinations.

Most of the students at the secondary schools refer to music as the 'white man's subject' because the music teachers have not been able to make music come alive in the classrooms. They are proffered theories without practice- music lessons without the sound of music, regrettably when music examples are used, they are English songs that have no bearing to the musical background of the learners. (Anya-Njoku, 2016:382)

Njoku's observation largely represents the perception of the majority of students in Nigeria that consider basic schools music programmes as Western.

On the contrary, depriving basic school children of music programmes, is detrimental to an all inclusive development of children. Brown (2019) registers the importance of music studies at a young age:

(i) it facilitates the learning of other subjects and enhances skills that students use in other areas;
(ii) growing up in a musically rich environment is often advantageous for children language development (music and brain development);
(iii) a small increase in the Intelligent Quotient's of six-year olds who were given weekly voice and piano lessons;
(iv) the brain of a musician, even a young one, works differently than that of a non-musician.

Children involved in music have larger growth of neural activity than people not in music training. Brown's submission underscores the importance of children's participation in school music programmes.

Notably, when the Christian missionaries brought Western music education to Nigeria, children born in homes with ecclesiastical music culture easily absorbed Western music tenets, because it is their community music. Several African art music pioneers, including the patriarchs/matriarchs of music education in Nigeria, i.e. T. K. E. Philip, F. Sowande, W.W.C. Echezona, A. Euba, A. Bankole, L. Ekwueme, Omibiyi-Obidike, D. Agu and R. Okerentie, were opportune to encounter Western music early, because of their parents, and relatives who were church affianced.

Indeed, it was Western culture of the missionaries that informed music in churches and schools. The missionaries founded both church and school that expressed Western culture. The symbiosis between church and school's music, barred indigenous Nigerian Music from churches and schools precincts. The missionaries and their followers were: clergy, catechists, musicians and teachers; thereby having monopoly over what was taught in schools.

Regrettably, most mission schools no longer offer music programmes in both primary and secondary schools, unlike in the colonial/post-colonial era. In spite, of music's absence from the basic school programme, Nigerian youths are musically talented in various genres. Nigerian popular musicians dominate the African music scene. In 2015, twelve Nigerian popular musicians were nominated for the Mama Music Television (MTV) African Music awards held in South Africa. "Nigerian musicians won seven of the awards. D'Banj defeated Tuface Dibia, P Square and three other Africans to win the premier award for creativity and the impact of African music on the globe. The MTV award is the most prestigious music award in Africa."(Akperi, 2015:355). Okafor (2019:103) record, that Wizkid a Nigerian, made history on the 26th of May, 2018 in the United Kingdom, when he "performed to a sold-out crowd of 20,000 at the *02 Arena* in London. With the feat, he became the first African-based artiste to perform at the arena, earning him a spot on a stage that had been graced by the likes of Drake and Beyoncé." Several popular musicians attained their Olympian heights in music with negligible contribution from the school music programme, while some were prepared by the church.

Nigerian children and youths are enthused by the music of these popular musicians than by any other music genre.

Music Replaced by the Cultural and Creative Arts Course (CCA)

The Cultural and Creative Arts (CCA) subject is an interdisciplinary field of study, which is a product of the synthesis of music, fine art, dance and drama. The CCA is an invention, intended to integrate and recreate the arts, in the African sense, as a subject in primary and junior secondary schools. The curriculum envisages pupils to be exposed to the elements of the various arts that make up CCA. In this regard pupils are guided through these elements to perceive, hear, explore, see, move, verbalize, touch, manipulate and recreate various symbols, experiences and activities in their own, creative ways. The general objectives of the CCA are stated as follow:

(1) to promote aesthetic education by enhancing learner's interest of aesthetic appreciation through knowledge of their own native music, art, dance and drama;
(2) to provide opportunities for pupils to see the usefulness and relationship among subjects that make up CCA;
(3) to provide opportunities for pupils to develop a language for expressing ideas, feelings, moods and action through CCA experiences;
(4) to nurture in pupils the ability to perceive the expressive qualities of music, art dance and drama;
(5) to acquire basic skills in these art forms;
(6) to develop ability, to explore, manipulate, improvise and experiment with sounds, colours and design, space and body movements.

The CCA is built around concepts, i.e. games and activities, festivals, folktales, legends, ceremonies etc. Elements from music, dance, fine art, drama and oral literature are integrated into concepts in the CCA. For instance, festivals in Africa, is an embodiment of drama, music, fine arts, dance, poetry and other cultural essentials. Teacher's competence/method is a challenge in articulating the essence of the subject and is the major drawback of the CCA.

Ajewole (2013:115) highlights some of the challenges of the CCA to include inadequate "human, physical and material resources…acute shortage of resourceful and professionally qualified CCA teachers and effective administrators…shortage of relevant CCA textbooks, journal and magazines…imbalance and lack of uniformity of the syllabus". The CCA is not a music course; in schools where the CCA is taught, the music teachers involved do not articulate the music of the various communities in the classroom.

Community Music

Community etymologically is derived from *communitas* which is a Latin word for fellowship or having something in common. Tracy (2009) gives five definitions of a community, which are diverse and complimentary:

> People who inhabit a certain geographic space (e.g., larger than family, but smaller than a state or nation; People who belong to a cultural identity group (African American, LGBTQ [lesbian, gay, bisexual and transgender], Pennsylvania Dutch); People who share an

interest or activity (i.e., folk musicians, vegetarian, distance runners); People who enact a sense of positive belonging (i.e., create a safe space, work toward group dynamic and benefit; nurture sense of belonging; fulfilment of human need) and People who are committed to the group good while also valuing and promoting individual rights within the group.

Community music entails a commonly shared musical experience between the members of a group or sub-culture. Community Music School (CMS), Trappe, PA, USA, (cmsmusic.org) defines their community music programme as a twofold mission "to enrich lives and communities by offering excellent, affordable music instruction to all people and to provide performance opportunities that contribute to the cultural life of the communities we serve. This dual mission is based upon the notion that music should play a central role in the life of any healthy community and that each and every individual has the capacity for music expression at some appropriate level of understanding and skill."

CMS provides opportunities for music education and performance experiences for 'all people of all ages [including a toddler's class], abilities and economic circumstances.'

Nwankpa (2013:1-2) defines a community music programme as "a community-minded arts curriculum in music. Community music programme may assume the function and meaning of a set of courses in music within a community setup." A Community Music Programme involves "traditional, cultural and contemporary musical activities involving instruction, education and performances organized under one umbrella of the community for the benefit of the members of the community and its environs" (Nwankpa, 2013:2)

Nwankpa's perception of a community music programme (a course at the University of Port-Harcourt) explicates three components: traditional, cultural and contemporary musical activities. In most parts of Nigeria contemporary music activities have supplanted traditional music activities. Nwankpa's position is in amity with CMS community music programme:

> The objectives of the CMS community programme include: to enrich lives and communities; give music instruction to all people; provide performance opportunities that contribute to the cultural life of the communities the institution serves. The community music programme considers that each and every individual has the capacity, for music expression at some appropriate level of understanding and skill, which tallies with the theory of 'musical intelligence'.

A community music programme, incorporates all the musical nuances, cultures (i.e. Western, African, Asian, Mexican etc.) which exist in the community it serves. The community music programme is of interest and satisfies the musical appetite of *all the members* of a community.

Likewise, Kerchner's (2019) music community is a place where, "they celebrated and grieved with each other, went to school together and sang fervent harmonized hymns on Sunday mornings together." In Kerchner's community, singing in harmony is a custom.

Similarly, in Nigeria till the early 1980s the morning and afternoon assemblies in basic schools was a daily occurrence; it was an avenue for the development of musical skills, because most schools had music bands, while others had sets of drums for parades and March past. Many popular music groups emerged during this era, prominent amongst them is *Ofege,* of St. Gregory College Obalende, in Lagos. Kris Okotie, Amas Grill, Eno Louis who became great popular musicians in the eighties, were members of Edo College Benin-City Music Band.

Some Popular Musicians in Nigeria: 2000-2020

At the dawn of the twenty first century, Nigeria witnessed a boom in popular music production. The boom is resultant on the return to a democratic system of governance, which arrived on the eve of the new century in 1999; the high exchange rate of the local currency (Naira) to the dollar spiked the prices of imported goods, including music compact discs, which forced Nigerians to look inward. In addition, Nigerian music was given more air play on television and radio, due to the restrictions on foreign content by statutory broadcasting authorities. The following table (1.) presents some of the major popular music and musicians of this era (2000-2020)

Table 1. List of some of Nigeria's popular musicians (2000-2020)

S/N	NAME	POPULAR SONG
	Burna Boy (Damini E. Ogulu Rex)	Killing Dem, On the Low
	Davido (David A. Adeleke)	Dami Duro, Skelewu
	Chidinma (Chidinma EkIle)	Jankoliko, Kedike
	D'banj (Oladipo D Oyebanjo)	Oliver Twist
	Don Jazzy (Michael C. Ajereh)	Gift
	Omawumi (Megbele)	Without You
	J. Martins (Martins J. Okey)	Cool Temper, Oyoyo
	P. Square (Peter & Paul Okoye)	No one like U, Chop my money
	Skales (John R Njenna)	Shake body, Fire waist
	Wizkid (Ayodeji B. Ibrahim)	Ojuelegba, Holla at your Boy
	Yemi Alade (Lawal)	Fimisile, Johnny
	Asa (Bukola Elemide)	Eyo, Fire on the mountain
	Tuface (Innocent U. Idibia)	African Queen
	Flavor (Chinedu O Izuchukwu)	Nwa Baby (Ashawo Remix),

		Adanma
	Phyno (Azubuike N. Cbibuzor)	Connect connect
	Iyanya (Mbuk I. Onoyom)	Iyanya (My story)
	TerryG (Gabriel O. Amanyi)	Koleto
	Olamide (Adedeji)	Eni Duro
	Tiwa Savage (Balogun)	All Over, Eminado
	Timaya (Enitimi A. Odon)	Dem Mama
	Frank Edwards (Ugochukwu)	Under the canopy,
	Sinachi (Osinachi Kalu)	Way maker
	Ty Bello (Toyin Shokefun)	This man, Ekundayo
	Lara George	Dansaki
	Mr. Incredible (Jude Abaga)	Mr Incredible
	Duncan Mighty (Okechukwu)	Fake love, Obianuju
	Kcee (Kingsley Chinweike Okonkwo)	Limpopo
	Patoranking (Patrick N. Okorie)	PM available
	IIIbliss (Tochukwu M. Ejiofor)	Can't Hear You, Chukwu Agozigo
	Naeto C (Naetochukwu Chikwe)	Ten over Ten
	9ce (Abolore Akande)	Glass House
	Dr. Sid (Sidney O. Esiri)	
	Waje (Aituaje. V. E. Iruobe)	No be You
	Waconzy (Anyanwu O. Kelvin)	Too much Money, Sweet like Tomato
	Sound Sultans (Olarenwaju Fasasi)	Bodmas
	Chinyere Udoma	Pure Praise, Ebenebe
	Eldee (Lanre Dabiri)	Today Today, Bosi Gbangba
	Harry Songs (Harrison T. Okiri)	Arabanko
	Kiss Daniel (Oluwatobi D. Anudugbe)	Pack N Go
	Niyola (Eniola Akimbo)	Go on
	Timi Dakolo	Iyawo mi
	Tekno (Augustine M. Kelechi)	Green Light
	Solidstar (Joshua Iniyezo)	Omotena, Oluchi
	Brymo (Olawale Ashimi)	Waka
	Muma Gee (Iyumane G. Eke)	Jekele
	Rugged Man (Michael Stephen)	Lessons, Give it up
	Sasha (Anthonia Y. Alabi)	Only One
	J' Odie (Joy E. Odiete)	I Lost My Mind
	Uche Agu)	
	Rapdibia (Omeje Ebuka)	Ifeolunye, Legacy

	Olu Maintain (Olumide E. Adegbulu)	Yahooze, Kowonje
	Marshal Morgan (Cynthia M. Ikponmwenosa)	
	Wande Coal (Oluwatobi W. Ojosipe)	Bumper to Bumper
	Vildee (Ngwu Victor)	
	Eva (Elohor E. Alordia)	Secret lover
	Raflee (Raphael Ugong)	
	Dj Xclusive (Rotimi Alakija)	Oyoyo ft. Burna Boy
	Nigga Raw (Okechukwu Oteke)	Obodo
	Ice Prince (Paushak Zamani)	Oleku
	Femi Kuti (Olufemi Anikulakpo)	Sorry sorry
	Banky W (Olubukola Wellington)	Strong Ting, Yes No
	Koredo Bello	Godwin, African Princess

The Music that Children Enjoy most in Contemporary Times

The musical choices of 200 secondary students in Benin City (Edo State) and Warri (Delta State) is assessed. The students were told to mention, the best five songs/music which they enjoy. The students are in primary and secondary schools, aged: 10-15 years; consisting of 125, males and 75, females. The participants were given two weeks to select their choices and were reminded twice on this assignment, before they submitted the following:

Table 2: Music choices of 200 Secondary School Students

MUSICIANS	SELECTED SONGS	SCORES
Burna Boy	Wetin Man Go Do, Anybody, Vanpaya, Dangote	70
Nathaniel Bassey	Air I Breathe, Imela	49
Roddy Rich	Project Dreams, Down low	48
Davido	Blow my mind	48
Mercy Chinwo	Excess Love, Chinedom, More than Gold	47
Sinach	Rejoice	42
Frank Edward	Ebube	42
Tim Godfrey	E dey work	42
Ema ft. Osinachi	You know dey use play	42
Teckno	Jogodo	38
Ada	Only you	38
Cardi B	Please me	38

Joe Boy	Beginning	38
Steve Crown	You are great	43
Juice wrld	Lucid Dreams	38
Tuface	African Queen	20
Flavour	Most High	20
Fire Boy	Jealous	20
Travis Green	Nara	20
Minister Excell	Bianlule	20
Kiss Daniel	Poko	20
Cacby B	Clout	20
Nasty C	Said	11
Falz	This is Nigeria	10

Picture 1: Burna Boy (Photo Credit: gettyimages)

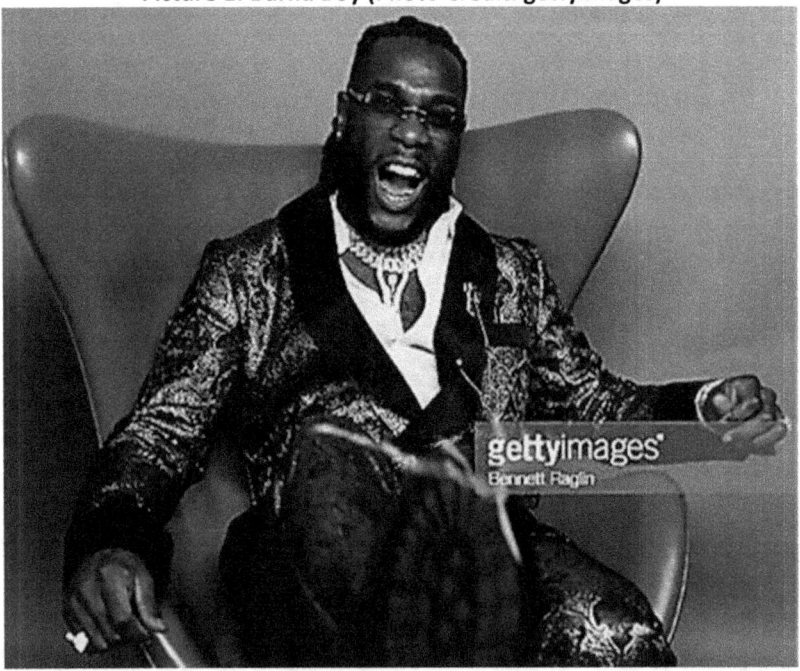

Burna Boy songs are the most popular (Table 2.) amongst teenagers in the two cities. Burna Boy won nomination for the 2020 Grammy awards; His song *My money, My Baby,* is amongst the four songs that Michele Obama (wife of Barak Obama) listens to during her daily aerobic workout.

Burna Boy was born on the 2nd of July, 1991 and named Damini Ogulu, he hails from Mbiama in Rivers State. He spent his early years with his parents in Port-Harcourt, where he attended primary school. His music is a combination of Afro-beat, Rhythm and blues (R&B), Hip-hop and dance hall genres.

Burna's youthfulness is an endearment to young people; he seems to be the youngest, amongst Nigeria's popular musicians that are making national/international impact. Burna Boy at 28 years is as young as Davido, and younger than Tuface, Wizkid and Olamide. His ability to combine different music genres seems to attract a crowd of adherents. The deployment of the Niger Delta variant of Pidgin English with its deep nuances to his song *Dangote*, arrests the sensibilities of Nigeria's South-South youths.

Dangote: by Burna Boy Translation

Dangote, Dangote, Dangote still they find money o	Dangote is striving for more wealth.
No level, no level…	Nothing to worry about.
It's Kel P vibes!	It's Kel P vibes.
Dangote, Dangote, Dangote still dey find money o	Dangote is striving for more wealth.
Who I be, who I be, wey make I no find money o	Who am I, not to strive for more wealth?
I no dey send anybody o…	I mind my business
Me I dey hustle gon, choko…	I am a real hustler
If you hustle ma loko…	If you hustle, it's your business.

In the song "Dangote" Burna Boy compares himself to Aliko Dangote who despite being the richest African (Forbes) for several years, is still searching for more wealth. Why should Burna Boy not search for money? The song is motivational for youths to relentlessly aspire for great goals in life. Niger Delta youths perceive Burna as their brother, hence the wide acceptance.

Interestingly most of the girls, choose female popular artiste such as Sinach, Mercy Chinwo as their musical heroine. The following musicians: N. Bassey, R. Rich, Davido, M. Chinwo, Sinach, F. Edward, T. Godfrey, Ema, Techno, Ada , Cardi B., J. Boy, S. Crown, J. World, occupy between 35-45% (see chart 1) of the research population. This indicate their popularity amongst youths, they form the middle spectrum of popular musicians in Nigeria.

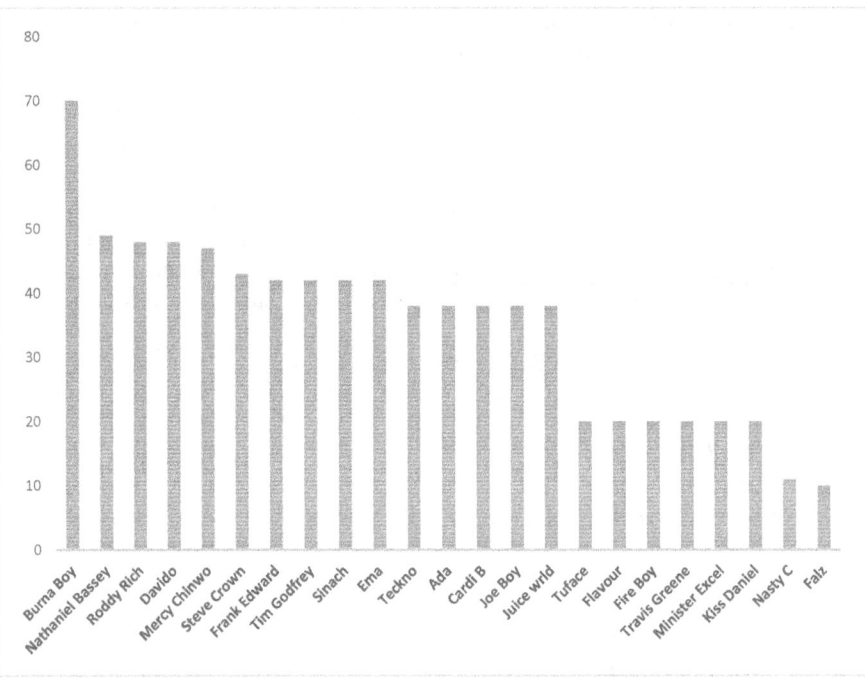

Figure 1: Bar chart showing ratings of musicians in the survey

Apart from church choruses and hymns none of the participants chose any anthem or classical music piece as their music of choice.

Table 3: Participants' Demographics

Pseudonym	Age	Gender	City	Ethnicity	Class
Abuach	14	M	Benin	Etsako	SSS 1
Esigbe	13	M	Warri	Isekiri	JSS 3
Mazuaye	15	F	Benin	Bini	JSS 3
Erobor	13	F	Benin	Bini	JSS 2
Aruke	14	M	Warri	Urhobo	JSS 3

The following research questions guided this aspect of the study:
Question 1: What attracts you to the music that you enjoy?
Question 2: Explain how you enjoy the music that you love?
Question 3: Why are other music genres not enjoyable?

Five students consisting of two females and three males living in Benin and Warri, were interviewed.

In response to the question: "what attracts you to the music you enjoy?" the entire students mentioned *text* as the major attraction; the message in the songs applies to their situations and experiences. Secondly, three of the interviewee chose *voice quality* as the second factor for their interest.

In response to the question: "Explain how you enjoy the music you love?' The answers are varied: "When I am alone I sing the songs I love" Sometimes unconsciously, "I sing the songs when I am sweeping, washing plates and clothes." Some sing the songs they enjoy with friends.

When asked to mention some Nigerian indigenous music they have heard, the entire students except a female participant claim that they do not enjoy indigenous music. The boy from Etsako complained that Etsako music has "no beat" saying "that music *ehn,* is terrible!" The writer hummed some Etsako songs, which the interviewee acknowledged; his response was that they were told that the texts of most indigenous songs and messages are incongruent with Christian doctrine, describing it, as worldly music. The girl that loves indigenous Bini music, usually listen to it, when visiting her grandmother; the songs are recorded in her grandmother's cell phone. When the writer sang *Joromi* by Victor Uwaifo to the students they appreciated it and did not contest the text. A major challenge to resuscitating indigenous music would be to promote it through contemporary mass media. With advancement in technology, indigenous musicians are unable to follow the trend, with a large amount of their music interred in long playing records (LP's) cassettes, compact discs (CD's).

The participant' music experiences in school (CCA course) are learning to play the recorder (three students). The repertoire of songs learnt in school, which they could recall, include: *Mary has a little lamb, Row, row your boat, London Bridge is falling down,* while one of the girls mentioned *unlimited favour* by Chinwo Mercy.

When asked about the following: T.K.E. Phillip, Sowande, and Akin Euba, that are listed in the Senior Secondary School (SSS) WAEC syllabus and CCA programme the participants were unaware of them. Similarly most of them said they have never heard of George Frideric Handel (1685-1759), Ludwig Van Beethoven (1770-1827) and Johann Sebastian Bach (1685-1750). When they were reminded of the 'Hallelujah Chorus' few of them nodded in acknowledgment and when 'A Fifth of Beethoven' and "Fur Elise" was hummed to them; one of the participants said the tune was his cell-phone ring tone. He chose it, because, "I love the sound" he claimed, but he was unable to specify why he loved it.

The students assert, that music programmes are absent in their schools and the Cultural and Creative Arts subject, does not emphasize music. The students encounter music sometimes during general assembly's and preparation for 'culture day', a day set aside in some schools for the celebration of the various ethnic cultures, in Nigeria, through music, dance, cuisine and drama.

Remarkably, one of the participants who attends a Christian mission school in Benin city, observe that the music of Nigerian popular musicians is employed on Fridays as background music for student's aerobics which is part of their physical and health education programme. It is the official occasion when students in the hostels listen to music, as they are barred from using cell-phones, iPod and tablets, while in school.

In spite of being in a mission, classical music and anthems are unfamiliar to them, apart from the school/national anthems. Participant's music choices are not included in the WAEC music syllabus. The curriculum/syllabus needs to be appraised annually to reflect this trend.

The participants listen to the music they enjoy through: television, radio, cell-phones, parties, churches and play. Some students living in school hostels do not have access to electronic music media of any kind, because such electronic devices are prohibited. Students in hostels, sources of listening to music are in church on Sundays (mission schools) and during aerobics classes on Fridays, in some schools.

The participants were asked why they enjoy the songs of their choices: some mentioned attraction to the music videos, the artiste's mannerisms on stage, voice, popularity, while others were unable to give any reason. Some of the participants selected Christian Hymns and choruses such as: The Solid Rock, Great is Thy Faithfulness, Amazing Grace, but the choices were minimal compared to the preferences of other students.

Incorporating Community Music into Basic Schools; Music Programmes

The Role of Mass Media/Information and Communication Technology (ICT) in Enhancing Community Music:

Mass media/ICT are the major organs of community music dissemination in contemporary times, they include: radio, television, internet, YouTube and live streaming, all these media are accessible through cell-phones. The cell phone, functions as a radio, TV, music player and computer; once the cell phone is charged, it is capable of supplying music from any part of the globe to the listener. As a mobile device, the cell phone owner, has access to music 24/7, wherever. Using the cell-phone with earphones, enable their holders, to listen to music while at work, home, in class, bus, without upsetting people around.

It is imperative to incorporate Mass media/ICT into education plans. It is a major source of discovering and communicating prevalent music in the community.

Undoubtedly, youths below thirty years enjoy Hip hop music more than other music genres. Hip hop is largely promoted by ICT and music entrepreneurs, who budget enormous sums of money to sponsor their artistes. Okpeki (2013:140) affirms that "Youths are the target of the marketing of rap and Hip Hop, they are always influenced by the media… and even the master mind behind the urge for fashion and indecent dressing are some of rap and Hip Hop artist"

Popular musicians encourage popular culture, through dress, mannerism, speech patterns, hairstyle, shoes and other social vices, which are copied by youths. For instance, Abraka youths have developed "the habits of seeking for guidance and mentoring from celebrities they see on television (TV) and pop stars on radio programs they view and listen to every day."(Okpeki, 2013:141)

Majority of the public primary/secondary schools do not have music instruments, do not observe assemblies, while some observe it once a week, music at such events are gospel music. Students after school periods are tied to extra classes, students get home at dusk exhausted, unable to play. They resort to ICT/Mass media, for entertainment.

Innovative Teachers and Classrooms
Evidently, children in basic schools are more attuned to popular music, which is largely excluded from the curriculum. It behooves teachers in the CCA and SSS programmes to be innovative by employing music resources in each community, into the classroom; thereby avoiding strict reliance on the curriculum. Music teachers, assisted by students, should source for existing music within school communities. The programme must be student centred. Students should be encouraged to form different bands, ensembles; i.e. brass bands, steel bands, indigenous ensembles and groups, depending on the form of music, common in their context. These groups should be afforded opportunities to perform, at school assemblies, concerts/competitions, culture days, Independence Day, Easter and yuletide celebrations.

The community music classroom is dynamic and multi-cultural. Each person contributes to the teaching/learning process. Apart from the keyboard which is unique as a melodic/harmonic instrument other music instruments in the community, should be members of the music classroom especially indigenous musical instruments. Every opinion, question, observation and suggestions should be considered important; teachers and students are learners, because everyone comes with his/her music.

The community music classroom must be receptive to all genres of music such as Christian, Islamic, classical music, hymns, indigenous African music and other derivatives, such as *Eyo* music which is a popular festival in Lagos; *Igue* in Benin, *Atilogu* in Igbo land; *Oye' Ekoro* in Warri, etc. Students should experience what music is, as presented by their instructors/classmates.

Community music teachers must recognize that students attend school to develop what is innate and acquire new knowledge that would help them to fit and contribute effectively to society. While some student would want to learn to play the keyboard, guitar, recorder, violin, trumpet and saxophone, others may be interested in Nigeria's music instruments and singing. The school music classroom should be empathetic to student's diverse interests and should not be kowtowed merely to the teacher's musical competence.

Indigenous/popular musicians that are available in most communities could serve as adjunct instructors to complement the full-time teachers. However, the basic school music teacher should be versatile in different music genres.

For instance Ken Worthy School in Houston TX advertisement for a music teacher, requested applicants to possess the following qualifications:

- The music teacher should have a comprehensive musical knowledge;
- Should be enthusiastic;
- Must have good communication skills;
- Flexibility and ability to teach children;
- To make student know the differences in music instrument as they look;
- Familiarize yourself with the basic concepts of music, such as notes, pace, symphony, composition, chords, scales, rhythm, etc.;
- How to coordinate songs with other musical instruments;
- Meet students with different music genres, like jazz, classical, techno, pop, folk, etc.;
- Collaborate with school management to organize musical programmes for civic tasks and school performances.

The above qualities, are for pre-school pupils, between the ages of 12 months and 5 years; Ken worthy admits infants that are six weeks old, while music lessons are taught when children attain one year. Notably, the job requisites is task is specific, the teacher is expected to possess the qualities enlisted and there is no requirement of a certificate/degree. The music teacher at the basic school level must be a versatile performer that is able to elicit curiosity and create vicarious interest in students. Teachers with these capacities are absent in Nigeria's basic schools.

Establishment of Local Government/Community Music Centres:
To promote music education at the basic schools, it is recommended that community music centres are established in each of the 774 Local Government Areas, in Nigeria. Nwankpa (2014:9) asserts that:

> Countries world over are known for their creativity, potentials, integrity and cultural expressions through their national and state ensembles and presentations. (In the developed countries cities and towns to own and run similar ensembles)...It is imperative that such ensembles should reflect the cultural elements, values, ethics, hopes and aspirations of the people. Consequently to achieve this ideas and

ideals and to bring their realization and impact to the grassroots, as well as encourage musical art education in creativity, entertainment, youth employment and productivity, we call for the establishment of community music programmes and centres

These community music centres would help to develop and stimulate interest in community music. Musicians would act as instructors. Children interested in African music instruments production for instance would be taught at such centres. The polytechnics at Ibadan and Ilaro, produces Yoruba drums and other Western instruments, lecturers/students on industrial attachment from these institutions could temporarily be employed to teach primary and secondary school students' music instruments production at the community centres.

Community centres could be established as an entity, in schools or in community centres/halls, but should be independent of school administration, while teachers in public schools are made coordinators.

Government/non-governmental agencies such as: State/Local Governments, Niger Delta Development Commission, Delta State Oil Producing Areas Development Commission, Edo State Oil Producing Areas Development Commission, including corporate bodies, such as The Central Bank of Nigeria and other commercial banks, The Nigerian National Petroleum Corporation and other multinational petroleum companies, should fund the project. Industrialists should be enlisted as patrons, the patrons would ensure that the centres are built and maintained, with the appropriate facilities/equipment for the performance of the music genres inherent in the community. The community centres should be administered by local government chairmen, through the Supervisor for Culture. The Musical Society of Nigeria centre in Lagos is an epic community music centre.

Community music centres would be venues for performances/exhibitions by visiting music bands/groups including tertiary students/musicologists. Such centres would on the long run, oblige the revitalization and inclusion of music as a subject in the school syllabus.

Discussions and Conclusion

Nigeria's extant music programmes are focused on producing people with versatility in Western music; this trend subsists due to the historical foundations of music programmes introduced into Nigeria, by the Christian missionaries. Students are forced to accept Western music as the ideal and superior music of all times, without consideration for the learner's choice/interest. In the West, community music such as Blues, Jazz, Reggae, Hip-hop and Rock, form part of the music programme, from basic school to tertiary schools. Students are allowed to specialize in instruments of their choice, while in primary school.

Some virtuosos in Western music instruments do not have a bachelor's degree in music, but, are experts in their various music instruments. Professor Agu, (2018) a notable Nigerian musicologist, narrated, buying a first class air ticket for a Ghanaian to fly from Ghana to Nigeria, to play the tenor saxophone, on a movie soundtrack, he was producing, because, none in Nigeria could perfectly play the tenor saxophone. There have been reported cases of bass guitarists being brought in from abroad to perform due to unskilled local musicians. These anomalies subsist because these musical instruments are not taught in schools.

Failure to systematically integrate the music that children/pupils enjoy, into the formal school music programme, would spell doom for the sustenance of music as a school subject, in basic schools, which has been the case, since Nigeria's independence. Majority of Nigeria's popular musicians never studied music in school.

Popular music is the most dynamic of all music genres, it is ever evolving, borrowing and shedding from within and without, the danger this poses to music scholarship if it is not quickly incorporated into the school programme, is that its speed of transformation, would be overwhelming to critical study, while on the other hand, it keeps attracting more audiences and followership. Art music is gradually being amalgamated into popular music genre. There are several popular musicians such as Michael Jackson, Lionel Richie, and Stevie Wonder, whose music are scored and performed by orchestras. Community music centres would serve as an outlet for the performance and promotion of all forms of music.

In the past some students learnt these musical instruments informally in school bands, but fail to hone their skills, because their musical instruments of choice are de-emphasized in schools. This writer learnt to play the guitar, including classical guitar, through private tuition, but lost traction, because the guitar was not an orchestral instrument and proficiency on it was not accorded any grade, in the NCE/BA music programmes, that position is unchanged in several tertiary institutions.

Community music ensures that learner's interests are considered in the curriculum. Despite the importance of orchestral instruments in music programmes, students should not be pressured by perennial philosophies that emphasize teacher's knowledge/skills. The piano should not be made compulsory, its historicity and dynamism over other instruments should be highlighted, but should not be a compulsory instrument in schools.

In conclusion, one of the most important components of developing musicianship is through listening; Cho (2019:133) affirms that: "listening is the basic skill required for both learning music and for developing good musicianship. Thus, listening plays a major part in the learning process. Through listening, students expand their musical understanding and increase their enjoyment of music" This study has revealed that Nigerian youths listen to hip-hop music more than other genres of music, the Christian artistes chosen by the research participants, likewise, compose in the hip-hop form, which presupposes that hip hop music, to a large extent determine their sense of musicianship. Cho (2019:133) summarizes that:

> Music listening is about understanding and enjoying the meaning, the aesthetics, and the beauty of music (Miller, 1968)It is an activity involving perceiving and understanding the characteristics and principles of the musical elements such as rhythm, melody, harmony, form, dynamics, tempo, and timbre (Reimer, 2003) Moreover, music listening activities include the process of exploring the aesthetic elements in music through understanding of the contextual factors related to music. (Elliot, 1995; Boardman, 1996)

Majority of Nigerian youths, apart from a few who are ardent Christians, listen to *Naija* jams, which is Nigeria's derivative of the global hip-hop. *Naija* jams form the core of Nigeria's youth musicianship, because that is what the various media broadcast more to the public. The school music programme must acknowledge this fact, that what an individual listens to, is a major component of the individual's musicianship.

The acoustic guitar and drums set, should be placed beside the piano/keyboard in every educational institution, because the guitar is cheaper to acquire, it is mobile, does not need power to play, it is both a melodic/harmonic instrument and it accommodates group performances between learners and instructors. The guitar emblematizes hip-hop music and Nigerian youths currently, *enjoy* hip-hop music, more than other music genres.

References

Ajewole, J. (2013). 'A Critique of the Cultural and Creative Arts Curriculum in Nigerian Secondary Schools'. *Nsukka Journal of Musical Arts Research.* Vol. 2.Pp: 108-117.

Agu, D.C.C (2018). 'Remarks during a Postgraduate Thesis Defence in December, 2018, at the Postgraduate Boardroom of the Delta State University, Abraka.

Agbidi, N. J. & Osayande, R. I. (2019). 'From Folk to Highlife: A Study of Sir Victor Uwaifo's Ebis, Ebis Sirrogbain and Joromi,' *Journal of the Association of Nigerian Musicologists. (JANIM)* No. 13. Pp: 254-267.

Akperi, Y. A (2016). 'The Challenges of Globalisation and Culture in Formulating Philosophies of Music Programmes in Nigeria'. *Music Scholarship, Culture and Performance Challenges in 21st Century Africa: A Critical Resource Book in Honour of Emurobome Idolor.* Kenneth Efakponana Eni (Ed.). Lagos: Bahiti and Dalila Publishers. Pp: 345-365.

Anya-Njoku, M. C. and Onu, S. O. (2016), 'Revamping the Unpopularity of Music as a School Subject in Nigeria through Indigenization: A Proposal'. *Journal of the Association of Nigerian Musicologists (JANIM)* No. 10.ANIM. Pp: 381-405

Chadwick, S. (2012) 'Teachers as Agents in Botswana's Music Education: Challenges and Possibilities'. *Music Education Research.* 14(4) p, 430-447.

Cho, S., Baek, Y., Choe, E. J. (2019). 'A Strategic Approach to Music Listening With a Mobile App for High School Students'. *International Journal of Music Education: Research and Practice. ISME Vol37/NO.1/2019.* Pp: 132-141.

Hess, J. (2019) 'Decolonising Music Education: Moving Beyond Tokenism'. Journal Code=ijma

Nketia, J. H. K. (2016) *Reinstating Traditional Music in Contemporary Contexts.* Akropong-Akuapem: Regnum Africa Publications. Print.

Kerchner, J. (2019) *Coming into the Music Community.* International Society for Music Education.Isme.org

Community Music School. *Welcome to the Community Music School Located in Trappe PA.*cmsmusic.org accessed11/9/2019

Nwankpa, O. N. (2014) Pasover Pedantry: Contesting the State of Musical Arts in Nigeria. *Nsukka Journal of Musical Arts Research. Volume 3.* Department of Music, University of Nigeria, Nsukka.

Nwankpa, O. N. (2013). *Community Music Programme: Development and Management.* Port-Harcourt: Celwil Publishers Nig. Ltd.

Okafor, R. C. (2019). *Popular Music in Nigeria* .Enugu: New Generation Books.

Okpeki, P. I. (2013). 'The Impact of Delta Broadcasting Service Music Programmes on the Speech of Youths in Abraka'. *Nsukka Journal of Musical Arts Research.* Vol. 2. Pp: 139-143

Reimer, B. (2003). '*A Philosophy of Music Education: Advancing the Vision, 3rd Edition.* New Jersey: Prentice Hall.

Simon, M. K., Goes, J. (2011). *What is Phenomenological Research?* www.dissertationrecipes.com accessed: 26/11/2019.

14

Popular Music and Skill Development in Tertiary Music Education

Precious Omuku, Ph.D

Introduction

Popular music is the most widely heard music with the largest fan based across Nigeria. On the other hand, the importance of skill development cannot be over-emphasized, as it is the bedrock for sustainable development. The objective of the study is to ascertain ways popular music could enhance skill development in tertiary music education. Popular music has been one of the most successful genres of music in Nigeria for years now. It is considered to be a veritable tool for developing musical skills, thus, harnessing it into the music education system, thus creating new possibilities of what popular music could offer students. An empirical research methodology was adopted for the study. The author found out that, most of the people who approach the University for Admission to study music, often come with the popular music background. The seriousness with which they approach their studies and the experience they already have make them great assets to the music business. More so, the acceptance of popular music in Nigeria cuts across various ethnic backgrounds as such, it is a veritable tool to harnessing the potentials of the youths in the society. The author concluded that a combination of a well-groomed musician with the popular music background coupled with a grounded understanding of music education is a huge advantage for the musical arts.

African popular music of today refers to the corpus of sounds, songs, and dance music crafted by African professional and non-professional musicians, at home and in the Diaspora, in response to the political, economic, spiritual, and social needs of the burgeoning modernity that started in the late nineteenth century, and is still ongoing. A basic characteristic of these 'new' sounds is that they keep adopting musical elements, properties, and instruments from any part of the globe that the musicians consider worthy of enhancing their creativity. This flexibility has given birth to today's World Music (also known as World Beat or Ethno-pop). Sometimes abbreviated to Afropop, African popular music exists in three sub-categories. They are the Ethnic pop, the Inter-ethnic pop, and the International pop (Agawu, 2003; Onwuegbuna, 2007).

The majority of the musical styles belonging to the recreational category of African traditional music have become popular. To this category belong those songs and dances that are neither culturally nor spiritually bound. They could be performed at any occasion and time for the entertainment of their audience; and they could also be hired or commissioned to perform in settings that are considered foreign to their home communities. They include children's games songs, age-grade music and dances, songs of satire, and folkloric songs. However, some songs belonging to the incidental category have equally emerged in the society to assume popularity. Incidental African music, generally, are not premeditated by their performers, but are performed on the incident of some traditional duties and activities. Work songs, performed either by a group of workers or individuals on domestic or occupational jobs, drive out fatigue and boredom from their tasks, using music made by themselves as they work. Some of these songs have found their way into the social arena, thereby becoming popular. Some of these songs have taken the centre stage in the public domain, and the community allows them because there are no rigid strictures for them. These songs and their accompanying musical activities fall within the ethnic pop category.

In the midst of the foregoing, some leading Nigerian music scholars and educators, like Agu (2008), Ekwueme (2004), and Onyeji (2002) seem to sound sceptical about the pedagogic possibilities of popular music in the country's academic curricula. However, their counterparts such as Mbanugo (1999), Okafor (2005), Adedeji (2006), and Vidal (2008) are of the firm opinion that the African music curricula would be incomplete and unbalanced without the inclusion of popular music studies to it. And amplifying the argument for the inclusion of popular music studies in the curricula, Agawu (2003) wonders why the most widely heard music on the continent is not also the most written about, the most taught in our institutions, and the most valued. The foregoing exposй, therefore, form the background against how 'African popular music can be used in the skill development of tertiary music education in Nigeria' because it is among the widely accepted form of music across various ethnic background. It wide acceptance can allow for various skill development to be designed around it.

The Concept of African Music

The term 'African music' has a long pedigree and is capable of various interpretations, both from historical and contemporary perspectives. From the account of early European travellers, sailors and explorers, the term African music represented the music of 'barbaric' tribes; it was devoid of any form of aesthetic consideration and existed outside the theoretical framework and aesthetic benchmarks of European musicology. According to Akpabot (1986, p.1), the idea of primitiveness, however, is a relative one: a group of African musicians listening to European jazz with its repetitive rhythm may term the whole process as primitive compared to their own complex rhythms.

Some scholars of African music sometimes refer to African music as music of sub-Saharan Africa only. Notable among these scholars is Ghanaian Professor Emeritus, J.H.K. Nketia. He holds the view that only African music south of the Sahara qualifies to be called African music. He excludes the music of North Africa and of white settlers in Southern Africa and parts of East Africa from the African music category on stylistic grounds (Nketia, 1975). This is, however, a contentious issue. While one may agree that some cultural differences exist between North Africa and sub-Saharan Africa, there have also been increasing interactions and unending streams of cross-cultural and trans-national influences from both sides of the divide. Some of these influences have come through migrations, the trans-Saharan trade, migrant labour, education, evangelical activities and other regional and trans-border collaborations. The direct impact of this is that the demarcation of Africa into two main cultural blocs, seeming to exist in isolation of each other, become all the more blurred in contemporary times.

To understand the parameters of African music, one needs to have knowledge of the conceptual framework of African music genres, understanding and appreciation of performance intentions and incentives and many other real and metaphysical dimensions including the role of language in performative contexts. For instance, most African music genres are in fact song-dance compounds. Song is often accompanied by dance and vice-versa. A song may be vocalised or played on an instrument, while dance is a bodily execution. The rhythm of song, which is usually enhanced or complemented by the drum, is responsible for instigating bodily responses or gestures the most elaborate and stylized of which being dance. Secondly, the dance, most often through its different stages of energy levels leads to some spiritual elevation. At the highest level of signing, instrument playing and dancing is a climax which manifest in numerous forms of incentives. Performer, at this level, often experience a sense of escaping all manner of physical and spiritual limitations.

Music Education

Music education can be defined as a process by which musical knowledge and skills are developed through learning at school, colleges and University and the informal traditional setting (Ogunrinade *et al.* 2012). It is the means that societies use in order to transmit music and musical skills from one generation to the next. However, music education also involves, implicitly, ideas about what music is (and is not), where music comes from, and what is the purpose or function of music. The most basic means of sustaining music from generation to generation is through informal or formal teaching and learning.

According to Ogunrinade (2015), music education especially in African setting shows differences and sometimes philosophical disagreement in three areas. The first area of difference involves the distinction between formal instruction with lessons and written musical notation in the schools versus informal learning that takes place in a family or neighbourhood setting by imitation and oral tradition, usually without lessons and almost never with notation. The second area of disagreement, which takes place in colleges, universities, and conservatories, is the balance in the curriculum and the structure of the musical institution between, first, practical instruction in performing music; second, theoretical knowledge in the history of music and how music is designed and structured. The third area, which takes place at all levels of formal learning, whether in elementary schools, high schools, colleges, universities, and conservatories, is the balance in the curriculum and the institution between Western art music and multicultural music, including folk music and world music (p. 84). Either formal (class room setting) or informal (Traditional) music gives opportunity to self discovery which helps in enhancing the productivity of such person thereby making the individual employable thus contributing to the economy of the society as well as self reliance.

Origin of Music Education in Nigeria

As stated by Ajayi, Goma and Johnson (1996), that it is difficult to precisely pinpoint the exact period of the origin of music education with respect to its historical context when considering the indigenous African and Islamic Systems in Nigeria. According to Kwami (1994), there are three major aspects on the origin of music education which are the indigenous/traditional African music education, Arabic and European music education (p. 544). Thus, to properly determine the origin of music education in Nigeria, these music educational systems must be considered separately as each of this music systems have influenced our music education separately in unique ways. However, in Nigeria, the origin of music education can be traced only to indigenous African and Islamic systems. These systems have continued the basis through which cultural values have been transferred from generation to generation including their musical concepts and beliefs (Ogunrinade, 2015).

The African Popular Music

The earliest form of popular music practiced by any human society is the ethnic pop. Ethnic pop are those styles that became popular within an ethnic environment where they are performed and appreciated by the folk of that region. They are, in the main, music and dances designed specifically for folk entertainment; whether they are recreational, occasional, or incidental, as long as there are no inhibitive strictures for them. Historical records of such forms are preserved in oral traditions. It is important at this juncture to observe that the development of urban popular music in Africa outlines a model in which musical resources mainly from Western Europe, America and the Islamic world are incorporated into traditional African music to produce new syncretic forms (Emielu, 2009). African popular music is, therefore, a product of the intermingling of African and foreign socio-musical resources as the West African Highlife has exemplified. The processes of its creation are idiomatic of the various styles of popular music on the African continent.

Popular Music and Skill Development in Music Education

Popular music has become the foremost tool for music education development as this genre of music promotes entrepreneurial skills that are readily applicable upon graduation from the university. This is so because; this genre of music appeal more to the youthful population of Nigeria as such, has created a huge market segment for its consumption. Beside, with the increase in demand for the consumption of African popular music across the country, it is pertinent that educational institutions take advantage of this opportunity to create a framework that will allow popular music to contribute to tertiary music education by developing a curriculum for popular music studies, which could be effectively applied in the teaching and learning of popular music at all levels in our tertiary institutions. More so, there are prospective learners who earnestly desire the formal training in popular music-making and research, and possibility of social, economic, and spiritual prospects for the graduate popular musician (Onwuegbuna, 2012) thus, creating a broader platform or field for musical studies that cuts across other fields of studies in tertiary institutions. They have so much experiences from the field where they have been and become masters in their own rights. With the mass revolution in the technological innovations around the world, popular music offers the opportunity to develop and enhance learning in the areas of ICT, sound engineering, mass media, linguistics, marketing, symbology, etc., among prospective music students. A typical example is the digitalization of sound files, beats production, etc., adding popular music to the curricula will allow students to not just have popular music knowledge but will also aid them in acquiring key technological and innovative skills required to succeed in the music world.

Conclusion

Popular music has been seen to attract a lot of attention among the youths of Nigeria. This genre of music has now become part of our lifestyle in Nigeria.

Therefore, harnessing its potential in tertiary music education via developing music education curricula to encourage students to pursue an academic career in popular music will allow for skill developments. This will allow music graduate to be fully prepared for the music world as popular music offers a lot of opportunity that cuts across all sectors of the industry.

References

Adedeji, Femi (2006). A critical appraisal of music scholarship in the contemporary Nigeria: Bridging the existing gaps between the practitioners. *Nigerian Musicology Journal*, 2, 246-257.

Adeogun, O. A. (2018). The Development of University Music Education in Nigeria: An Outline. SAGE Open April-June 2018: 1–14.

Agawu, Kofi (2003). *Representing African Music*. New York: Routledge.

Ajayi, J. E. A., Goma, L. K. H., & Johnson, A. (with Mwontia, W.). (1996). *The African Experience with Higher Education*. Accra, Ghana: The Association of African Universities; London: James Currey; Athens: Ohio University Press.

Akpabot, S. E. (1986). *Foundation of Nigerian Traditional Music*. Ibadan, Nigeria: Spectrum Books.

Ekwueme, L. E. N. (2004). *Essays on African and African-American music and culture*. Lagos: LENAUS.

Kwami, R. (1994). 'Music Education in Ghana and Nigeria: A Brief Survey'. *Africa*, 64, 534-559.

Mbanugo, C. E. (1999). 'The effect of the language of Nigerian Popular Music in Promoting National Consciousness in Youths of Anambra State. *Unizik Journal of Arts and Humanities,* 1(1), 198-206.

Ogunrinade, D. O. A. (2015). 'Music Education as a Pillar to Sustainable Development in Nigeria'. *Journal of Economics and Sustainable Development. Vol.6*, No.3.

Ogunrinade, D.O.A, et al. (2012) 'The State of Music Education in Nigerian Secondary School Programme' *Journal of Educational and Social Research* (Sapienza University Italy), Vol. 2 (3): 391- 403.

Okafor, R. C. (2005). *Music in Nigerian society*. Enugu: New Generation.

Onwuegbuna, I. E. (2007). *Trends in African Pop Music: A Survey of the Reggae Genre in Nigeria*. An Unpublished Master of Arts Thesis, University of Nigeria, Nsukka.

Onwuegbuna, I. E. (2012). *The Instructional Value of African Popular Music: Its Application in Nigeria Music Education*. Lambert Academic Publishing. Deutchland, Germany.

Onyeji, C. (2002). 'Popular music: Facts about the Music and Musicians'. In E. Idolor (Ed.), *Music in Africa: Facts and Illusions* (pp. 24-36). Ibadan: Sterling-Horden

Vidal, 'Tunji (2008). 'Music education in Nigeria: Entering the 21st century with a pragmatic Philosophy'. *Journal of the Association of Nigerian Musicologists (JANIM),* Special Edition. 1-19.

SECTION IV

Nigerian Art and Church Music

Ekundayo Phillips and the Development of Modern Yoruba Music

Professor 'Bode Omojola[*]

Introduction

Ekundayo Phillips (1884-1969) contributed perhaps more than anyone else to the growth of Yoruba Christian Church music in the twentieth century. Through his numerous works, creative and academic, he helped to lay the foundation for the emergence of a culturally relevant tradition of Church music in western Nigeria. In 1953, he published a pioneering study on Yoruba music in which he describes key identity-defining features of the music and how such elements could provide the basis for developing a modern musical idiom for use in the Christian church (Phillips 1953). Phillips locates the origin of Yoruba music in the inherent musicality of the language. The Yoruba language, according to him, has innate rhythmic and tonal qualities that provide the basis for understanding how Yoruba music evolved from speech. Phillips also draws parallels between traditional Yoruba music practices and the music of medieval Europe of roughly from the tenth to the fifteenth century with a view to showing how medieval Europe could provide important models for composers of Yoruba Church music.[1] The study is thus particularly significant because it is conceived as a treatise on composition with guidelines for modern composers of Yoruba music. His discussion relies extensively on music examples drawn from traditional Yoruba repertoires as well as from his own compositions.

My objective in this study is to investigate the musical and cultural principles that underline Phillips's work as a composer and musicologist. I will also highlight the impact of his work on modern musical composition in Nigeria. My methods here are simple and straightforward, defined mainly by a descriptive reading of his treatise and a brief reflection of its impact, supported with modest analytical references to selected works. Born in 1884,

---

[*] University of Massachusetts, Amherst, U.S.A
[1] For studies focusing on church music practices from the Eastern part of Nigeria, see Ekwueme, 1981.

Phillips received his first organ lessons from his uncle, the Reverend Johnson. In 1911, he proceeded to the Trinity College of Music, London to study organ, thus becoming the second Nigerian to study music in Europe.[2] Upon his return to Nigeria, he became organist and choirmaster at Christ's Church, Lagos, a position he held till 1962 when he retired. In 1964, five years before his death, he was awarded an honorary doctorate degree by the University of Nigeria, Nsukka. Phillips is generally regarded as the most influential twentieth-century church music composer and musician in western Nigeria.[3]

An Examination of Phillips's Study of Yoruba Music

Phillipsr book, *Yoruba Music* (1953) describes many important elements of traditional Yoruba vocal music, including the prominence of the pentatonic scale, parity of melodic and linguistic contours, and prevalence of parallel harmonies conditioned by linguistic inflection (Omojola, 1995: 30-31). Based on the similarities between Yoruba and European medieval musics, he encourages composers of Yoruba music to pay more attention to the music of medieval Europe for compositional models and procedures that could aid the development of Yoruba music. A summary of his observations on this topic is provided below.

Similarities between Yoruba and European Medieval Musics
Pentatonic Scale

The typical Yorùbá anhemitonic pentatonic scale, which, as we know, precludes the use of the perfect fourth and the major seventh (labelled by Phillips as "fah" and "te"), is, in his opinion, conceptually related to the modal scales of medieval Europe. Phillips explains that these two intervals were rarely used in medieval music, at least not in the same way as they are in baroque and post-baroque Western tonal music. According to him, "Although the seven-note scale was used in Europe at that time, yet so sparingly were the notes *fah* and *te* used that the music of the period could almost past as the pentatonic. On the other hand, as I have already mentioned, the Yorùbás (sic) occasionally use extra notes-*fah* and *te* in particular. Putting these two facts together, it is easy to see that there is really very little difference in the scales, and also to understand the similarity of the two kinds of music."[4]

---

[2] The first Nigerian to study music formally in Europe was Reverend Coker who studied in Germany in 1871.
[3] For more information on the life and work of Phillips, see. Michael Olatunji, 2005 and Godwin Sadoh, 2019.
[4] Phillips, *Yoruba Music,* 9.

Singing in Unison, Parallelism, and Magadizing

Other musical similarities identified by Phillips between medieval Europe and Yorùbá culture include the use of unisons, madagizing, and descant. He explains that the simplicity of both the Yorùbá pentatonic scale and the modal scales of medieval Europe becomes apparent when the two are compared to the major, minor, chromatic scales of post-medieval Europe. The predominance of unisons in Yorùbá music attests to the relative lack of harmonic thought in Yorùbá culture, although Phillips admits that there are occasional instances of harmony in Yorùbá vocal music. Yorùbá music and European medieval plainchants are nonetheless quite similar: unison singing is "the rule" in Yorùbá music, while part-singing "the exception" in both traditions. He explains however that both traditions of music employ parallel singing at the fourth and fifth in the form of "magadizing and descant." This procedure consists of the adding of harmonizing phrases above the main melody. According to him, the "music of the Yorùbá is purely melodic and what is part-singing in it is simply a duplication of the melody at certain intervals which differ with various tribes. The most commonly used of the intervals is the third, not the European tempered third, but the peculiar thirds sometimes described as imperfect in the broad sense."[5] Evaluation of Yorùbá music here resonates with those of Western scholars like W.E. Ward (1927) and Hornbostel (1928) who ascribe similar heterophonic qualities to African music. Hornbostel, for example, once observed that the use of organum in parallel fourths in African music is comparable to the music of medieval Europe, and is not based on any harmonic principle.

Cadential Points

Cadential points also highlight the modal similarities between the two traditions of music, none of which makes use of semitonal leading-note and its associated functional dominant chord. To illustrate the general absence of semitonal leading tones in Yorùbá music, Phillips refers to the compilations made by the Rev. Canon Ransome-Kuti, another prominent composer and compiler of Yorùbá music of the period.[6] Phillips advises that harmonic procedures of medieval Europe should be employed in composing Yorùbá songs. He opines that Yorùbá composers who treat their songs to Western tonal (major-minor key) harmonies destroy the music in the process. Semitonal cadences based on "te-doh" (the perfect cadence) and "fah-me" (the plagal cadence) are, according to him, "particularly objectionable especially when harmonized by a dominant seventh followed by tonic triad chords; and all students of musical history know that dominant sevenths were neither in existence in medieval times nor are up till now admissible in

---

[5] Phillips, *Yoruba Music*, 26.
[6] This compilation is part of the appendix in *Yoruba Hymn Book*.

Plainsong." He continues: "If then as I have endeavoured to prove, there is a close similarity between our present Yorùbá music and the Plainsong of the Europeans, should we not be proud of it and regard our music as a noble heritage worth preserving. This is exactly what should be our aim in planning our church music."[7]

The "Development" of Yorùbá Music

Phillips's concept of musical development entails the enlargement and embellishment of Yorùbá vernacular materials into larger forms. For example, short and repetitive melodies could be developed into longer pieces through the use of borrowed developmental techniques. Likewise, Western harmonic procedures could be used to transform melodies into part-songs. To achieve these musical objectives, composers should take advantage of the similarities earlier identified between Yorùbá and medieval European musical traditions. It is instructive to briefly explore Phillips's suggestions as to how these objectives could be achieved.

Rhythmic Development, Folk-Tune, and Dance

Phillips expresses some general views regarding the incorporation of African rhythmic elements into Christian worship. He begins by correcting the erroneous but widely held view that the best of African music exists only in its pulsating, dancing-inducing rhythm. Reacting to this misjudgment and writing as a converted Christian, Phillips remarks that there "is no doubt that the idea that any kind of drumming would do for worship arose from ignorance about the custom in local heathen worship. It is not commonly known that these worshippers, at some moments in their worship, either change the style of singing and drumming or stop the latter altogether."[8]

Phillips urges caution in bringing folk tunes and dance elements into the church so as to avoid infiltrating Christian worship with what European missionaries considered to be profanity. He explains though that songs whose "pagan" connotations have waned over time, could be adapted for Christian use. He reminds us that the introduction of secular and folk melodies into the early European Christian church led to negative results especially in the fourth and fifth centuries. It took the intervention of Saint Ambrose, and later Saint Gregory, to check the "menace." But while Phillips objects to the "tendency to introduce current secular—sometimes profane dance tunes into our services, under the cloak of religious words, I cannot see anything wrong in using certain dignified tunes whose original words are neither immoral nor profane such as *Ohun a fowy ṣe kòlè bàjẹ́* (a folk song

---

[7]Phillips, *Yoruba Music*, 14.
[8]Phillips, *Yoruba Music*, 47.

about the value of money) and *A ṣé gi lóko èrò ya wá wŏ* (a folk song about rural life)." [Translations in brackets and tone marks are mine].[9]

Part-Singing and Accompaniment

As I have earlier mentioned, Phillips argues against the use of European baroque and post-baroque tonal harmonies in composing or arranging Yorùbá music because contrary motion and other harmonic features which characterize the music of these periods generally work against the inflectional patterns of Yorùbá speech. Phillips explains this issue thus:

"The question has often been put to me, whether or not parts may be added in modern harmony. The answer is an emphatic No, so long as (Yorùbá) words are sung…Harmony requires frequent use of contrary and oblique motion which is opposed in principle to the idea of parallel parts (or similar motion) as demanded by the Yorùbá language…Substitute *te* for *lah* and you spoil and Westernise it at once; accompany the *te* with dominant seventh chord, and you make it worse still. This is exactly the kind of absurd thing being indulged in at present by certain enthusiastic but misguided reformers.[10]

Phillips, however, recommends the use of contrapuntal procedures, which can help to guarantee the retention of the tonal inflections and meanings of Yorùbá words. Thus, he notes:

> Attention has been drawn to the fact that our songs and part-singing belong to the medieval and fifteenth –sixteenth-century styles…what can be more fitting than to study the European style of harmony of that period and adopt it…Chromaticism must be avoided in the melodies, so it must also be avoided in the accompaniment. Besides the extent to which we may go in the chords, there is also the style and method of use, and this involves the study of modal harmony, namely the harmony of the period of the old modes, beginning with plainsong and culminating in the sixteenth century.[11]

Form

Regarding form, Phillips explains that Western procedures can be adopted effectively to compose Yorùbá music and to avoid the monotony that results from excessive repetition. He explains that certain elements of Western musical forms are inherent in indigenous Yorùbá music. For example, the

---

[9]These two songs employ the same tune, and were later adapted for Christian worship. A new composition resulting from this adaptation is entitled *Iṣẹ́ Olúwa kт lн bajй* (the work of God endures for ever), which is one of the most widely performed Yorùbá Christian songs in Nigeria today. Other similar songs sung originally in praise of Yoruba deities but later adapted for Christian use include *Тунgнyigм Ọta Omi* (later changed to *Тунgнyigм lỌlyrun wa*) and *Ọlyfun Idanigbo Niye*. For more details on these, see Phillips, *Yoruba Music*.

[10] Phillips, *Yoruba Music*, 26-28.

[11]Phillips, *Yoruba Music*, 28.

principle of repetition and variation, which is germane to the European rondo form, also exists in traditional Yorùbá performances in which instrumental interludes alternate with singing, especially whenever a significant part of the singing is repetitive. In such performances, instrumental sections perform roles comparable to those of rondo episodes. In addition, forms like binary and ternary are already present in Yorùbá music. Summing these points up, Phillips observes that although "Yorùbá music at present may seem to lack form and may not be able to boast of all the attributes (of form), yet there are traces of form and design in our simple music just as much as in the beginnings of European music which developed and eventually reached great heights in the music of Haydn and Mozart and was perfected by Beethoven. It took Europeans centuries to develop their musical form into the present state of perfection and the fruit of their labour is at our disposal."[12]

Phillips explained that forms like the rondo, binary and ternary could, therefore, be used with great effects in new Yorùbá compositions. Large-scale ones like "theme and variation" and the fugue are also potentially effective in such new compositions. According to him, there "may be no fugue in Yorùbá music but the essence of it, that is, dominant answering tonic and vice-versa, is evident in it. The fugue, which is a product of the centuries immediately preceding the sixteenth and perfected in the following century, provides a suitable meeting ground between European and African music."[13]

Expression
According to Phillips, expression marks such as soft, loud, are not apparent in Yoruba music, although *accelerando* and *rallentando* are used in Yoruba drumming. But this should not be taken to imply that Yoruba musicians perform without creative interpretation. Phillips observed that "[e]xpression in Yoruba music is something deeper than mere artificial means —that lies in those indescribable things summed up under the term nuances —and it consists in the rspirit of the musicr. It is emotional rather than mechanical."[14]

He believed that expressions of intensity such as *forte, piano, crescendo,* and *diminuendo* are not used deliberately in Yoruba music, and that loud singing is particularly common. 'If sometimes soft singing comes in, it is due more to the nature of the medium of tone than to any deliberate style of production' (Phillips, 1953: 32). In spite of the above, Phillips did not see any reason why expression techniques covering intensity as well as speed and borrowed from Western sources could not be effectively used in modern Yoruba music.

---

[12]Phillips, *Yoruba Music*, 31.
[13]Phillips, *Yoruba Music*, 31.
[14]Phillips, *Yoruba Music*, 32.

Conclusion: The Significance of Phillips's Work

Phillips's perspectives on Yoruba music and his ideas about musical "development" must be understood within the context of the British colonial era in Nigeria, especially the period between 1900 and 1960 when he was active as a composer and church musician. We must remember that the British employed the concept of "development" to disguise their real motive for colonizing the African continent. Also relevant to Phillips's discussion of development is the power dynamics of colonial rule, which, as we know, was defined by an asymmetric relationship that was disadvantageous to colonized countries. In accordance with the power equations of colonial domination, European cultural practices, including music, were presented as the epitome of modernism, which African societies and individuals were expected to embrace. The notion of development was thus constructed in ways that encouraged African societies to gauge the significance of their own cultures in terms of how they (the cultures) measured up to European practices.

The impact of Phillips's ideas extends far beyond the artistic and cultural circles of his own generation. Younger composers like Fela Sowande, Ayo Bankole, Sam Akpabot, and Dayo Dedeke followed many of his compositional guidelines.[15] Dedeke's simple piece, "Kérésìmesì Odún Dǔ" (Christmas Song), for example, uses the pentatonic scale, shuns modulation, and embraces parallel harmonic movements that follow the tonal inflection of its Yoruba texts (Ex 1).

---

[15] For examples of studies on the works of modern African composers, see: Omojola, 1995; 2000; Johnson Njoku, 1997; and Mensah, Atta Annan, 1997.

Ex. 1: Fairly quickly and gaily

"Kérésìmesì Ọdún Dé" by Dayo Dedeke

As expected, however, many younger composers have deviated from some of the style elements prescribed by Phillips. Such deviations, which often manifest in the realm of part-writing, is illustrated in Christopher Ayodele's "Olúwa LOlùṣọ́ Àgùntàn Mi" (SATB, and organ), a Yorùbá setting of Psalm 23 (The Lord Is My Shepherd). In the piece, the logogenic movement of the melody is jettisoned in the process of harmonizing the soprano melody (Ex. 2).

Ex. 2:

"Olúwa LOlùṣọ́ Àgùntàn Mi" by Christopher Ayodele

It is also instructive to note that, although Phillips repeatedly draws affinities between Yoruba and medieval European music practices rather proudly and recommends the use of European-derived elements, the ways he weaves such elements into his compositions are often original and effective. This can be observed in his piece, Èmi Yíó Gbé Ojú Mi Sókè Wọnnì, a Yoruba setting of Psalm 21, which is highly remarkable for the skillful balancing of speech tones, melodic movements, and harmonic progressions. This piece demonstrates Phillips's ability to incorporate European-derived musical elements and techniques creatively and forge a compositional style that helps to chart a new and original pathway for the development of Yoruba church music. As shown in this piece, Phillips's compositions often problematize the concept of musical development away from its colonialist resonances and in ways that negate the condescending evolutionist discourses of development that colonial powers imposed on Africa.

References

Church Missionary Society, 1923 *Yoruba Hymn Book.* Lagos: *CMS Bookshop.*

Ekwueme, Lazarus (1981), 'African Music in Christian Liturgy: The Igbo Experiment,' *African Music* (5) 3: 60-75.

Hornbostel, Eric M. von. 1928. , African Negro Music, *Africa: Journal of the International African Institute* 1 (1): 25-26.

Mensah, Atta Annan (1997), 'Compositional Practices in African Music,' *Africa: The Garland Encyclopedia of World Music, Vol. 1,* edited by Ruth Stone, 208-231. New York: Garland Publishing Inc.

Njoku, Johnston (1997), 'Art-Composed Music in Africa,' *Africa: The Garland Encyclopedia of World Music Vol.1*, edited by Ruth Stone, 232-253. New York: Garland Publishing Inc.

Olatunji, Michael. (2005), 'The Biography of T.K.E. Phillips: Nigeria's Foremost Contemporary Art Musician,' *Research Review of the Institute of African Studies,* 21 (2): Online.

Omojola, Bode (1995), *Nigerian Art Music* Ibadan: Institut Francais de Recherchŭ de Afrique (IFRA).

_____.(2000), Africanische und europanische Elemente in neuer nigerianische Musik," *Musik Texte* 86/87: 16-27.

Phillips, Ekundayo (1953), *Yoruba Music.* Johannesburg: *African Music Society.*

_____. (1926), *Vesicles and Responses,* Lagos: *CMS Bookshop.*

Sadoh, Godwin (2019). 'Thomas Ekundayo Phillips: Prelude to Early Twentieth-Century Hymnody in Nigeria,' *The Hymn* 70 (1): 11-18.

Ward, W. E. 1927, 'Music in the Gold Coast,' *Gold Coast Review*, III: 2I4. 21.

16

Tensions between Ecclesiastical Authority and Musical Creativity in Nigeria:
Methodist Church Nigeria Example

Isaac E. Udoh, Ph.D[*]

Introduction

Religious Organisations (Churches) in Nigeria today make use of music whether vocal or instrumental or both in their worship services or related services. Methodist Church Nigeria is used as an example because she is united in ecclesiastical or doctrinal matters. Inclusive also, are Churches that are united in ecclesiastical or doctrinal matters. These Churches are not tied to one type of music, they do not only use music composed by Westerners, but also use various types of music composed by indigenes. In the process of music creativity in Churches in Nigeria, there seems to be a battle between Ecclesiastical authority and artistic expression. Artistic expression here equally includes the creative work of composers. This is the problem this paper wants to address. This chapter seeks to discuss how to create a balance between ecclesiastical authority and artistic expression. The method used in this work includes interviews, library review, collection of songs and the researcher's personal involvement as a composer and Reverend Minister in Methodist Church Nigeria. This research will bring to the fore the way out between ecclesiastical authority and artistic expression by composers of religious (Church) music in order to create better relations between members that will in turn bring sanity and morality to the Nigerian society and beyond. It will also help composers, researchers and academicians in a further study of religious music and with a view to creating a sound

---

[*] Reader, University of Uyo

relationship; a marriage of convenience between ecclesiastical authority and artistic expression.

The argument for the primacy of the so-called serious music has come under a heavy attack at the dawn of the twenty-first century (Wilson-Dickson, 1992; Flynn, 2018). Opinions on meaning and value of music diverge sharply, resulting in a compromise that instead of a unitary global typology, there is a plurality of discrete music types that constantly engage stakeholders in musical creativity, performances, research, education, technology, polemics and even governance. Religious organizations (Churches) are not left out in this development. They engage in plurality of discrete music types especially in the area of music creativity and performances. Religious Organisations (Churches) in Nigeria today make use of music whether vocal or instrumental or both in their worship services or related services. These Churches are not tied to one type of music, they do not only use music composed by Westerners, but also use various types of music composed by indigenes, that is, indigenous music.

In this work, the researcher's idea of religious organizations refers to Churches or it is limited to Churches – the Christendom. Therefore, this paper discusses music creativity in Churches. Udoh (2004:165) defines, Church music 'as music composed, adopted or deemed suitable for church use, or for Christian worship, prayer, meditation, thanksgiving, or commemoration, public or private'. Again, Udoh (2003:1) discloses, 'Church music is a compendium of all the tenets, doctrine, principles, belief, etc, of the Christian faith'. Church Music may be defined as music written for performance in Church or any musical setting of liturgy, or music set to words expressing propositions of a sacred nature, such as hymn. Church music can also be regarded as Christian music. Christian music, therefore, is music that has been written to express either personal or communal belief regarding life and faith. Common themes of Christian music include praise, worship, penitence and lament and its forms vary widely across the world.

History has it that Methodism was the first Church to arrive Nigeria in 1842. Familusi (1992) discloses that on 24th September 1842 and 1843, the Wesleyan (now Methodist) Missionaries and Church Missionaries Society (now Anglican) both landed in Badagry respectively. This they did with the importation of European Christian religious institutions and Christian music into Nigerian society. That was the beginning of the spread of Christianity in Nigeria. Other Churches came later, were founded or were off shoots of Methodists.

The missionaries' importation of Christian music was mainly the primacy of hymns (and Western oriented works) mostly rendered in English, a foreign language to Nigerians. With this, the Nigerian worshipers did not grasp the true meaning and value of music rendered in a foreign language. There was, therefore, need for a divergence (against the primacy of hymns) to a plurality of distinct music types. One of which was indigenization. There was need to create music types that were meaningful to worshippers. That was the proliferation of Church music types apart from hymns – that was a divergence. In order to touch lives at the grassroots level, and make singing meaningful, and in the name of indigenization, indigenous composers emerged with their indigenous compositions, coupled with the translated hymns to local languages. A very good example is a general hymnbook, *Nwed Ikwo,* translated into indigenous language (Efik) by the early missionaries to Eastern Nigeria for the Efik speaking people of Nigeria. Some of the translators included Miss M. B. Gilmour and Rev. C. S. Benington (*Nwed Ikwo*, 1955). Other ethnic groups did so to their hymnbooks, like the Yoruba and the Igbo. In 2016, Very Rev. Dr. Isaac Udoh spearheaded, translated (with four others) and edited *Nwed Ikwo Methodist* (a complete translation of Methodist Hymnbook into Efik) for Methodist Faithfuls (Nwed Ikwo Methodist, 2016).

Studies (Idowu, 1973, Ekebuisi, 2010) reveal that until 1842, Church music was alien to Nigeria while Nigerians were practicing and enjoying their traditional religious music, based on her cultural setting. When Nigerians eventually were exposed to Church music from the missionaries, it was with mixed feelings since Church music did not really fit into the Nigerian culture, hence the need for indigenization of Church music. It was the desire for indigenization, adaptation and assimilation that led to several stages of developments of Church music from its original stage to other stages.

A new category of church music emerged as a result of a search for an African identity (indigenization) and the subsequent processes of acculturation, adaptation and assimilation. Vidal (1993) rightly labelled it 'Western and Africanized Church music'. Vidal (1993) observed:

> ...Therefore, the various splinter groups from orthodox churches formed their own Native African Churches during the last decade of the nineteenth century. It was not surprising that these native African churches gave church music an African idiom through the use of native airs and indigenous musical instruments as accompaniment; a development that was later introduced into the orthodox churches during the first three decades of the twentieth century to prevent the drift of people from orthodox churches (p.4).

It consisted of European hymns translated into Nigerian languages and sung to European melodies, in the name of indigenization. As Udoh (2013) has rightly observed:

> From this period (1960s) to the 1990s, church music developed from its original state to Western and Africanized church music. It also witnessed the emergence of indigenous church musical compositions

with indigenous musical instruments. Singing of choruses in vernacular was also witnessed in church music. The composition of native airs, musical entertainment and emergency of church musicians gave rise to more developments in church music (p. 226).

Udoh (2013) also discussed the different levels of development of Church music. In order words, the departure from the primacy of hymns to discrete church music types. The following were pointed out:
1. **The original stage:** That is Church music, as the Missionaries brought them;
2. **Western and Africanized Church Music:** A new category of church music that emerged as a result of a search for an African identity and the subsequent processes of acculturation, adaptation and assimilation;
3. **Indigenous Compositions and use of Accompaniment:** Various splinter groups from Orthodox churches started their indigenous music composition in their dialect and accompanied such music with indigenous musical instruments;
4. **Emergence of Church Musicians:** The composition of native airs and musical entertainment within the Christian communities led to the emergence of a new breed of musicians called church musicians;
5. **Use of Foreign Musical Instruments:** From late 1980s, many churches (both the Orthodox and Pentecostals) opted for the use of foreign musical instruments in their church band instead of the previous indigenous musical instruments used;
6. **Emergence of Church Music Artistes:** These are talented Christians who own their personal bands or own a group for the purpose of propagating church music. With the advent of modern technology, some of these church music artistes have produced their gospel cassettes, CD, VCD, or DVD. They commercialize their music;
7. **Contemporary Christian Music:** Contemporary Christian music (CCM) and occasionally 'inspirational music' is a genre of modern popular music which is lyrically focused on matters concerned with the Christian faith.
8. **Pentecostalism in Church Music:** Presently, in the name of Pentecostalism, there seem to be proliferation of church music in its different forms including extravagant use of church bands with or without indigenization. Some Church music styles today defy definition since three types of music may be combined to produce something new. Pentecostal church music is steeped in English language- a global communication language which becomes the defining principles of the new religious phenomenon in our country, Nigeria.

From the above discussion, it is noticed that Church music has moved from the primacy of hymns to discrete (Church) music types. They include Western and Africanized Church music, indigenous compositions (e.g. native airs, choruses) and use of indigenous musical instruments, use of foreign musical instruments. Others include Contemporary Christian music (CCM) and occasionally 'inspirational music' which is a genre of modern popular music which is lyrically focused on matters concerned with the Christian faith. Examples include Funk, Rhythm and Blues (R&B), Calypso, Reggae, and Negro Spiritual. High Life music is equally used in Church today.

These different (Church) music types were and are musical creations of composers or song writers with artistic expression. The crux of the matter, therefore, is, 'Is there a marriage of convenience between Ecclesiastical authority and artistic expression?' In order words, are the music compositions in line with biblical standards/church approved doctrines? There seems to be a battle between Ecclesiastical authority and artistic expression.

Theoretical Framework

A theory is not a wild guess. It must be consistent with known experimental results and it must have predictive power. Theory is a well-substantiated explanation of some aspect of the natural world; a plausible or scientifically acceptable general principle or body of principles, an organized system of accepted knowledge that applies in a variety of circumstances to explain a specific set of phenomena. Theory is also a belief, policy, or procedure proposed or followed as the basis of action. Therefore, the belief (the doctrines and tenets inclusive) of the Church is the theory of the church, I mean the binding principles. The belief of the Church forms the theoretical framework for this study.

According to Encarta (2009) Dictionary, the word 'ecclesiastical' is derived from or has its root in the Greek word *ekklēsia,* meaning assembly and later Church. *Ecclesiastica* is the same thing as 'Christianity'. Ecclesiastical means 'of church: belonging to or involving the Christian Church or clergy'. Ecclesiastical Authority, therefore, refers to the rules, authorities and belief of the Church. The Church has a stand on Sacred Music- its texts (lyrics) must be based on the Bible (Holy Scriptures) either directly or paraphrased in line with the accepted doctrine and tenets of the Church. The Catholic Encyclopaedia on Ecclesiastical music (Gietmann, 1911) provides the rules required in creating and performance of sacred music. It discloses the interest taken by the Church in music and is shown by her numerous enactments and regulations calculated to foster music worthy of Divine worship. The document (Catholic Encyclopaedia) states, 'The Church, however, does not despise artistic means of a more elaborate nature... but which, nevertheless, conform to every liturgical requirement...' Again it (Catholic Encyclopaedia) submits:

Church music has in common with secular music the combination of tones in melody and harmony, the division of time and rhythm, measure, and tempo, dynamics, or the distribution of power, tone-colour in voice and instruments, the simpler and more complicated type of composition. All these, however must be adapted to the liturgical action, if there be such, to the words offered in prayer, to the devotion of the heart they must be calculated to edify the faithful, and in short must serve the purpose for which Divine service is held.

Udoh (2004) commenting on the qualities of original Church music submits:

> It had a distinctive character that differentiated it from secular music, the ministerial aspect (it ministered to worshippers by way of touching their hearts to serve God the more), holiness (lyrics mostly derived from the bible and tenet/belief of the Christian faith) and solemnity (performed with all amount of awesomeness and humility) were expected from such music (p. 166).

Church music (sacred music), among other things, should possess these principle qualities: i) the ministerial aspect, ii) the holiness aspect, and the solemnity aspect. This is the theoretical framework on which this study rests. In support of regulations on Church music, Vatican II Document states:

Holy scripture has bestowed praise upon sacred songs (cf Eph. 5:19; Col. 3:16) ... Therefore, sacred music increases in holiness to the degree that it is intimately linked with liturgical action, willingly expresses prayerfulness, promote solidarity and enriches sacred rites with heightened solemnity. The church indeed approves of all forms of true art, and admits them into divine worship when they show appropriate qualities (p.171).

Another Document, Second Vatican Ecumenical Council *MusicamSacram* Instruction on Music in the Liturgy (http://Vatican.va...), supports the ministerial, the holiness and the solemnity of Church music.

Ecclesiastical Authority and Artistic Expression

Church music creativity and performance today in Nigeria is not without high level of artistic expression, coupled with globalization. Church music composers are allowed by Ecclesiastical authority to use the techniques of composition, the combination of tones in melody and harmony, the division of time and rhythm, measure, and tempo, dynamics, or the distribution of power, tone-colour in voice and instruments in their simpler and more complicated type of composition as are also found in secular music. But the lyrics (text) must be based on the scriptures, which is, the Bible either directly or paraphrased – this is one of the major differences between sacred music and secular music.

Truly, various types of music are also allowed in Church music today in Nigeria and no longer the primacy of hymns (Western works). Such include **Western and Africanized Church music, indigenous compositions** (e.g.

native airs, choruses) and use of indigenous musical instruments, use of foreign musical instruments. Others include Contemporary Christian music (CCM) and occasionally 'inspirational music' which is a genre of modern popular music (Funk, Rhythm and Blues (R&B), Calypso, Reggae, and Negro Spiritual, High Life music) which is lyrically focused on matters concerned with the Christian faith. Despite the Church's allowance of artistic expression and various types of music for use in Church toady, some composers of Church music still break Church rules in their music creations and performances. This brings a constant fight or disagreement between Ecclesiastical authority and artistic expression. To buttress this point as regards Church music creativity and performance, Udoh (2013) notes:

> In Pentecostal churches, noise, excitement, aggressiveness, loud singing with accompaniment drowning the voices are considered as qualities of true worship. 'Rapping', a kind of speech rhythm is also brought into church music with or without biblical background. Pentecostals do not really mind the Nigerian tonal language. Any word in vernacular could be used without minding the tonal levels, thereby distorting the meaning of the words. Their concern, mostly, is to sing as the American or European gospel artistes like Don Moen, T. D. Jakes, etc. (p. 227).

Offiong (2001) points out that:

> It can be observed that all the external influences affecting our liturgical music, the worst is from the presence of Pentecostalism in our society...The Pentecostal sects pose strong attractions to the youths in particular through excessive noise making, excitable gestures and the use of sophisticated 'band sets' for their conventions (p.3).

Offiong (2001) has really pointed out a major problem, especially in the area of performance. Sometimes the music is written in line with the accepted rules/principles, but during performance, it takes a different shape. Excessive noise making, playing/singing music at the loudest volume is an abuse. It is not common to discover that one goes to Church well and sound but comes back with temporary deafness because of the heavy/too loud sounds from box-speakers/band set. Sometimes the instruments drown the vocals/texts and nothing is heard during performance except the loud sounds of the instruments. Words are the main-stay of vocal music and it is the words that minister to the soul/individual. Doing otherwise is not acceptable. It does not mean that Pentecostalism should be avoided, but should be practiced in a way to build the Church and Church Music. Udoh (2004) also submits:

> It is a pity, entertainment music and celebration have entered the church from the start of the worship service to the end of the entire service - little or no attention is paid to the ministerial aspect of sacred music. One of the reasons being that the artistes or choristers /musicians need the praise of men and possible 'spray' of money in the church, even during worship to the detriment of sacred ministration (p. 170).

It is not only on the issue of Pentecostalism, many Church music composers today base their texts on mundane issues, on local/African proverbs and sometimes on self pity. This is not acceptable because it is not in line with biblical standard and it is not the stand of the Church.

Another area where composers of Church music derail is in 'local compositions'. What the researcher means by 'local compositions' are those ones in indigenous languages – the composers may be (formally/informally) trained or not. There seems to be no check in these areas – composition of native airs, choruses and Negro spiritual. Most times, the texts of these compositions are not scripturally - based or are performed out of context. Let the researcher present one example. On Sunday, February 10, 2019, in Methodist Church Nigeria, Abiakpo Ikot Essien in Ikot Ekpene Local Government Area of Akwa Ibom State, a chorus leader was called upon to lead in praise/worship session. The chorus presented went thus (in Efik language):

> *Ami ndi itiat, asua mi edi ekpeme. Ekpeme ama oto k'itiat, eyebomo.*
> Meaning (in English language) I am a stone and my enemy is the bottle. When the bottle hits the stone, it will break.

Some worshippers were not comfortable with the lyrics of the chorus. A careful study of the composition above, considering the context it was performed, is questionable. The composition sounds proverbial (not based on the scripture) and above all, was performed out of context. This is a clear example of a clash between Ecclesiastical authority and artistic expression. Even if this was to be acceptable (I mean the performance/ the composition), it should not have been performed during praise/worship. Praise/worship (as enshrined in the Church's Order of Service/worship) is a time all adoration, all praise, all honour, all thanks, all glory is given to the Almighty God for who He is and for His blessings/faithfulness upon our lives. It is not a time to attack the enemy or go on self-pity.

Compositions and performances that are at variance with ecclesiastical demands (the ministerial, holiness and solemnity) are many and are quite alarming. The Church should not be reduced to another 'social gathering'. There should be a difference between sacred music and secular music. Secular music cannot fulfil the spiritual needs of worshippers and it is not acceptable in the church (http://Vatican.va...). In other words, Church music composers/performers should not bring secular music into the church either in the name of composition/performance or in the name of plurality of music types. The Church should not be troubled with secular compositions/performances. There are clear guidelines to be followed.

The Way Out

Though some compositions/performances are at variance with ecclesiastical demands, there is still a way out. The researcher wishes to itemize the points here:

i. Church music composers/performers should clearly know that they are the image of the Church or that they represent the Church through their compositions and their performances. That their works/performances can either make or mar the Church.
ii. Church music practitioners (composers/performers) should have a level of training formally or informally to acquaint them with the nitty-gritty or the fundamental of the work. This will provide a clear vision and a difference between sacred and secular music.
iii. Church music practitioners (composers/performers) should be closer to God and be well vested in the Scriptures. They should allow the Spirit of God to lead them in their compositions and performances in line with ecclesiastical demands. No room should be given to the 'flesh' to dictate to the leadership of the Holy Spirit or the ecclesiastical demands.
iv. There should be a cordial relationship between Ecclesiastical authority and church music practitioners.
v. Church music practitioners should submit to Ecclesiastical authority. In the other way round, Church compositions/performances that are found wanting should be sanctioned before it degenerates/goes out of hand.
vi. The Church should always take her stand whenever it comes to sacred music. It should not be watered down. It is this clear stand that will bring sanity to Church music compositions and performances. This will give a positive boost to the image of the Church.

Church Music and Relations in Nigeria

The researcher recalls that a few years ago, Methodist Church Nigeria had a striking theme that read, 'The Church in a Troubled World.' That theme meant so much as several truths were revealed out of it. Yes, the Church is in a troubled world. It is the Church that will maintain her stand without compromise and possibly lead the world out of her troubles. The role of the Church in Nigeria cannot be over-emphasized. The Church preaches peace and advocates for cordial relationship and brotherhood in Nigeria. One of the areas of manifesting the good relations in Nigeria is through Church music (compositions and performances).

The Church points to the Almighty God as the Creator of the universe and urges all to trust in Him. The Church equally points to God as the only true solace, protector and a sure hiding place. This proves why many people are worshipping God today. Let us have a look at the words of this hymn, 'How Sweet the Name of Jesus Sounds' (Methodist Hymn Book No. 99, V1-4). This composition meets Ecclesiastical demands.

1. How sweet the name of Jesus sounds
In a believer's ear!
It soothes his sorrows, heals his wounds,
And drives away his fears.
2. It makes the wounded spirit whole,
And calms the troubled breast;
'Tis manner to the hungry soul,
And to the weary rest.
3. Dear name! the Rock on which I build,
My Shield and hiding-place,
My never-failing treasury filled
With boundless stores of grace.
4. Jesus, my Shepherd, Brother, Friend,
My Prophet, Priest, and King,
My Lord, my Life, my Way, my End,
Accept the praise I bring.

This hymn is a clear indication of the Christians' belief and such is presented to Nigerians and the entire world through music.

The Church preaches repentance and change of attitude from bad to good. The Church is truly against corruption, inhumanity to man, wanton destruction of lives and property, nepotism, bribery and corruption and against all social vices. These messages, apart from preaching, are relayed to the Nigerians and the entire world through her music.

The Church points to God as the true source of happiness, it also teaches contentment. Lack of contentment is one of the major problems of Nigerians. The nation's funds are looted heavily by unpatriotic Nigerians and diverted to their personal and family uses to the detriment of the suffering masses without considering the future of Nigeria. The Church is against these evil acts and they are sinful before God and man. Again these messages are put across through Church music which warns against evil and encourages good deeds. This adds to national development. Let us have a look at this hymn, 'Turn back, O man..' (Methodist Hymn Book No. 912, verse 1.)

1. Turn back, O man, forswear thy foolish ways:
Old now is earth, and none may count her days,
Yet thou, her child, whose head is crowned with flame,
Still wilt not hear thine inner God proclaim:
Turn back, O man, forswear thy foolish ways.

Whenever and wherever this hymn or the likes (sacred music) are performed – in the Church, outside the church, in the radio, through television or at burial ceremonies, the needed message is surely passed across. It is left for the individual to heed the message or not. The Church contributes in no small measure to the development of Nigeria.

The Church advocates for mutual existence, brotherly love, care and safety for one another and general welfare of everybody. The Church preaches hope in this time of economic recession in Nigeria – that all hope is not lost, it shall be well again. Let us take a look at this contemporary sacred popular composition by Bill & Gloria Gaither (Jan 6, 2015) (www.metrolyrics.com>lyrics) entitled, 'God on the mountain'. It admonishes and gives hope. This is a message to all.

> Life is easy, when you're up on the mountain,
> And you've got peace of mind, like you've never known,
> But things change, when you're down in the valley,
> Don't lose faith, for you're never alone.
> For the God on the mountain, is still God in the valley,
> When things go wrong, He'll make them right.
> And the God of the good times
> is still God in the bad times,
> The God of the day is still God in the night.
> We talk of faith way up on the mountain,
>
> Talk comes so easy when life's at its best,
> Now down in the valleys, of trials and temptations,
> That's where your faith is really put to the test.
> For the God on the mountain, is still God in the valley,
> When things go wrong, He'll make them right.
> And the God of the good times
> is still God in the bad times,
> The God of the day is still God in the night.

Conclusion

In Nigeria today, Church music is practised in various types and no longer through hymns or Western compositions only. Compositions in Nigerian languages are encouraged as a way of indigenization. This paper advocates that sacred compositions and performances should meet the demands of the Church. This is where the correct message(s) is/are passed to worshippers and beyond. Church music adds to National development as earlier discussed above. It condemns social vices, encourages brotherly love and calls for national unity amongst others. There should be a marriage of convenience between Ecclesiastical authority and artistic expression – this is the way forward.

References

Bill & Gloria Gaither (Jan 6, 2015). *God on the Mountain*. Retrieved on 27th April, 2017 from www.metrolyrics.com>lyrics.

Ecclesiastica. Microsoft® Encarta® 2009. © 1993-2008 Microsoft Corporation.

Ekebuisi, C. C. (2010). *Renewal Movements within Methodist Church Nigeria*. Nigeria: Soul Winner Publications.

Familusi, M. M. (1972). *Methodism in Nigeria 1842-1992*. Ibadan (Nigeria): NPS Educational Publishers Limited.

Flynn, W. T. (April 26, 2018) 'Christian Liturgical Music'. *Oxford Research Encyclopaedia of Religion*. doi:10, 1093.

Gietmann, G. (1911). Ecclesiastical Music. In *The Catholic Encyclopedia*. New York: Robert Appleton Company. Retrieved April 28, 2017 from New Advent: http://www.newadvent.org/cathen/10648a.htm

Idowu, E. B. (1973). *Towards an Indigenous Church*. Lagos: Literature Department, Methodist Church Nigeria.

Nwed Ikwo (1955). Nigeria: Thomas Nelson (Nigeria) Ltd, Ikeja, Lagos.

Nwed Ikwo Methodist (2016). Ikot Ekpene: Manue Nigeria Enterprise. © Methodist Chuech Nigeria, Ikot Ekpene Diocese.

Second Vatican Ecumenical Council Musicam Sacram Instruction on Music in the Liturgy (5 March,1967). Retrieved on 27th April, 2017 from pttp://Vatican.va/archive/histp_councils/ii_vatican_council/documents/vat-ii_instr_19670305_musica m-sacram_sn.html

The Methodist Hymn Book (1962). 34th Edition. London: Novello and Company Limited

Udoh, I. E. (2003). *A Practical Guide to Choirmasters and Choirs*. Nigeria (Ikot Ekpene): God's Power Singers.

Udoh, I. (2004). 'The Challenges of Church Music in Contemporary Nigeria'. *Awka Journal of Research in Music and the Arts (AJRMA)*. Vol. 2, October, 2004. Pp: 165- 73.

Udoh, I. E. (2013), 'Church Music in Nigeria since the 1960s: The Journey so far' in *Journal of Nigerian English and Literature (JONEL)*. Vol. 9, January 2013. Pp. 223-230.

Vatican II Document on the Sacred Liturgy, Chapter VI, par. 2 and 3, p. 171.

Vidal, T. (1993). "From Traditional Antiquity to Contemporary Modernism: A Multilateral Development of Music in Nigeria". *A Seminar Paper* Presented at the Conference of Music and Social Dynamics –The Nigerian Situation. January 26th - January 29th, 1993.

Wilson-Dickson, A. (1992). *The Story of Christian Music: From Gregorian Chant to Black Gospel*, Oxford: Lion Publishing.

17

Reflections of Traditional Music in the Anglican Communion: *Samples from Churches in Iju-Ishaga Archdeaconry, Lagos West Anglican Diocese*

Opeyemi Adeyinka Asaolu, Ph.D[*]

Introduction

The chapter examines the use of Nigerian traditional music in Anglican Churches in Iju-Ishaga Archdeaconry in the Diocese of Lagos-West in the Church of Nigeria Anglican Communion and its environs in order to identify the traditional songs used and highlight the need, nature, structure and impact of this practice on liturgical music as well as growth and development of the Church. Using oral, observatory and bibliographic methods, this paper relies on cultural theory as its focus for discourse. The research findings revealed that drums, rattles, horns and whistles were used. Handclapping was seen to act almost as a metronome, which steadily maintained the tempo. It was concluded that introducing Nigerian traditional music into the services in Anglican Churches in Iju-Ishaga Archdeaconry has increased attendance and participation of church members. This paper concludes that the introduction of traditional music elements and instruments should be considered for other Anglican Churches in Nigeria and in Africa.

Singing is linked to religious experience and expression. In both the Lutheran and Reformed traditions – to name but two – music plays an important part in worship. Luther accepted music as part of the true church, and as an expression of faith itself. It is clear that there are fundamental links between singing and life. In fact, singing is (a mode of) life – an expression of

---

[*] Olabisi Onabanjo University, Ago-Iwoye, Nigeria

the existential dimension of life. This fundamental link entails, *inter alia*, the following:
i. singing as ritual (liturgical dimension);
ii. singing as worship and confession;
iii. singing as spirituality (and therefore shaping of God-images);
iv. singing as hermeneutics, that is, as a mode of giving meaning.

However, the intention of Nigerian rhythm is not (as the word 'discontinuity' may suggest) to 'disrupt' the flow of the music; rather it means that the emphasis is not necessarily on melodious coherence, but on the impetus for life that rhythm can provide. In Nigerian spirituality singing is all about bringing people back to the right rhythms of life. Music and dance provide an opportunity for people to participate emotionally and physically in prayer and worship. There is a growing body of evidence to support this view; for example, Maboee (1982:131) observes that 'traditionally, when Africans worship, they sing and dance together. They have a tendency to become emotionally or spiritually involved in the service'.

It is noteworthy in this context that music is an intrinsic part of everyday life, as well as in religion. One could even argue that music in all its forms is the central theme, which runs through all aspects of life, including the church. Along similar lines, it is worthwhile to mention here Kubik's (2001:199) view on music and movement; according to him, music in Africa is almost naturally associated with movement and action, such as playing African musical instruments and clapping of hands or dancing.

From a cultural point of view, Nigerian people do not always feel comfortable in a controlled and/or solemn church environment where emotions are not expressed freely. In Independent Churches popularly known as Pentecostal Churches singing is always accompanied by the clapping of hands, and the whole church service is turned into a more colourful experience for the members of the congregation. Where traditional music is seldom used, Churches may lose members to Pentecostal Churches, because of passive their participation in divine worship. African music generally is not contemplative in nature but participatory in nature.

The focus of this chapter is to examine the use of African traditional music in Anglican Churches in Lagos West and its environ in order to identify the traditional songs used and highlight the need, nature, structure and impact of this practice on liturgical music as well as growth and development of the Church.

Theoretical Framework

The premise for discourse in this work shall rest on Cultural theory in Sacred Musicology advanced by Adedeji (2014) posits that, the cultural theory considers cultural context and hermeneutics in understanding and application of theological/Biblical and musical principles. According to him, the denial of this dimension was responsible for unnecessary tension that arouse from the domination of Western ideals and their superimposition on non-Western musical practice. 'The cultural dimension seeks to understand God, worship God and communication with him in indigenous languages, musical ideals and worldview. Thus, the linguistic approach in its diverse dimensions is imperative.' (Adedeji 2014: pg.111)

Adedeji (2004) while discussing on the Nigerian Gospel music styles described the indigenous style as those music who derived their musical elements mainly from indigenous musical sources. They include 'native' traditional 'classical' and 'spiritual styles. 'This category differs from others on the basis that they originated here in Nigeria and hence sound more African because of their closeness to the root-traditional African music.' Adedeji 2014)

Since music in the Nigerian context is experienced physically as it anticipates movement in the form of dance motivated by the use of drums and other melo-rhythmic instruments and hand-clap. Church members therefore have the opportunity to have a taste of their traditional musical elements as part of music in Christian worship. This practice intends to fuse the religious worship in the Churches with the people's familiar musical culture.

Need for Traditional Music in Churches

Schrag (1989:313) explains that each music system is governed by its own set of rules for creation and comprehension, and creates emotional responses in those who know it, which no other music can do. This fact makes it so vital for a missionary to first understand her or his own musical heritage and only then encounter the other musical traditions. According to him, music is an important key to understanding a culture that enables the missionary to communicate the gospel more accurately and sensitively.

Hunt (1987:33) argues that, our choice, if we are to be effective missionaries, is not whether we will use music. Our choice is how we will use it: effectively, efficiently, spiritually, or slovenly and carelessly. This practical approach to the missionary-functional quality of music, as done by Hunt, has doubtlessly to be appreciated. Protestant theologians such as Friesen (1982), Nelson (1999) and Kraft (1980) often focus on the subject from the ethno-musicologist's point of view; for example, Friesen (1982:83–96) expanded a methodology in the development of indigenous hymnody.

In Friesen's (1982:92–94) discussion of the development of contextualized music, he distinguishes several basic 'missionological principles', linked to the development of contextualized music for an Africanized Lutheran liturgy. Friesen (1982:85) describes his methodology as consisting of two parts: the 'ethno-musicological' (the study of forms and functions of song types, instruments, singers, instrumentalists and technical characteristics of any culture) and the 'psycho-ethno-musicological' (the study of the person's relationship to the native music). He argues that ultimately, everything in every culture must be evaluated in the light of both biblical principles and ethno-theology of the society.

In his article 'Crossing the Music Threshold', Nelson (1999:152:155) examines how culturally attuned music fosters communion with God. Nelson (1999:152–155), for example, examines the role of 'ethnomusicological' research in the mission context, herein stressing the importance of the bonds between music and culture, and arguing that God can and will use whatever we have for his kingdom and service. Kraft (1980:211–236) promotes his 'dynamic equivalent model' to describe the position and task of 'The Church in Culture', claiming that his model is the best approach to enable the church to convey the message of God most faithfully in its surrounding culture (Kraft 1980:230); included in this culture is music.

The aforementioned arguments are wholly convincing, simply because there is no music or religion, which is superior to the other. The point we want to make, and the first conclusion to be drawn from the aforementioned arguments, is that it would be convenient if not entirely accurate to describe the approach (of the models of the three protestant theologians) to musical meaning as the focus on the development of music and mission. Friesen's point of view stated earlier links closely to what Darby (1999:66) terms 'African spirituality'. Darby gives the example of the mode of worship whereby worshippers are afforded the opportunity to worship God the way they like.

Dierks (1986:37) endorses this observation by stating that early missionaries were not in the position to compile indigenous hymnbooks, catechisms or liturgical formulas. Dierks supports his position by noting that the important and positive role music and liturgy could play regarding indigenization, is not considered. Other scholars clearly feel the same way.

Amalorpavadass (1971:11) also states that a truly Indian liturgy has been shaped through the implementation of Indian instead of Western music. He suggests that, considering the cultural impact on liturgy (including its music), the future of worship and its music should be written by both the church and society. On a similar note, Friesen (1982:92–94) believes that continuity of culture is vital to a smooth transition and thus an indigenous development of Christianity. In his view, an analysis of the indigenous music system is necessary in order to develop an intelligible, theological and cultural hymnody for the church.

From the arguments of the scholars cited above, there is general agreement amongst scholars that, in the African context, music is an intrinsic part of everyday life, as well as in religion. They assert that creativity provides the window through which music reveals with singular clarity just how the congregants can worship together. The issue of cultural relevance (to their liturgy) has therefore always engaged their attention.

Nigerian Traditional Music in Anglican Churches in Iju-Ishaga Archdeaconry of Diocese of Lagos West

With regard to the Anglican hymnal as well as the appendix at the back of its Yoruba Hymn Book, the enquiry revealed that it has worthy poetic hymns, but in most cases, the emotions are suppressed and restrained. Even though the music is well arranged, the cultural blend is lacking. This shows that the missionaries did not consider the traditional African religious background. It has emerged from this study that the question of culture is instrumental in liturgical church services, whereas its consideration has been generally neglected in the past.

With reference to the cultural dimensions of liturgy, During the field investigation, it was observed that the connection between culture and religion results in as many liturgical forms as there are congregations and church choirs build a repertoire that is characterized by a cultural blend, polyrhythm, improvisation and four-part harmonic setting, which compel the whole congregation to dance to the music, and hence increase attendance and participation. A typical example in this regard is the Sam Ojukwu's song Eucharist for Holy Communion. The musical part of the sung Eucharist has been adopted by most churches in the Church of Nigeria, Anglican Communion. The part of "The preparation of the gifts" is laced with musical accompaniments that are characterized by African musical instruments like *Agogo* (gong), *Gangan* (talking drum), *Shekere* (rattle) and other melo-rhythmic instruments. When the service gets to the point of taking the offertory hymn, a hymn or choruses with or without musical accompaniment and dancing would follow as the bread and wine are brought by the representatives of the congregation to the Deacon or President. The people stand as the offerings are presented and placed on the Holy Table. After the offering prayers might have been said, the congregation anticipates the next part which brings in the music and as this time approaches, an unspeakable joy is observed on the faces of the congregants waiting to move their bodies to the beautiful music. The President and the congregation led by choir would sing with African musical accompaniments:

"Yours, Lord, is the greatness, the power, the glory, the splendour, and the majesty; for everything in heaven and on earth is yours. All things come from you, and of your own do we give you.

It was also interesting to learn from one of the church elders of the Anglican Churches in Iju-Ishaga Archdeaconry of the Diocese of Lagos West, Papa Olátúnjí Aremu Aina (during the Community Hymn Singing in 2018) that if the congregants were giving the opportunity during the church service to express their own feelings in praising God, when it comes to Sunday offering, they will offer more because they are happy. I personally had a conversation that centres on this in the year 2002 when I was the Director of Music of Cathedral Church of St. Phillips Ayetoro, Ile-Ife with the Chairman of the Music committee, Prince J.B. Adeyeba, who said "Opeyemi, anytime the choir does not sing well with the *gángan* playing distinctly, I don't get encouraged to drop any offering". When participants were asked whether the integration of traditional African religious music into Anglican Church services respects the Anglican tradition, they were all in tandem. They felt this approach produces a liturgical form, which respects both the Anglican tradition (with its emphasis on theological teaching) and African culture (with its deep affinity to music and rhythm). It seems obvious from the results that such an African – Anglican liturgy, faithful to both Anglican theology and African culture, has the potential to increase participation and attendance in Anglican liturgical church services.

Reflections of Traditional Music in the Anglican Communion

And of Your own do we
You
all things come from You, and of Your own do we
You
all things come from You and of Your own do we
give You, Your, Lord Lord is the great - ness
give You Yours, Lord is the great - ness
give You Yours Lord, is the great - ness O yes My
All - things come from You
All things come from
Lord, All things come from

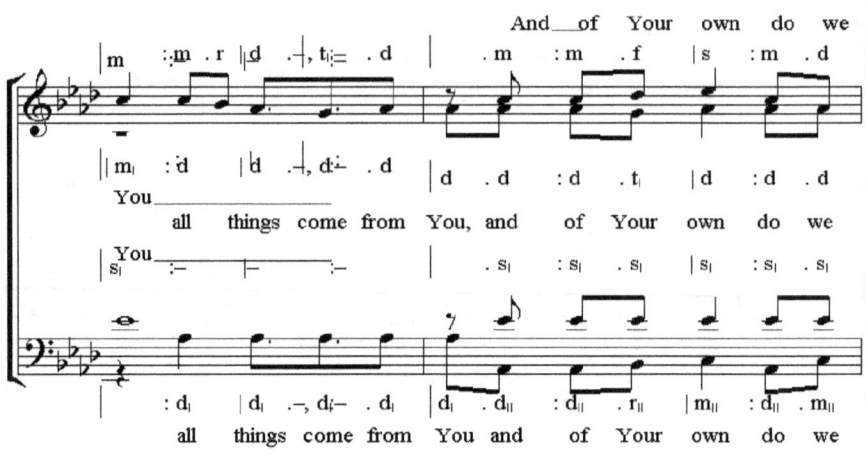

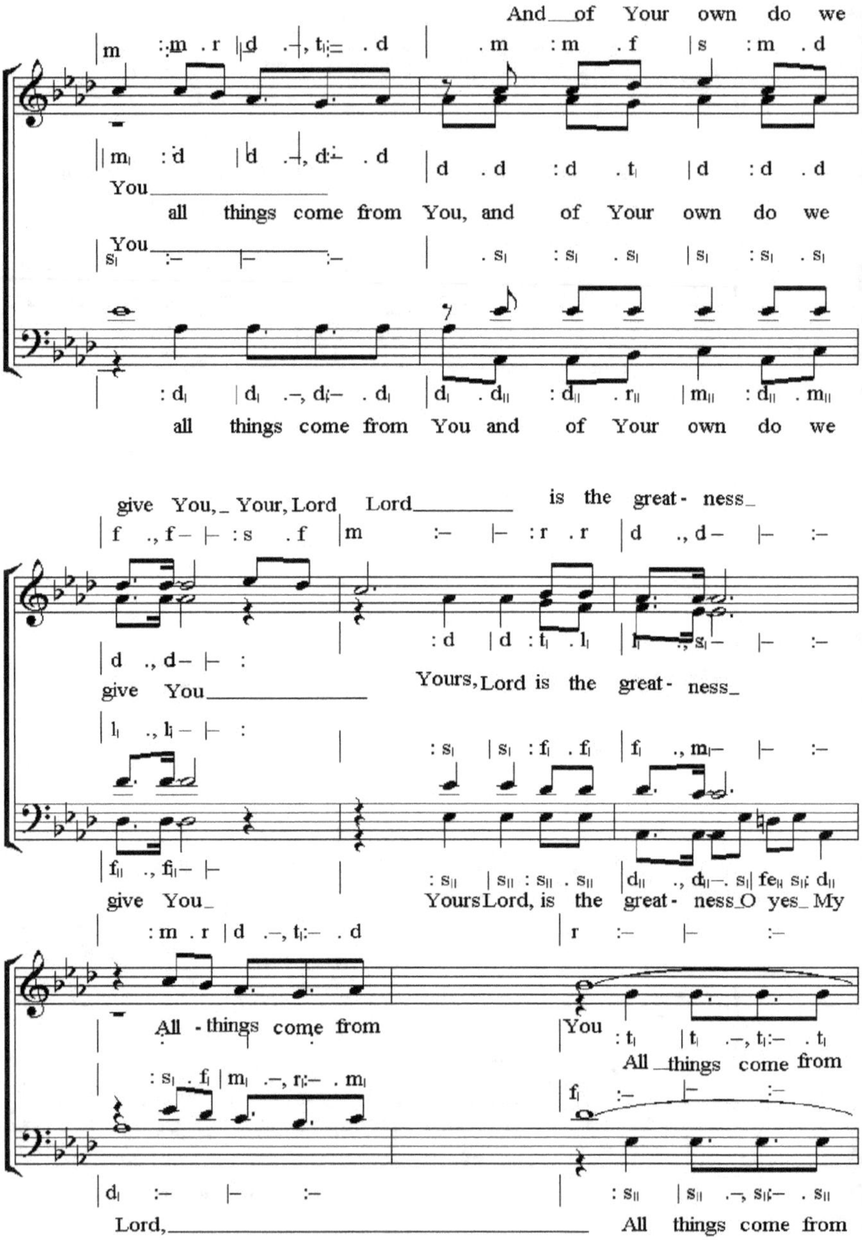

The following is an example of Yoruba traditional songs otherwise known as 'Native Air' incorporated into Anglican churches in Lagos:

It is also generally believed that drumming, clapping, playing other percussions and dance constitutes major musical culture of the people of Nigeria and Africans in general. This culture has also been adopted by Anglican Churches in Iju-Ishaga Archdeaconry in the Diocese of Lagos West of Lagos and other communities since over a hundred decades. This involves the use of local musical instruments which includes drums like Akuba, Ogido, Samba, Gangan and Bata; as well as other melo-rhythmic instruments like Sekere, and Agogo. These drums provides accompaniment to the native airs for people's enjoyment and dance.

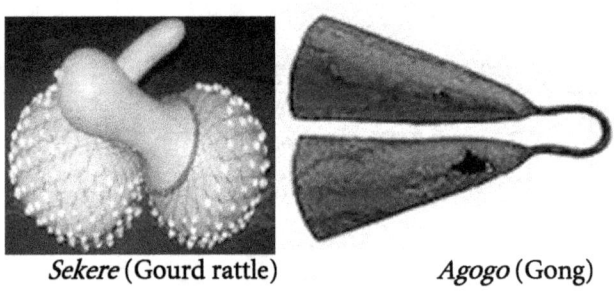

Sekere (Gourd rattle)   *Agogo* (Gong)

Nketia (1974:15) is of the opinion that the fact that drums and other percussion instruments were used in the Ethiopian church, which had been established in the fourth century AD, did not affect the evangelistic prejudices. Noteworthy is the fact that even the mission churches, such as the Anglican, Roman Catholic and Dutch Reformed Churches, have incorporated similar music into worship. Since the introduction of such musical forms, the massive movement of their members to Independent Churches (because of passive participation) seems to have abated. The results thus far suggest that the missionaries should have encouraged their converts to express their own feelings in praising God. However, further research needs to be undertaken in order to more fully understand the possible connection between traditional African religious music and liturgy.

Research Findings

After critical study of the practice of incorporating Nigerian traditional musical culture into the Service session of Anglican Churches in Iju-Ishaga, it was observed that this practice in general has a great impact on Yoruba congregation of Anglican Churches in Iju-Ishaga Archdeaconry in the Diocese of Lagos West. It is noticeable that whilst traditional African music are perfectly accompanied with the help of traditional musical instruments (e.g. *gangan* [talking drums], *shekere* [rattles] and [ululation], melo-rhythmic instruments in worship enables the congregants to be in communion with God in the context of a divine service.

It was also adhered that the positive impact of traditional Nigerian religious music on Anglican liturgical church services. This is evident in the fact that majority of all the Church members participated in the singing and dancing with zeal. This invariably responsible for the noticeable increase in new members of the churches and the return of the members who have refused to attend Church services in the past.

Conclusion

The evidence from this study should help to provide more definitive information in terms of the cultural impact of introducing traditional Nigerian religious music into liturgical church services. It is concluded that introducing Nigerian traditional religious music, whilst maintaining the Anglican liturgy, will increase member participation and attendance. It is therefore suggested that other Anglican congregations in Nigerian (that are losing church members because of poor attendance) could potentially consider introducing Nigerian traditional religious music as part of their church services. The study contributes to the notion that traditional religious music has a positive impact on mission work in the South-Western Nigeria context. This knowledge may help us understand the relevance of traditional African religious music in terms of mission and liturgy. Based on the findings of this study, it is suggested therefore that mainstream churches in Nigeria i.e. the protestant churches and Anglican churches in particular – ought to recognize and accept Nigerian traditional religious music as intrinsic to missionary work. Recommendations for future research include investigations surrounding contextualization and the importance of liturgy – with special emphasis on musical-liturgical forms. Other investigations could include the creative potential of Nigerian traditional religious music in liturgy. With further research leading to a greater understanding of this area, we may be in a position to develop a liturgy that expresses the joy and liberation of the gospel, which is appropriate for the Nigerian context, and will reflect Anglican theology, encourage maximum and unimpeded participation in worship by members.

References

Adedeji, S.O., 2014, African Musicology: Developments and Challenges in Contemporary Times, in C. O. Aluede, S. Kayode and F. Adedeji (Eds.), *African Musicology: Past, Present and Future: A Festschrift for Mosunmola Ayinke Omibiyi-Obidike*. Ile-Ife: Timade Ventures.

Amalorpavadass, D.S., 1971, *Towards Indigenization in the Liturgy*, St. Paul Press Training School, Dasarahalli.

Bosch, D.J., (2005), *Transforming Mission: Paradigm Shifts in Theology of Mission*, Orbis Books, New York. NY.

Calvin, J., 1(960), 'Institutes of the Christian religion,' in J.T. McNeill (Ed.), *Library of Christian Classics*, p. 894, Westminster Press, Philadelphia, PA.

Chenoweth, V., (1984), 'Spare them Western Music!', *Evangelical Missions Quarterly* 20(1), 31–37.

Chernoff, J.M., (1979), *African Rhythm and African Sensibility: Aesthetics and Social Action in African Musical Idioms*, The University of Chicago Press, Chicago, IL, and London.

Chupungco, A.J., (1994), 'Die liturgie und bestandteile der kultur,' in A. Stauffer (ed.), *LutherischerWelthund: Gottesdienst und Kulturim Dialog, LutherischesKirchenamt*, pp. 151–163, EvangelischeHaupt-Bibelgesellschaft, Berlin.

Darby, I., (1999), 'Broad differences in Worship between Denominations', in C. Lombaard (ed.), *Essays and Exercises in Ecumenism*, pp. 64–71, Cluster, Pietermaritzburg.

Dargie, D., (1989), 'Die kirchenmusik der Xhosa', transl. K. Hermanns, Concilium: Internationale ZeitschriftfbrTheologie 25, 133–139.

Dargie, D., (1997), 'South African Christian music: Christian music among Africans', in R. Elphik & R. Davenport (eds.), *Christianity in South Africa: A political, social & cultural history*, pp. 319–326, University of California Press, Berkeley, CA. http://www.hts. org.za doi: 10.4102/hts.v71i3. 2761 Page 6 of 6 Original Research.

Dierks, F., (1986). Evangeliumim afrikanischen kontext: Interkulturelle kommunikationbei den Tswana, Gutersloher Verlagshaus GerdMohn, Gûtersloh.

Friesen, A.W.D., (1982). 'A Methodology in the Development of Indigenous Hymnody,' *Missiology: An International Review* 10(1), 83–96.

Hunt, T.W., 1987, *Music in Missions: Discipline through Music*, Broadman, Nashville,

TN. Khuzwayo, L.B., (1999). 'Bodily Expressions During Worship,' in Minutes of Church Council No. 90, pp. 17–19, Evangelical-Lutheran Church in Southern Africa, Lutheran Church Centre,

Kempton Park. Kraft, C.H., (1980). 'The Church in Culture: A Dynamic Equivalence Model', in R.T. Coote & J. Scott (Eds.), *Down to Earth. Studies in Christianity and Culture – The Papers of the Lausanne Consultation on Gospel and Culture*, pp. 211–230, William B. Eerdmans Publishing Company, Grand Rapids, MI.

Kritzinger, J.J., (1988), *The South African context for mission*, Lux Verbi, Cape Town.
Kubik, G., 2001, 'Africa', in *The New Grove Dictionary of Music and Musicians*, 2nd Edition., Macmillan London.
Lieberknecht, U., 1994, Gemeindelieder: Probleme und chanceneinerkirchlichen Lebensäußerung, Vandenhoeck & Ruprecht, Guttingen.
Lilje, D.R., (1992), 'The Path of our Lutheran Church into the Future,' in H.L. Nelson, P.S. Lwandle & V.M. Keding (eds.), *Dynamic African Theology: Umphumulu's Contribution*, pp. 94–113, Lutheran Theological Seminary, Umphumulu.
Maboee, C., (1982), *Modimo Christian theology in Sotho context*, Lumko Institute, Pietermaritzburg.
Mashiane, M.A.B., (2005). 'An Assessment of the Constitution of the Evangelical Lutheran Church in Southern Africa within the Bill of Rights as Enshrined in the South African Constitution Act'. Master's Thesis, Department of Church History, University of Pretoria.
Mugambi, J.N.K., (1989), *The African heritage and contemporary Christianity*, Longhorn, Nairobi.
Nelson, H.L., (1996). 'Holy Spirit and Lutheran Belief,' in H.L. Nelson (ed.), *Calls, Gathers and Enlightens. Lutheran Views on the Holy Spirit – Festschrift*, Gert Landmann, pp. 23–56, Christian Literature Publishers, Kranskop.
Nelson, D., (1999). 'Crossing the music threshold – Culturally attuned music fosters communion with God,' *Evangelical Missions Quarterly* 35(2), 152–155.
Nketia, J.H.K., (1974), *The Music of Africa*, W.W. Norton & Company, New York.
Rapetswa, P., 2001, 'Towards holistic mission, with special reference to the Evangelical Lutheran Church in Southern Africa, Northern Diocese,' Master's thesis, Dept. of Mission and Religious Studies, University of Pretoria. Reed, L.D., 1947, The Lutheran Liturgy, Fortress Press, Philadelphia, PA.
Schrag, B.E., (1989), 'Becoming Bi-musical: The Importance and Possibility of Missionary Involvement in Music,' *Missiology – An International Review* 17(3), 311–319. http://dx.doi.org/10.1177/009182968901700306
Scott, J., 2000, *Tuning in to a Different Song – Using Music as a Bridge to Cross Cultural Differences*, University of Pretoria, Pretoria.
Triebel, J., (1999). 'Mission and culture in Africa – A Working Report on Tanzanian Experience,' *Africa Theological Journal*, 21(3), 232–239.
Whelan, T., 1990, 'African ethnomusicology and Christian Liturgy,' in T. Okure & P. Van Thiel (Eds.*), 32 Articles Evaluating Inculturation of Christianity in Africa*, pp. 201–210, Association of Member Episcopal Conferences of Eastern Africa, Gaba Publishers, Eldoret.

The Bible as an Invaluable Source and Inspirational Archive for Church Music Composition

Justina Enoh Okafor, Ph.D[*]

Introduction

Through historical epoch, church music composers of all ages beginning from medieval period to the Baroque period down the lane to the twenty-first century, have resorted and relied on the pages and verses from the Bible as a resource material for their compositions. Literatures related to the subject matter were reviewed and in order to achieve intended objective, fifty church music compositions with titles and composers/arrangers were randomly cited. Also ten musical excerpts with Biblical passage(s) were randomly selected. Though the genre, style or type is not the focus of the chapter, the paper acknowledged that church music compositions are in various genre, style and or type. The paper also noted that the Bible is not the only source of inspiration but maintained that the Bible is a reserve and archive. The paper advocate that music composers irrespective of their compositional leanings should search the pages of the Bible for inspirations since it touched on all subject and aspect of human life therefore recommend they tap from the interminable reserve of the Bible.

The Bible cannot be divorced from the church and the church from the Bible - from sermons, Sunday school teachings, and Bible studies, preachers often attest to the fact that the Bible is the compass of the church and hub of all Christian gatherings and activities including music used in the church. Music is part and parcel of the church because music used in the church extols the virtues of the Bible by simply incorporating the titles and texts into the music and in so doing help to impress and etch each message(s) in the mind and hearts of both performers and listeners. According to Adeleke (2018) 'Church music is written or performed to express people's religious

---

[*] College of Education, Agbor, Delta State, Nigeria

experiences, common belief regarding Christian faith, as well as giving a Christian alternative to mainstream of secular, popular or folk music idiom' (p.252). On the other hand, Schuter (1990) quoted in Ossaiga (2015:76) opined that:

> Church music is a vast repertoire that spreads across centuries, a product of many nations and languages, composed by greatest musicians in human history; these constituting the product heritage of the human race. Church music is both instrumental and vocal; embracing many forms and styles; and that it is an ecumenical art.

Composers of church music have composed songs from many themes in the Bible. From themes on prayer, forgiveness, repentance, consecration, humility, thankfulness, joy and gladness, to service, followership, obedience, providence, protection, God's Greatness, ascription of the Godhead and or Trinity, the birth of Jesus, resurrection, after-life, and faithfulness to mention a few.

The Bible has acted as an inspirational resource to composers of church music; from the book of Genesis in the Old Testament to the book of Revelation in the New Testament. Thousands of church music of various genres, types and styles has evolved. While the names of many church music composers are known, there are others whose names are unknown. One of such compositions with the Bible as a source of inspiration is a composition titled 'Israel in Egypt' taken from Exodus chapter 15 composed by George Fredric Handel and the other composition titled 'Jesus of Nazareth' taken from the book of Mark chapter 10 verses 46 to 51 whose composer is unknown or anonymous. There are also church music composers who arrange and or compile other composers' works known and unknown. Worthy of note is Arugha Aboyowa Ogisi who compiled a list of 248 (two hundred and forty eight) Nigerian church music of various genres, styles and types which he tiled 'Praise the Lord: a collection of Nigeria Spirituals'.

It is a truism that the sole purpose of any genre of church music composition irrespective of the type or style is to direct men to the power of the Almighty, reconcile men to their creator, serve as viable tool of encouraging the hearts of men, serve as a healing balm, to redirect wandering feet, extol the greatness and power of God, worship, praise, adore, to show man's incapability and reliance upon an invisible hand who can stir the affairs of men. Corroborating the purpose of church music composition, Aluede (2009) alluded that the Bible reveals that the use of music is of many functions; for praise and worship of God, merry making, mocking, thanksgiving, surprising and terrorizing enemies, warding of evils, coronation, confession and admonition, suiting troubled mind, prayer and supplication to God, prophesying, as accompaniment to work and healing of people'. (p. 159)

Down through the century titles and texts including inherent messages of church music compositions coined from the Bible often reflect and express the purpose and function of music used in the church while the compositional processes employed by church music composers which also include the genre, type and style shed light and or reflect the individuality of each church music composer right as evidenced from earliest epoch of church music composition to contemporary times.

The Bible avails an array of verses on praise and worship as exemplified in the song of Moses found in the book of Exodus chapter 15; Judges chapter 5 the song of Deborah and Barak and 1 Samuel chapter 2, the song of Hannah. There are also instances in the Bible were singers and instrumentalists appointed to sing and play instruments for the worship of God. An example is found in the book of Nehemiah chapter 7 verses 1. The scripture according to the book of 1 Chronicles chapter 15 recorded thus; 'So the singers, Heman, Asaph, and Ethan, were appointed to sound with cymbals of brass' (1 Chronicles 15:19). 2 Chronicles 20 also recorded that:

> 'And when he had consulted with the people, he appointed singers unto the LORD, and that should praise the beauty of holiness, as they went before the army, and to say, Praise the LORD; for his mercy endureth for ever' (2 Chronicles 20:21).

Sometimes, church music composers coin music composition around a Bible character an instance is Zadok the Priest and Nathan the Prophet found in the book of 1 Kings chapter 1 verse 32 to 34; Matthew chapter 21 verse 9, Hosanna to Jesus. Okafor (2018) noted that 'many hymns/sacred songs, air, traditional gospel songs and compositions (vocal and instrumental) to mention a few have been coined from Biblical themes relating to the gospel' (p. 280). Onwuekwe (2018) also corroborate that 'many of these compositions are based on the Biblical text with emphasis on the Gospel of our Lord Jesus Christ' (p.161).

Haldor Lilenas a church music composer described the astuteness of the Bible with the following prose:

> The Bible stands like a rock undaunted
> 'Mid the raging storms of time;
> Its pages burn with the truth eternal;
> And they glow with a light sublime
>
> The Bible stands though the hills may tumble,
> It will firmly stand when the earth shall crumble;
> I will plant my feet on its firm foundation,
> For the Bible stands.

> The Bible stands and it will forever,
> When the world has passed away,
> By inspiration it has been given,
> All its precepts I will obey

Another church music composer (Anonymous) penned a beautiful prose describing the Bible as Holy God's inspired Word. The Bible is believed to be an inspired Word of God, a 'sacred writing' not in the sense of being the works of genius or of supernatural insight, but as "breathed into by God" in such a sense that the writers were supernaturally guided to express exactly what God intended them to express as a revelation of his mind and will. The testimony of the sacred writers themselves abundantly demonstrates this truth as found in the book of 2 Timothy chapter 3 verses 16 which clearly expressed that 'All scripture is given by inspiration of God, and is profitable for doctrine, for reproof, for correction, for instruction in righteousness' (2 Timothy 3: 16). Although there are many sources of inspiration from which music composers whether traditional, secular or religious may avail themselves which according to Adedeji (2008:69-70) opined thus:

> The four common approaches identifiable in terms of compositional inspirations are the one that rises from determination to compose or when composing by method, inspiration through intuition, inspiration through meditation on nature, philosophical/religious issues or unique experiences and inspiration through spiritual sources.

Adedeji further implicated that although distinct, the four are interwoven. The first approach is based on the need to compose. The composer has the need and sits down under 'musical' inspiration to figure things out. In intuition, the composer may not even think of composing, thus by passing predetermination and pre-compositional processes. It occurs like a spark; a kind of an illumination from the sub-conscious. Yet it is noteworthy that church music composers through the ages have sought inspiration from the pages of the Bible. Below are five examples of church music compositions with Bible passage(s).

(a) Musical Examples of Church Music Composition(s) with Bible Passage(s)

1. Title: And They Remembered His Words
Bible Verse: Luke 24:1-8
Composer: Walter A. Shawker
Song Texts: Now upon the first day of the week,
Very early in the morning, very early in the morning,
They came to the sepulchre.

And they found the stone roll'd away,
And they found the stone roll'd away,
And they found the stone roll'd away,
Roll'd away from the sepulcher,
And they entered in,
And they entered in,
And they entered in,
And they found not the body of the Lord.
He is not here, but is risen,
He spake when in Galilee,
The Son of man must be crucified,
And the third day rise again.
He is not here, He is not here, but is risen.
Musical excerpt below:

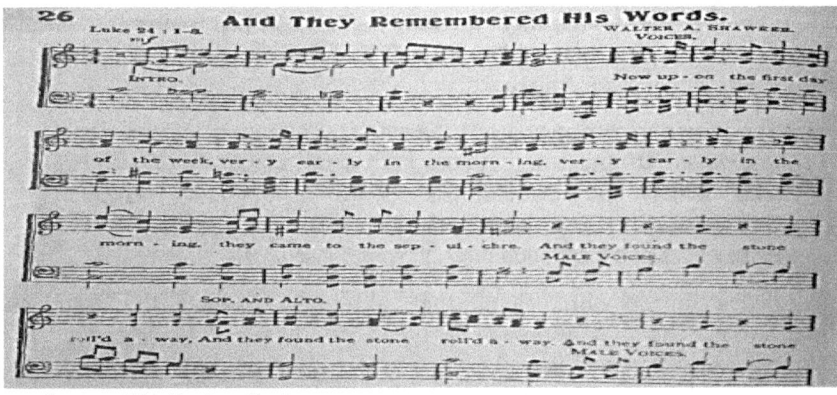

Source: *The Easter Choir*

2. Title: The Lord is My Strength

Bible Verse: Psalm CXVIII: 14, 19, 22, 24
Composer: Caleb Simper
Song Texts: The Lord is my strength,
The Lord is my strength,
The Lord is my strength and my song,
And is become, and is become, and is become my salvation.
Open me the gates, the gates of righteousness,
Open me the gates, the gates of righteousness, that I may go into them,
That I may go into them, and give thanks unto the Lord, unto the Lord.
The Lord is my strength, my strength and my song.
The same stone which the builders, the builders refused,

The same stone which the builders,
The builders refused is become the head stone, the head is the corner.
This is the day which the Lord hath made.
This is the day which the Lord hath made,
We will rejoice,
We will rejoice, we will rejoice, we will rejoice.
This is the day which the Lord hath made,
This is the day which the Lord hath made,
We will rejoice, we will rejoice,
We will rejoice, we will rejoice and be glad in it, Amen

Musical excerpt below;

Source: Best Anthems

3. Title: Rejoice in the Lord Always

Bible Verse: Philippians 4:4
Composer: Anonymous
Arr: A. A. Ogisi
Song Texts: Rejoice in the Lord always, again I say, rejoice
Rejoice in the Lord always, again I say, rejoice
Rejoice, rejoice
Again I say rejoice, rejoice, rejoice,
Rejoice, rejoice,
Again I say rejoice
Rejoice in the Lord always, again I say rejoice

Musical excerpt below:

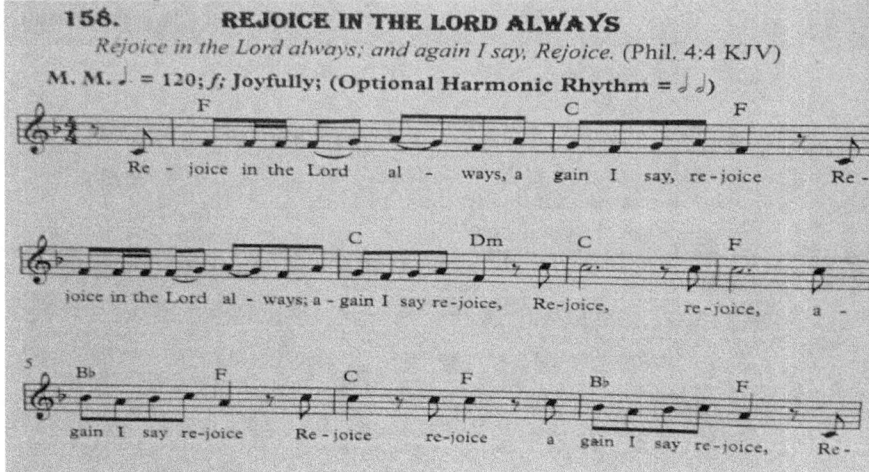

Source: *Praise the Lord: A Collection of Nigerian Spirituals* by Arugha A. Ogisi

4. Title: Make a Joyful Noise

Bible Verse: Psalm C
Composer: R. A. Smith
Song Texts: Make a joyful noise unto the Lord, all ye lands
.   Make a joyful noise unto the Lord, all ye lands
             Make a joyful noise unto the Lord, all ye lands
             Come before his presence, before His presence with singing,
             Know ye that the Lord He is God,
It is He that hath made us, and not we ourselves
We are His people, we are His people, and the sheep of His pasture.
Enter into His gates with thanks-giving, and into His courts with praise;
Be thankful unto Him, be thankful unto Him, and bless His name.
For the Lord is good: His mercy is everlasting;
And His truth endureth to all generations.
Musical excerpts below:

The Bible as an Invaluable Source and Inspirational Archive

Source: *Empire*

5. Title: While Shepherds Watched Their Flocks By Night

Bible Verse: Luke 2:8
Composer: Words: Nahum Tate
Music: George Frederic Handel
Song Texts: While shepherds watched their flocks by night,
All seated pm the ground;
The angel of the Lord came down,
And glory shone around,
And glory shone around.
Fear not, said he; for mighty dread had seized their troubled mind,
Glad tidings of great joy I bring,
To you and all mankind,
To you and all mankind.
To you, in David's town, this day is born of David's line
The Saviour, who is Christ the Lord;
And this shall be the sign:
The heav'nly babe you there shall find to human view displayed,
All meanly wrapped in swathing-bands,
And in a manger laid.
All glory be to God on high,
And to the earth be peace"
Good will hence-forth from heav'n to men,
Begin and never cease!
Begin and never cease!
Musical excerpt below:

Source: *Carol of Christmas*

Also see below five musical examples of church music compositions without Bible passage(s) but related to themes from the Bible.

Musical Examples of Church Music Composition(s) without Bible Passage(s)

1. Title: Thanks to Calvary

               (I DON'T LIVE HERE ANYMORE)
Composer: Words: W. J. G & Gloria Gaither
               Music: William J. Gaither

Song Texts: Today I went back to the place where I used to go,
Today I saw the same old crowed I knew before,
      When they asked me what had happened,

      I tried to tell them "Thanks to Calv'ry I don't come here anymore"
         Thanks to Calv'ry I am not the man I used to be,
         Thanks to Calv;ry things are diff'rent than before,
         When the tears ran down my face, I tried to tell them
         "Thanks to Calv'ry I don't come here anymore:\"
Musical excerpt below:

The Bible as an Invaluable Source and Inspirational Archive   247

Source: *Sing and Be Happy (GREAT GOSPEL FAVORITES)*

2. Title: He Was Despised
    Composer: George Frederic Handel
    Song Texts: He was despised, despised and rejected, rejected of men,
       A man of sorrows, a man of sorrows, and acquainted with grief,

    A man of sorrows, and acquainted with grief,
    He was despised, rejected,
               He was despised and rejected of men,
                  A man of sorrows, and acquainted with grief,
       A man of sorrows, and acquainted with grief,

       He was despised, rejected,
    A man of sorrows, and acquainted with grief,
    And acquainted with grief, and acquainted with grief,
    A man of sorrows, and acquainted with grief.
    He gave His back to the smiters,
    He gave His back to the smiters,
    And His cheeks to them that pucked off the hair,
    And His cheeks to them that pucked off the hair,
    And His cheeks to them that pucked off the hair,
    He hid not His face from shame and spitting
    He hid not His face from shame, from shame,
    He hid not His face from shame, from shame and spitting
    He was despised, despised and rejected, rejected of men,
       A man of sorrows, a man of sorrows, and acquainted with grief,
                  A man of sorrows, and acquainted with grief,
                  He was despised, rejected,
                  He was despised and rejected of men,

A man of sorrows, and acquainted with grief,
A man of sorrows, and acquainted with grief,
He was despised, rejected,
A man of sorrows, and acquainted with grief,
And acquainted with grief, and acquainted with grief,
A man of sorrows, and acquainted with grief.
Musical excerpt below:

Source: *Messiah (G. F. Handel)*

3. Title: Kyrie Eleison
Composer: W. A. Mozart
(Excerpt from song texts)
Song Texts: I will call upon the Lord, and complain unto my God,
I will call upon the Lord, and complain unto my God, I will
I will call upon the Lord, and complain, complain unto my God,
I will call upon Him, upon Him, I will call upon Him,
And complain unto my God
I will call upon Him, upon Him, I will call upon Him,
And complain unto my God;
Lord in Thee is my hope, Lord in Thee
Lord in The is my hope, quicken me, quicken me, as Thou art wont
Lord in Thee is my hope, Lord in Thee
Lord in The is my hope, quicken me, quicken me, as Thou art wont
I will call, I will call, upon the Lord, upon the Lord
And complain unto my God.
Musical excerpt below:

The Bible as an Invaluable Source and Inspirational Archive   249

Source: *Mozart's Twelfth Mass*

4.   Title: When Upon Life's Billows
Composer: Words: Rev. Johnson Oatman, Jr.
      Music: E. O. Excell
Song Texts: When upon life's billows you are tempest tossed,
      When you are discouraged thinking all is lost,

      Count your many blessings, name them one by one,
      And it will surprise you what the Lord hath done.
          Count your blessings, name them one by one,
          Count your blessings, see what God hath done,
          Count your blessings, name them one by one,
          Count your many blessings, see what God hath done.
Musical excerpt below;

Source: Collected Gospel Songs

5. Title: We Praise Thee O God, Our Redeemer
   Composer: Anonymous
   Song Texts: We praise thee, O God, our Redeemer, Creator,
   In grateful devotion our tribute we bring.
   We lay it before thee, we kneel and adore thee,
   We bless thy holy name, glad praises we sing.

Musical excerpt below:

Source: *Baptist Hymnal*

Furthermore, lending credence to the discourse, twenty five (25) song titles with Bible verse(s) and composers' names and twenty five (25) song titles and composers' name portraying various themes from the Bible were cited respectively. See list(s) below:

(c) **Song Titles, Bible Verse(s) and Composer(s)**

Lists of twenty five (25) song titles, with Bible verse(s) and name of composer(s)

S/N	TITLE	BIBLE VERSE	COMPOSER
1.	Come Unto Him and Rest	Mark 2 verse 4	B. B. McKin
2.	Come, Ye Sinners	Matthew 9 verse 13	Anne W. Waterman
3.	Fill My Cup, Lord	John 4 verse 10	Richard Blanchard ASCAP
4.	Seek Ye First the Kingdom of God	Matthew 6 verse 33	Rev. W. McCrea
5.	Oba Oluwajo Balo	Revelation 4	Timothy Oladunmomi
6.	Let Him In	Revelation 3 verse 20	Emmanuel & Lazarus
7.	Worthy is the Lamb that was Slain	Revelation 5 verse 9	George F. Handel
8.	The Sinner and the Song	Malachi 3 verse 7	Will L. Thompson
9.	There is A Balm in Gilead	Jeremiah 8 verse 22	William L. Dawson
10.	Dare to Stand like Joshua	Numbers 14 verse 6	Bilhorn P. P.
11.	By Grace Are Ye Saved	Ephesians 3 verse 8	James McGranahan
12.	The Lord Will Provide	Philippians 4 verse 9	Words: Mrs M. W. Cooke Music: Philip Phillips
13.	I Am the Lord that Healeth Thee	Exodus 15 verse 26	Don Moen
14.	Ore-ofe mi tofun o	1 Corinthians 12 verse 3	Anonymous
15.	Hosanna in the Highest	Matthew 21 verse 9	Anonymous
16.	In the Beginning was the Word	Genesis 1 verse 1	W. Sharrott
17.	Paul and Silas	Acts 16 verse 25	Anonymous
18.	Out of the Depths	Psalm 130 verse 1	Arranged from G. Verdi Words: Elsie Duncan Yale
19.	Sing O Ye Heavens	Isaiah 44 verse 23	Enoh J. Okafor
20.	Thou Wilt Keep Him	Isaiah 26 verse and Psalm 1 verse 3	Enoh J. Okafor
21.	Israel in Egypt	Exodus 14 verse 24 and 15 verse 1	George F. Handel
22.	Jesus of Nazareth	Mark 10 verse 49	Anonymous
23.	To Him that Overcometh	Revelation 2 verse 3, 17, 26; 3 verse 5, 12 and 21	Words: Fanny J. Crosby Music: M. Upham Currier
24.	You Are the Mighty Man in Battle	Exodus 15 verse 3	Words & Music: Anonymous Arr: Arugha A. Ogisi
25.	The Lord is my Light and my Salvation	Psalm 27 verse 1	Austin Miles C.

(d) Song Titles and Composer(s)
Lists of twenty five (25) song titles and name of composer(s)

S/N	SONG TITLE	COMPOSER(S)
1.	Kabiyesi O Hossana	Dapo Taiwo
2.	I Can Almost Hear the Sound of the Trumpet	Ted L. Frieson
3.	O yo winor	'Mudiakevwe Igbi
4.	Urinrin k'Oghene	'Mudiakevwe Igbi
5.	Oghene Fejiro	'Mudiakevwe Igbi
6.	Turn Your Eyes Upon Jesus	Helen H. Lemmel
7.	Jesu, Joy of Man's Desiring	J. S. Bach
8.	He is Risen	Walter A. S.
9.	I Will Rejoice	Enoh J. Okafor
10.	In God is Our Trust	Anonymous
11.	Asi Na Madu	Moses O. Ehiwario
12.	Tata Mary	Elsie E. Nwoko
13.	Utibe Abasi (Ima Abasi Okpon)	Moses
14.	Funiali Funicula	Luigi Denza Jivan Daffel
15.	Fly to the Moon	Bart Howard
16.	Hallelujah	Jeff Buckley
17.	ODo Ben Ni	James Varnick Armaah
18.	Fall On Your Knees	Andrea Bocelli
19.	You Raise Me Up	John Goban
20.	Worthy is the Lamb	Darlene Zschechlf
21.	If Jesus Comes Tomorrow, What Then?	Vern Goshdin
22.	God You are my God	Joan Rosario
23.	A Night Watch	Jim Reeves
24.	Jesus is at the Door (Someone's Knocking)	Nathaniel Bassey
25.	He is God	Lara George

Conclusion

The Bible as an archive and a source of inspiration to church music composers was the main focus of the chapter. Though other sources of inspiration are available for compositional considerations, the paper alludes that for many decades thousands of church music compositions has emerged through the use of various scriptural verses and themes from the Bible - often created in various styles, types and genres. Given instances so far indicate that the Bible has proven to be a well of unfathomable water of inspiration which church music composers and of course composers of all climes and musical preferences may draw wealth of knowledge from.

References

Adedeji, F. (2008). Compositional Techniques in African Art Music in Meta-Musical Dimension. *African Musicology Outline* 2(2), 60 - 80

Adeleke, A. (2018). Re: Conceptualizing Contemporary Gospel Music in Nigeria: A Tribute to Professor 'Femi Adedeji'. In Samuel Olufemi Adedeji (Ed.)

Music, Musicology and theGospel in Nigeria: A Festschrift in Honour of Samuel Olufemi Adedeji. Pp: 252-264).Ile-Ife: Association of Nigerian Musicologists

Aluede, C. O. and Ekewenu, D. B. (2009). Healing Through Music and Dance in the Bible: Its Scope, Competence and Implications for the Nigerian Music Healers. *Ethno-Medicine* 3(2), 159 - 163

Jack Taylor (1977). *Sing And Be Happy (GREAT GOSPEL FAVORITES).* Dallas, Texas: STAMPS-BAXTER MUSIC

John, W. Peterson (1965). *CAROL OF CHRISTMAS (S.A.T.B) A CHRISTMAS CANTATA.* Michigan: Singspiration Inc.

Ogisi, A. A. (2017). *Praise the LORD (A Collection of Nigerian Spirituals).* Apapa-Lagos: AMFITOP BOOK COMPANY

Okafor, J. E. (2018). Music and the Gospel: An Account of Adam Cornelius Igbudu and thepropagation of the Gospel. In Samuel Olufemi Adedeji (ed) *Music, Musicology and the Gospel in Nigeria: A Festschrift in Honour of Samuel Olufemi Adedeji.* Pp: 279-291. Ile-Ife: Association of Nigerian Musicologists

Onwuekwe, I. A. (2018). Compositional Techniques and Guidelines for the African Contemporary Choral Music Composer. In Samuel Olufemi Adedeji (ed) *Music, Musicology and the Gospel in Nigeria: A Festschrift in Honour of Samuel Olufemi Adedeji.* Pp: 147–168) Ile-Ife: Association of Nigerian Musicologists

Ossaiga, U. P. (2015). The Use of Music in Burial Services of Warri Baptist Association. In Arugha A. Ogisi (Ed) *Studies in Nigerian Music (Music and Society in Nigeria),* Pp: 75-81. Apapa-Lagos: Amfitop Book Company

Anonymous (2018). *Collected Gospel Songs Orchestration.* Lagos: Apostolic Faith Church

_____ (1975). *Baptist Hymnal.* (ed) William J. Renolds. Nashville, Tennessee: CONVENTION PRESS

_____ (1992). *Mozart's Twelfth Mass.* Ibadan: Damson Graphic Production Company withthe permission of NOVELLO & CO.

_____ (1951). *Tabernacle Hymns Number Four.* Publisher: Tabernacle Publishing Company

_____ (1947). *MESSIAH.* New York: Published by Carl Fischer

_____ (n/d). *Best Athems.* Chicago, USA: Hope Publishing Co.

_____ (n/d). *The Easter Choir for Volunteer Choirs and Special Choruses.* Indiana, USA: THE RODEHEAVER HALL-MACK Co.

_____ (n/d). *The Empire Anthem Book.* A Collection of Original and Selected Anthems.London: F. PITMAN HART & Co. LTD.

_____ *(n/d) The Holy Bible (King James Version).* London: Cambridge University Press. The Queen's Printer under Royal Letters Patent.

Internet Source(s)
https://www.bibledictionary1567784970902 Retrieved: September 3rd, 2019.

SECTION V

General Readings

19

Performance Arts and Societal Transformation: A Case Study of Footprints of David Academy, Bariga, Lagos, Nigeria

Albert Oikelome, Ph.D[*]

Introduction

This chapter explores the use of performing arts as a transformation agent among young people in the slums. Using the Footprint of David Academy, Bariga, Lagos State, Nigeria, as a case study, the paper investigates the dynamic relationship between performing arts and the activities of young people in disadvantaged settings. Through detailed analytical lenses, the study provides a comprehensive description of the academy's activities and developments over the years. By examining their musical practices, it argues for a relational indigenous perspective that brings together ideas about the children's' involvement, the group's relationship with the audience and other groups in the community, and the influence of the academy on the children and the immediate society. It concludes by proposing a framework for analysing further projects that help children in the discovery and harnessing of talents thus keeping them off the streets and engage them in worthwhile activities.

I sat before the television one evening to watch and listen to the news broadcast. There I saw a group of young children in performance at an event in Bariga, Lagos State. They sang, danced, and played on traditional musical instruments so well that one would pass them for professionals in the field. They are not professionals. The children are from the Footprints of David Arts Academy, Bariga, Lagos State. These children were handpicked by Seun Awobajo, the Performance Director, from several slums and dark spots in Bariga, Lagos State. Being a product of the slum himself, Seun scouts around for children that are disadvantaged, vulnerable, and from poor backgrounds.

---

[*] Associate Professor, University of Lagos, Lagos, Nigeria

He aims to discover their innate potentials in the arts and direct their energy towards meaningful performance through mentoring and tutelage. His expertise and knowledge in indigenous performance practice are not in doubt. As a graduate of Theatre Arts from the University of Lagos, He honed his talents in dance, drama, and ensemble performance. Through painstaking efforts, he has raised them from the squalor of societal degradation to great stars of repute. Today, their stories have turned out to be something of an inspiring tonic to millions of youths struggling in several ghettos sprawled all over Lagos and even beyond. It is an inspirational story from the slums to stardom. They have now become arts ambassadors travelling across the globe. This story brought back memories of a song, 'Brand from the burning'. The excerpts below:

> Polluted, and vile, and burning away. To list, sin and hell, I made me a prey. Sure I must admire that merciful hand which I from the fire plucked out as a brand. Am a brand plucked out from the burning (Thomas, 2019).

As conveyed in this text, the short lyric demonstrates the transformation of children from the 'fire' of social ills to a 'great brand' through performance.

There is unprecedented growth in the urban population in Nigeria. Lagos is one of the fastest-growing states with rural migrants coming in daily. Interestingly, young people make up to a third of people living in these slums. A major reason for the large population of people in these slums can be attributed to the migration of people from rural areas to large cities. However, the cities cannot take the influx of migrants. Coupled with the expensive state of the city, the poor have no clue there alternative than relocating to these remote areas thereby slums. A slum has been defined as a "contiguous settlement where the inhabitants are characterized as having inadequate housing and basic services" UN-HABITAT (2002). This is characterized by overcrowding, high levels of unemployment or underemployment, deficient urban services (water, sanitation, education, and health), and widespread insecurity (UN-Habitat 2003b). Young people raised in these slums feel a disconnect from the larger society. The result of this is a sense of neglect, isolation, rejection, and inferiority complex. Life expectancy is high in the slums, leaving lots of children orphaned and vulnerable. This can become a major threat to social cohesion and economic prosperity (Donnelly and Coakley 2002). The study, therefore, examines the use of performance arts as a social transformation mechanism in the slums in Bariga, Lagos State. Furthermore, we need to examine music as a positive and purposeful transformative music engagement. Therefore, the paper examines the program of the footprint of David Academy, the students, the trainers, and the experiences of the students in the academy. The paper also discusses the multifaceted ways that performance is being taught the members of the academy and how the members are being prepared to engage in both multimodal and participatory forms of music-making. The paper explores the musical world of the members, their view about the world, and the goals we pursue to empower learners as active agents in their musical development. Using the Footprints of David Academy, Bariga, Lagos State as a case study, I examine performing arts as key to an integrated perspective that helps the children in terms of self-esteem, mastery, critical awareness, expression of inner voice, propensity to perform on stage, and collective empowerment Music, Dance, and Drama have served as viable tools for engagement with young people. This, according to Cheong-Clinch (2009), is 'pertinent at this time of changes and development of the young person's self-image, sexual identity and peer relationships'. The performing arts, therefore, serves as a medium of self-expression and a means of integrating the external world with their impulses (Schalkwijk, 2015).

Primary data for this study was collected through in-depth interviews of the leaders and young people in the academy. I also conducted a series of interviews with the trainers and observed them working with young people during rehearsal sessions. The questions for the interviews were both structured and unstructured to allow for more flexibility.

The theoretical framework for this study is based on Femi Adedeji's theory of transformative musicology. According to Adedeji (2006), transformative musicology encompasses all musical activities that focus on transformative purposes, a product of intercultural musicology. He postulated that music could be used as a vehicle for the transformative process needed in a society and that composition constitutes its major tool. He opined that musical compositions could be used to meet contemporary social challenges. This is in tandem with the works of Umenyilorah (2014) who believe that 'performing artists speak to the people in their language and idioms that deal with issues of direct relevance to their own lives'. Development is achieved by, with, and for the community through the dialogue once the awareness is created and the community in question is involved. Hence, learning becomes transformative when the learner not only acquires a skill or knowledge, but also experiences a profound effect on his/her notion of self and relationship with society (Qi, and Veblen, 2016). It is necessary to consider not only the music learners and their dynamic potentials, but also the social affiliations that promote music learning.

Over the years, studies have shown that music, theatre, and dance have been proven to have the transformative power to change lives of the young people in underprivileged areas of the country. Furthermore, it opens up endless opportunities to tap from the wealth of the knowledge of mentors and teachers in the field thereby creating great opportunities in developing their innate talents. Art has been described as a tool for development. Apart from improving academic performance and student discipline (Fiske, 1999) it also revitalizes neighbourhoods and promotes economic prosperity (Walesh, 2001). The arts provide a catalyst for the creation of social capital and the attainment of important community goals (Goss, 2000). Research has shown that performing art activities develop brain capacity among young people. Art also 'engages children's senses in open-ended play and supports the development of cognitive, social-emotional, and multi-sensory skills'. As children progress into elementary school and beyond, art continues to provide opportunities for brain development, mastery, self-esteem, and creativity. This article, therefore, explores ways by which the Footprints of David Academy seek innovative ways to employ the arts to improve and strengthen communities in Bariga, Lagos State Nigeria.

Members of Footprints of David Academy in action at an event

Source: **Footprints of David Academy**

Figure 1: Members of Footprints of David Academy in action at an event
Source: *Footprints of David Academy*

Footprints of David Academy: Beginning and Early Development

Footprints of David Art Academy started as a community project in Bariga at Olanrewaju Street by Ilaje Bus-stop in Lagos state Nigeria (Obalola). It was established in 30th December, 2005 by Seun Awobajo. The school is made up of young boys and girls between ages 8 to 14 residing within the suburbs of Bariga, a slum in Lagos Nigeria. The city is marked by deep inequality and pockets of poverty, especially, in the mainland regions. This is exacerbated by limited access to education, cultural participation, and opportunities for economic advancement. Most children in this area attend public schools, which often experience limited enrichment opportunities due to paucity of fund. From the streets as hawkers, scavengers, destitute, more than 400 children who were literally picked from the streets and transformed into great performers of music, dance, drama and movies. Recounting the spark that led to the establishment of the academy, Yemi Obalola in an interview observed:

> On several occasions, when the adult dance group go out for performance, these so called 'street children' who watched rehearsals of the dance group, will group up to imitate the dance group as they coordinate themselves to render dance performance in their way. They use any object like tin of milk, broken buckets, bottles, sticks etc to form beats for their dance steps. The activities of these children used to amaze everyone including the dance group using the ground for rehearsals but it was an exposé for Seun Awobajo, one of the pioneer members of the dance group. While he derives pleasure seeing these children do their stuffs, he discovered 'inner ability' of an African child. He later developed a strong interest in children performance theatre based on charity (Obalola).

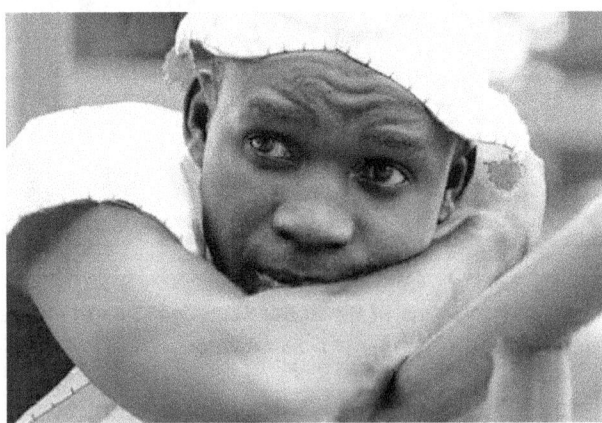

Figure 2: Seun Awobajo: Founder/CEO of Footprints of David Arts Academy
(Courtesy: Footprints Academy)

Since inception, the academy has executed lots of outstanding art projects independently as well as worked with many Nigerian icons in the entertainment industry. In an oral interview, the founder stated the reason for the establishment of the academy:

> Footprints was born out of a revolution. The antecedent of my growing up propelled the need to start footprints in Bariga. This area is one of the dis-advantaged areas of Lagos state with young people roaming the streets for want of nothing doing. But with the eagle's eye and hindsight, you will see that the young people in this area have great talents unexplored. Truly, diamonds exist in rough places. Hence, 'footprints academy' is my way of saying 'there are better things we can achieve with these raw talents' (Awobajo).

Describing the humble beginning of the academy in an oral interview, Seun Awobajo explained:

> 'I started with three boys and a girl. Over the years, we started having more children join the group with the attention from both public and the media on our performances.

The academy is located in Bariga, a slum in Lagos State. This community is known for the high rate of crime among young people. Unfortunately, these youths are victims of these heinous crimes. The academy serves as solace for some of these youths. It is an avenue for them to divert their talents to profitable use. The academy, therefore, helps young people to harness their gifts in music and dance. By providing the programs of artistic engagement among young people in the community, the academy is taking the youths off the streets. The students in the academy expressed the positive influence the school has on their lives. John Lakuku, a member of the academy expressed this in an oral interview:

> If it were not for footprints, I should be a street boy moving aimlessly on Bariga road. Footprints helped and gave me new meanings to life. I really didn't think much about my future before. But with footprints, I have a future to look forward to' (Lakuku).

John Lakuku is one of many boys and girls that has received some form of transformation through active engagement in the academy. A major task in the academy is to teach the children music and theatre. Thus, their leaders carefully crafts into stories into an artistic performance.

Footprints of David Academy, Bariga, has changed the lives of several students, many of whom would never have studied music or dance. Since its inauguration, the academy has grown in leaps and bounds with the enrolment of over four hundred (400) students, who have dance and music lessons, and participate in the popular music ensembles. Through the numerous programs and activities, students are taught to actively take control of their lives, which is an important tool for social justice among such a disadvantaged community. Subsequently, music had become an essential activity to them, something that they could not stop doing, even as they pursue other career paths in life.

Figure 3: Rehearsal Procedure at the Academy
(Courtesy Footprints Academy)

Figure 4: **Performance at an International event** (Courtesy Footprints Academy)

Inculcation of Moral Values at the Academy

The Footprint of David Academy, Bariga, has a holistic program that caters to other aspects of the children's lives. The academy provides a platform for the inculcation of moral values like discipline, teamwork, and respect for the elders. Discussing this in an oral interview, Awobajo states:

> Some of these children have imbibed the wrong values all their lives from the streets and bad gangs. The academy becomes the best place to reform and inculcate the right mode of behaviour in them. It has not been an easy feat but over time, and with resilience, the task is becoming achievable.

As part of their contribution to community development, the academy organizes extra mural classes for children in the Bariga community. All the teachers in the academy are volunteers whose passion for the community project has brought them to the academy. Their activities involve preparing the children for the Junior and senior secondary examinations. This will help to keep their academic performances in check as they concentrate on the activities of the academy.

Membership Requirements for the Academy

The membership in the academy entails the desire to learn and willingness to work with other members of the group. The leader of the group stressed that the structure of the academy reorganizes the social order by putting together children from diverse ethnic class, young people and adults, experienced and non-experienced musicians, in the same space, which is sometimes reconciling, sometimes conflicting, but ultimately keeping them together in the search for the pleasure of making music (Joly and Joly, 2011). The act of music-making together is definitely a potential source for disorienting dilemmas among the participants; their narratives corroborate how their meaning schemes were changed through participation and collaboration. For, Esther Balogun, her membership of the dance troupe has been an exhilarating experience:

> I was seven years old when I joined footprints. I saw them dancing beside my grandpa's house. So I told my mother that I wanted to join. At first she was hesitant. But my father gave his blessing and the rest is history (Balogun).

In communities like Bariga that is bedevilled by serious social problems, participation in a social project gives youngsters a sense of self-importance (Qi, and Veblen, 2016). This testimony is evident in the life of Chidera Nwobodo. In an interview with the researcher, he stated that his participation in the academy has brought him fame and fortune and opened doors of opportunities to travel to different parts of the world with the group.

Figure 5: Members in traditional costumes (Courtesy Footprints Academy)

Rehearsal Procedure at the Academy

Rehearsals are normally done in the evenings on weekdays (Wednesday and Friday from 4 to 6 pm) and Saturdays. A typical rehearsal session at the academy starts with a warm-up session where all members are put on a drill in the large hall with no seats. They have been drilled on all forms of African dance steps with the instrumentations made by the children. The dance movements are divided into segments, derived from the theme. The common division is three which are the preparation, main motion, and climax. One common feature of their performance is the total art concept of music, dance, and drama with elaborate costumes to complement them. Every movement on stage has its meaning and significance. The dance steps are choreographed by the artistic director to fit into the mood of the event. Here we see exertion of intense energy and heat at rehearsals as the children strive to outdo one another in performance. At the end of the rehearsals, the director gives a talk on the need for discipline and commitment to the task ahead. A major observation at the rehearsal is the fact that there is no gender segregation or discrimination during the performance. All the boys and girls are made to pass through the rigorous dance moves, regardless of gender. You find the members positioning the hands and legs in acrobatic display with dexterity in performance. Commenting on the performance practice of members of the group, Seun Awobajo explains:

> When we are invited to perform at any event, we put all of our strength to ensure we give our best. No event is considered small or insignificant. I coordinate, choreograph and ensure it is in synchrony with the songs and instrumentation.

Communal Development and Interaction through the Arts

Another goal of the academy is to create human development through interaction among people from different social, cultural, and economic classes, so the attention to the musical development of the group has a larger meaning than simply developing their techniques" (Joly and Joly 82). The group routinely offers trips, parties, social activities, and concert situations that encourage dialogue and shared learning among its members. Furthermore, it endeavours to develop a repertoire that is relevant to the participants with personalized arrangements and compositions that integrate and explore each of the musicians' abilities, character, and potential. Footprint academy is now an international phenomenon. The children have been able to take part in both global and local events with their great performances in Germany, Switzerland, Turkey, Netherlands, Austria, and England. They have also performed before the president of the federal Republic of Nigeria, Dr. Goodluck Jonathan, Prof. Wole Soyinka and most State Governors in Nigeria at the "Bring Back the Book project" initiated by Mr. President. Members of the group have been involved in film productions like: DE STREET by Blue Star Entertainment, MAAMI & ALO IYA AGBA by Mainframe production, FOLKS by DSTV; a television series on Yoruba movie magic directed by Tunde Kelani of Mainframe Production (Obalola).

Figure 6: Photograph with Prof. Wole Soyinka (Courtesy Footprints Academy)

Conclusion

The performing arts of Footprints of David Academy has become an alternative to violence and crime in Bariga community in Lagos State. Activities in the academy has helped liberate the children from the negative influences in the community and ultimately given them a new lease of life. With a mentor or guardian like Seun Awobajo to show them the way, the young people in the academy have found succour in the numerous performances organized by the academy. Through the performance engagements, the students have developed a positive mindset to life. Some have also enjoyed the good will of well-meaning personalities through the award of educational scholarships. Interestingly, activities of Footprints academy have not gone without any notice from corporate organizations and international bodies. That has opened more opportunities for growth and development in the academy. The success story of Footprints of David Academy comes as a living testament the transformative power of performance art in the hands of a man with a will. It brings clarity to Kleber's statement that 'bring a boy or girl from the street back to a decent life is considered the greatest conquest and goal. The inner transformation that the students experienced is thus intrinsically connected to an outer transformation in their life conditions' (279). It is therefore pertinent to state that the government should support the non-governmental organizations that are promoting the performance arts in the slums. Furthermore, they should develop a comprehensive programme that will cater for the musical needs of the vulnerable and underprivileged young people in the major slums of Lagos state. Through this programme, young people in the slums area will actively engage in the processes that constitute creation and performance in the arts (dance, music, theatre, and visual arts) and participate in various roles in the arts. Ultimately, it gives credence to the fact that music, dance and drama can indeed be used to change the world around us for good.

References

Adedeji, Femi (2006). 'Transformative Musicality: Recontextualizing art Music Composition for Societal Transformation', in Dan Agu (Ed) *Nigerian Musicology Journal* 2006.Vol 2 (Pg.137-156).

Awobajo, Seun (2018). 'Arts for Development: The Grace to Grace Story of Bariga Youths' *Interviews with TVC News* by Ola Awakan. 2018

Balogun, Esther (2018). 'Arts for Development: The Grace to Grace story of Bariga Youths' *Interviews with TVC News* by Ola Awakan. 2018

Cheong-Clinch, C (2009), 'Music for Engaging Young People in Education,' *Youth Studies* Australia, 2009 28(2), Pg. 50-57. Print

Daniella Ben-Attar, 'Youth Participation in Development: Strategies & Best Practices'http://www.weitzcenter.org/uploads/1/7/0/8/1708801/youth_participation_for_development_daniela_ben_attar.pdf Retrieved 4/12/2018

Donnelly, Peter & Coakley, Jay (2002), *The role of Recreation and Promoting Social Inclusion.* The Laidlaw Foundation

Fiske, Edward (1999), *Champions of Change: the Impact of the Arts on Learning,* Washington, DC: Arts Education Partnership President's Committee on the Arts and the Humanities.

Goss, Kristin. (2000), Better together: the report of the Saguaro Seminar on Civic Engagement in America, Cambridge, MA: Saguaro Seminar Civic Engagement in America, *John F. Kennedy School of Government Harvard University*, 1999. http://www.bettertogether.org/bt%5Freport.pdf.Accessed March 10, 2019

Kleber, Magali O. (2006). A Prática de Educação Musical em ONGs: Dois Estudos de Caso no Contexto Urbano Brasileiro [Music education practice in nongovernmental organizations: Two case studies in the Brazilian urban context]. Instituto de Artes, Universidade Federal do Rio Grande do Sul, Porto Alegre, Brazil.

Joly, Maria, and Ilza Joly (2011). Práticas musicais coletivas: um olhar para a convivência em Uma orquestra comunitária *[Collective Musical Practices: A Look at Coexistence in a Community Orchestra].* Revista da ABEM V19 26): (Pg79–91) Print

Lakuku, John. (2018). 'Arts for development: The Grace to Grace story of Bariga Youths' *Interviews with TVC News* by Ola Awakan.

Mincemoyer, Claudia (2019). 'Art – an Opportunity to Develop Children's Skills' The Pennsylvania State University. May, 2016 http://bkc-od-media.vmhost.psu.edu/documents/HO_Art_AnOpportunity.pdf. Accessed on 24th March, 2020.

Obalola, Yemi (2019). Meet Seun Awobajo -Founder, Footprints of David Art Academy. Nigerian Gems March 2018 https://nigeriangems.com.ng /2018/03/17/meet-seun-awobajo-founder-footprints-of-david-art-academy/ Accessed 24 March,

Schalkwijk F. (2015) *The Conscience and Self-Conscious Emotions in Adolescence: An integrative approach. Hove.* New York, NY: Routledge,

Qi Nan, and Kari Veblen (2016) 'Transformative Learning through Music: Case Studies from Brazil' in *Action, Criticism & Theory for Music Education.* Vol 15 (2) 100-125. Print

Umenyilorah Chukwukelue Uzodinma (2014), 'Theatre as Tool for Development in Nigeria' *IOSR Journal of Humanities And Social Science (IOSR-JHSS)* Volume 19, Issue 6, Ver. II (Jun. 2014), PP 34-40 Print.

Thomas, Tom (2019). 'John Wesley: Brand Plucked from the Burning' in Moral Apologetics https://www.moralapologetics.com/wordpress/2019/9/18/john-wesley-brand-plucked-from- the-burning retrieved August 13, 2020.

Walesh, Kim and Doug Henton (2001). *The Creative Community--Leveraging Creativity and Cultural Participation for Silicon Valley's Economic and Civic Future.* San Jose

The Relevance of Music in Nollywood

Philo Igue Okpeki, Ph.D[*]

Introduction

The chapter examined the relevance of music in Nollywood. Not much of music features in critical and scholarly studies on Nollywood. Film critics and scholars engage themselves more on socio-political, economic and technical issues when Nollywood is discussed as a means to promote cultural art form. It is against this backdrop of the unconscious neglect of sounds; especially music in Nollywood in critical discourses, that this paper attempts to examine the relevance of music in the realization of the composite sense of realism in the Nigeria film practice; although the paper examines the relevance of music in Nollywood. It equally pays attention to how music makes the message of film apt and precise. Invariably, this article noted that music and actions play complementary roles in the realization of message in films.

The video film industry in Nigeria, which is now labelled as Nollywood is arguably the most popular platform for cultural expression in Nigeria today. It is produced at a rate which makes Nigeria the hot sit of the genre across the world. However, because of certain technical flaws and the peculiarities of the economy of screening, critics and scholars continue to doubt the possibility of its development at the level of technicalities. However, regardless of its limitation Nollywood remains the best media of retelling the Nigerian story.

Nollywood remain Nigeria's most formidable film industry in the twenty-first century. This film enterprise makes available to its enthusiastic public the drama of everyday life in a post-colonial space. The audience watch their lives being played out on silver screen what Okuyade (2006:2) describes as "the realities of life staring at them screen to face". Nollywood

---

[*] Delta State University, Abraka

provides most Nigerians dreams, especially those who are scared of having one.

Although, video film in Nigeria is still a nascent phenomenon, scholars and critics have linked its emergence to Yoruba popular theatre and serial narratives. The trail blazing film in Nollywood tradition is Kenneth Nebue's living in Bondage 1 and 2. Lasode (2004), Adesanya (1997), Ogundele (1997), Haynes (1998), Okome (1997) accentuate the above assertion.

Objective of the study

The main objective of this study is to examine the relevance of music in Nollywood. Specifically, the paper sought to evaluate the application of music in Nollywood to ascertain the effect it has on films.

Music and Film

Music in films serves several significant roles in the film industry; amid them, it helps shape emotional responses, creates rhythm to scene as segments and comments on the action of actors. Music is crucial to the experience of scene and sometimes as iconic as the movies themselves. This is typical in films in Nigeria such as 'Living in Bondage', 'Dumabi the Dirty Girl', 'Kings of Boys', 'Oma, the Village Girl', amongst others. Music serves many purposes that are relevance to emotion and helps enhance the storytelling. According to Adam (2020), music, not only is it helpful to film making, but also essential for any director and producers to keep the music in mind when planning or shooting the movie. Music therefore add so much to the experience and emotional drives of film making.

Music can put a judgment on certain movie scenes; it can state that a certain battle is heroic or a certain dialogue is sad. In the early days of film making, the function of music was to comment on the images; but presently, music serves many purposes in film. It can portray emotions, developed a character, create social and cultural and geographic references (Hoffmann, 2020).

Emotional music is used to create the perfect atmosphere in film scene by setting the right tone and mood for the scene movement and the characters. Music also help to understand and develop character through the texts of the song used. For example, in the 'she loves me' in *kiddiswink*, Oghenerugba from an interview discussion, revealed that he was able to learn and understood the sad story of the character of 'Jesse'. Music in film likewise create and reveal the social, cultural and geographical references, thereby reflecting on the cultural heritage and geographical setting of the character. According to Irorovwo Eguridu, the kind of music heard during a certain scene can enable one to tell where it is taking place without the need of establishing the location.

The Application of Music in Nollywood

The subject of this article is specifically to examine the relevance of music in Nollywood. Although, the Nigerian video film has provoked a robust scholarly attention, Nollywood is usually appraised from the cultural perspective, the economics of production and distribution and most occasions criticism on it bothers more on its socio-political dynamics without much discussion on the use of music. It is against this background that this study attempts a reading of the film tradition in Nigeria in order to foreground the place of music in popular cultural practice designated as Nollywood. The study does not insist on the utilitarian function of music in the film, but its significance.

Brockett (1997) in his magisterial work, *The Theatre: An introduction*, distinguishes, total theatre sound into three categories: the actors' voices, music and abstract sound and realistic noises. In the realization of film production, numerous sounds are deployed to create effect in film. For the purpose of our study, we shall only address one of the categories of sounds Brockett distinguishes above. The study, therefore attempts to appraise the relevance of the application sound, or music in Nollywood films. Music is not used arbitrarily in film production; its function is specifically to make the meaning of the message of the film clear to the viewers. Ejeke (1994:46) contends that "the audience may get glued to a film if music is recorded to function as an adjunct in realizing its composite meaning: "the sound crew must find the appropriate type of music for a suitable musical piece when and where it is needed in the production even if it is live music that is needed".

Classical Greco Roman Dramatic and theatrical tradition was dominated by songs and dances, not because they were whole in themselves, but as an ancillary which leads the audience to the subject of the play. Thus, in the classical production the dancers were reduced to movement with musical accompaniment especially the chorus in ancient Greek drama sang choral odes with appropriate dance movements. Music was an important part of classical drama. Bowskill (1979) remarked that, music can help the audience retain, the mood, meaning and atmosphere of a play long after the last word has been spoken. It can quietly pursue their thoughts and feeling until they are outside the theatre. Invariably, the audience of Nollywood does not watch the action of the films which are usually protected by the rhythmic pattern of the sound track, they equally place premium on the development of sounds especially music. Music remains undoubtedly, the most potent weapon in filmic production which creates amazing effect on the audience if properly articulated to correspond with the thematic thrust of the film. The visual element of films is ordered towards achieving maximum dramatic filmic impact. The auditory complements are the human voice and speech. Consequently, music in film production functions to indicate the locale, advance the plot, create and sustain audience or anticipate the thematic thrust of a film. This is so because the visual elements and the musical are not at variance; they are what make films a composite whole.

From the discussion so far, it becomes glaring that music is deployed in films because it appeals to our sense of listening as it create an appeal which helps us reconcile the technicalities of screening and the act of filming. This will in turn place the audience at a vantage position to appreciate the finesse of production. Thus, Akpan (2020) insist on the synergy and visual and music and explained that the musicians must be able to combine the video and audio. He also explained that we must structure, a video-audio gestalt which is a production rather than a mere sum of pictures and sounds.

Akpan's (2020) argument aptly captures the complementarity of both in the realization of the total wholeness of filmic production. Music can equally be used before, during and after the enactment as functional, supportive and decorative element. Our discussion so far covers the significance of music as background in film production especially sound effect.

On some occasions, music can supplement action in film, a good example of this, is the use of music in ushering in a character by creating rhythm to fit a character's behaviour. If properly deployed, music can equally help the audience to predict character's intention, thereby creating an atmosphere whereby the audience becomes a participant in the entire filmic process.

Music in Nollywood most times performs the function of the chorus in classical drama. At this level, music functions as a means by which the filmmaker makes philosophical commentaries. This function is strictly a direct address to the audience so that they do not get carried away by the action of the film realized through music. This function is popular with Christian video films. However, the city/urban film magic money both produced by Helen Okpabio.

This study attempts an analysis of a religious film in order to make lucid our argument about the relevance of the use of music in film production. Helen Okpabio's *Highway to the Grave* will be briefly analysed to make practical our argument. Of the four recognizable genres in the Nigerian video film, the religious film seems to be the only genre that makes music function as part of a composite whole in film production. The Christian video films are not screened for mere entertainment purpose, they function beyond mundane bondage created by the Devil. Hence, Oha (1997:94) describes the struggle between the just and the forces of evil or darkness as "the war paradigm". The films are to help man realize their spiritual potentials and return to God. Thus, it is because of this utilitarian function of the film, that filmmakers offer their audience a significant proportion of sound track as gospel music.

Nollywood prioritizes heavily on music, even on occasions when the plot structure is shoddy. The deployment of sounds in films is usually magnificently organized. Music as an integral part of film production arouses the imagination of the audience and creates aesthetic pleasure. Beside the function of entertainment it performs during and after the production, music is like a compass which gives action and dialogue direction. By this function, music helps to sustain and articulate the changing mood of a film. Music sometimes effect action, if the gulf between silence, dialogue and music is bridged.

The Relevance of Music in Highway to the Grave

In *Highway to the Grave,* music functions as the pulse of the film. It helps to sustain and adjust the temper of the film. The music which introduces the film does not only function as prelude, it equally functions as prologue especially as the characters do not use speech to express their emotion, but action. The music gives the film its threnodic essence. Through the deployment of music in the film, a conscious audience would no doubt come to understand that the film is not only grotesque in temper; it equally has a tragic subject matter which is signified in the sound. The film details how the marine spirit from the water world, torment man on earth. A large chunk of the film eloquently demonstrates how man has been totally subdues to the supernatural world and it appears there is no rescue from this spiritual existential impasse.

As noted earlier, it is through music that this atmosphere of fear is sustained and asserted. The music equally demonstrates the powerlessness of mere mortals because they seem hunted and as such they are terrified and always on the run. When the scene changes to the supernatural world, the music which activates the scenic switch caries the tone of celebration, where we see the supernatural forces dancing and celebrating their destruction of the human world. The importance of music in creating and sustaining the filmic atmosphere and scenic switch cannot be over stated. It functions as a guide which replaces the popular role of narrator on stage. The film aptly performs this role albeit unconsciously. Music in the film equally functions to prepare the audience for a dramatic action, reinforce it or elongate its impact. This is obvious, hence the inclusion of music in the film.

The function of music in the film becomes easily discernable when, the world of the supernatural is eventually destroyed by a man of God through the resources of the power of God. Before the eventual triumph of the pastor, the music equally demonstrates the change of the direction of the film, signifying that God will certainly triumph over the forces of the darkness no matter how long it takes.

Another very formidable utilitarian function of music in Nollywood is it moralistic agenda. Every artistic piece usually has didacticism as an important message to the audience. This function of music in Nollywood is not strictly peculiar or particular to religious film. It runs across the other genre. According to Okuyase (2006:18) "the soundtrack of the film, Highway to the grave is very functional it does not only propel the film to an evangelical standard it unequivocally articulates the massage".

Music in Nollywood helps to accentuate the sense of realism in films. Life is music and music is life. Mankind relies on memory for existence especially on issues of documentation. Music on the other hand gives man the opportunity of capturing the essence of life in melodious form. Man expresses his joys, pains, anger and triumph in songs, invariably, music in films help to communicate the realities of existence, it adds plausibility to film thereby making it look realistic. Music do not function in isolation in the realization of realism in a film, but its sound is amplifies for the benefit of the audience.

Conclusion

The undue emphasis paid to dialogue and action in films has made the place of music in Nollywood seem subordinate. A critical examination of the Nigerian video film will not only establish the fact that filmmakers have excelled basically in deployment of the resources of sounds, especially music in the articulation of their message to the audience. The major concern of this paper has been to establish the fact that music is part of the compound and composite whole in film production. However, because of the undue emphasis on action and dialogue, the audience continues to fail to recognize the singular indisputable fact that music is important and a recognized aspect of the total process in the realization of realism in film production.

On the whole if we consider the manifold importance of music in film production, we will realize that music is not only an important auxiliary in film production, it could equally function as a map which can lead the audience to the heart of the message. Our argument is therefore a vindication that music is by no means a peripheral prop, if its potentials are holistically engaged in film production, bringing to bear Paz's contention, that music is not indefinite, but a concrete item which give movement and rhythm to action and dialogue.

References

Adam, G. (2020), *Film Music inside and outside of Hollywood.* https://rider.edu
Adesanya, K. (2002), Roll tape. *Saturday Tribune. 17th August.*
Akpan, G. (2020), A look at Creating Concept Art Environments. https://africandigitalart.com
Bowskill, D. (1979), *Acting and Stagecraft made Simple,* London: W.H. Allen.
Brockett, O.G. (1974), *The Theatre: An Introduction,* (3rd edition), New York Holt, Rinehart and Winston, Inc.

Ejeke, O.S. (1994), The Play and Sound Application some Principles, in O. Onookome and M. Enedu (Eds.), *The Sight of Sound: Sound in the Media and Theatre,* Ibadan: Kraft Books.

Haynes, J. (1998), *Nigeria Video Film,* Ibadan: Kraft Books.

Hoffmann, R. (2020), *What is the Function of Film Music?* https://robin-hoffmann.com

Lasode, D. (1994), *Television broadcasting: The Nigeria Experience,* Ibadan: Caltrop Publications Nigeria Limited.

Ogundele, W. (2000), From Soap Opera to Folk Opera: Improvisations and Transformations in Yoruba Popular Theatre, *Nigeria Video Film*, (Ed). Jonathan Haynes, Jos: Nigerian Film Corporation.

Oha, O. (1997), *The Rhetoric of Nigerian Christian Videos: The War Paradigm of the great Mistake Nigeria Video Film Corporation.*

Okome, O. (1997), Onome: Ethnicity, class, gender, *Nigeria Video Film* (Ed.). Jonathan Haynes, Jos: Nigeria Film Corporation.

Okuyase, O. (2006), Selling God with woman: The Word and the Women in the Nigeria Filmic Enterprises, *Ugo Journal of Humanities,* 11

Paz, O. (1992), *Collected Poems,* New York: New Direction Books.

Interview
Iroroevwo Eguriduon the relevance of music in films 20th August, 2020
Ogherugba on the relevance of music in films 20th August, 2020

A Bibliographic Classification of Music in African Total Theatre

Adegboyega Ayodele Samuel* & Olusegun Edward Oluwagbemiga, Ph.D*

Introduction

The onerous endeavour of rendering a taxonomic prescription or description in African theatrical forms come to fruition with musical identities. European canon has long remained the defining "heritage" of African theatre. However, the idea of "total theatre" which accommodates the use of music in secular, sacred and popular performance arts have since given new identities to African performance arts. This paper therefore attempts a classification of the symbiotic role of music and theatre in Africa. The write-up makes use of extant dramatic forms from different areas of Nigerian theatre adopting sociological delineation, personal interviews and literary approaches. The paper concludes that the symbiotic relationship of music and theatre has given an identity and a nomenclature to African theatrical forms.

Analysts, critics and different schools of thought have variously defined the terms 'music' and 'theatre' in line with their background and experience. The aftermath of imperialism with its attendant mental conditioning has greatly affected the perception of the average African about himself and his arts. Art, to the African mind, in its various forms, guises and descriptions is a communal activity, heritage and possession. Apart from its entertainment and aesthetic qualities, art is highly functional. To the initiate, African art has a 'soul' which, though, covert to the outsider, is overt to the initiate. Art therefore opens the window into the worldview of the creators, crafters, designers, moulders, trimmers, composers, shapers, etc.

The arts of theatre and music are complementary. Social life is highly centred on these twin-sister arts. Agawu (2003:23) notes that "in African society, it is difficult to separate African social life from drums." Thus, in traditional African societies, performance in its various forms and

---

* College of Education, Ikere Ekiti
** College of Education, Ikere-Ekiti

colourations, are embedded in rituals, liturgies, festivals and activities like puberty, funeral, chieftaincy conferment, work-songs, etc. All the engagements listed above form part of the African culture. It must however be noted that culture is one of the means of giving an identity to a people. In his observation about culture, Ajewole (2010:13) asserts that:

> Countries can be distinguished one from another because of the peculiar cultures they possess. Culture in this regard entails every aspect of music, dance, drama, fashion, culinary, painting, linguistics, architecture, ideology, religion, etc.

On the issue of identity, Ajewole (2010:14) states:

> the study of music in cultural context can also play a crucial role as an analytical lynchpin between music and culture. Identity can be seen in many ways such as national identity, political identity, religious identity, ethnic identity, cultural identity, etc.

In the same vein, Anoemete in Ajewole (2010:13) notes that:

> scholarly works must address both the social and musical layers of performance in order to understand the overall meaning of music in culture. In this way identity is negotiated, often constructed and sometimes stylized.

Africa depends on the west for definition, signification and identity of most life activities. In Arts, the canon is still that of Aristotle, Plato, Horace, Shakespeare, etc. The gap could be located in the dark years of colonial encounter. Giving an identity to theatrical genres therefore is still a movement in transition.

Conceptual Framework

Theatre experience to the African mind if restricted to fictive and imitative roles is unfulfilled. Attempts have been made to give an identity to the art of performance in Africa, away from the western canon. Theatre in Africa is all embracing resulting in the classification of this art form as Performance Art. In his summation, Obafemi (2008:63) asserts that:

> in sum, the dominant informing aesthetic of Nigerian theatre, long established in pre-literate, pre-colonial indigenous tradition, and one which summarizes the basic taxonomic propositions in modern scholarship of Nigerian theatre is the concept of total theatre.

The initiator of this concept is Adedeji (1968 and 1972) quoted in Obafemi (2008:63) who he affirms:

initiated this concept as a defining principle of Nigerian drama... arrived at that conclusion through a historical study of the masque dramaturge as a courtly theatrical form comprising song, dance, music, costume and spectacle emerging in a stagist process from ritual, festival and theatre.

Ogunbiyi (1981) also quoted in Obafemi (2008:63) describes the dominant aesthetic appeal in African theatre as the "incipient focal point of most-traditional drama in Nigeria." In the same vein, Orioloye (2006:97)claims that "Africans have long recognized music as the language of the gods. In the same vain, Olusegun (Book Series) affirms that each major Yoruba divinity has a particular rhythm associated with such divinity. Such rhythm depicts the personalities of each divinity as fiery, violent, peaceful and uncertain and these characteristics set the correct mood of worshipers during public worship. They therefore worship the gods with music and express their religious sentiments in music and dance." Also, Hastings cited in Oriloye (2006:97) in his observation on the use of music in performance arts concludes that "Africa is a continent of song, dance and musical instruments. Here lies the heart of their communal artistic inheritance."

Arising from the above observations, this paper highlights the symbiotic nature of theatre and musical experience in Africa. It also attempts to show how music has given a new identity in theatre experience away from the western canon. Thus, a uniquely African identity in the world of theatre is now "total theatre".

The primal dramatic thrusts, in terms of theme and form, of ritual performance and indigenous performances of itinerant troupes such as the Alarinjo and early theatre groups of Ogunde, Ladipo and Ogunmola, relied heavily on music to emphasise their inherent homologous. In his own view on the structure of *Oba ko so* by Duro Ladipo, Obafemi (2008) notes that:

> Structurally too, this drama, and others in a similar frame, borrows extensively from early ritual performances assembling all the ingredients of indigenous arts – the drums, dance, music, chants, cult poetry, panegyrics, proverbs; in short the total theatre.

Corroborating the idea of total theatre in African traditional performance, Dasylva (2004:6) opines that:

> the significance of *egungun* festival is the visiting spirit of the ancestor. It calls for reverence and worship. There are such ceremonials as drumming, songs, dancing, acrobatic display, poring of libations, exchange of gifts and prayers (evocatory and ivocatory), ushering in the new years' blessings, prosperity, peace, etc.

However, he observes that structural elements of ritual drama, visible in festivals and ceremonials have been imposed on or transferred to secular drama; he thus asserts that:

> ...Some of these traditional roles like dancing, drumming, singing, chanting and even masquerading which hitherto have been an exclusive preserve and significant constituents of traditional rites and religious worship have since been employed in secular 'festivals'...

Also contributing to the idea of total performance in indigenous performance, Ogundeji (2000) in Dasylva (2004:12) claims that:

> Communication among performers on the one hand, and between performers and the audience on the other hand is enhanced through music, chants, songs, drumming, dancing, acrobatics and miming. The mythological background that foregrounds the plot is also not usually elaborate. It is mainly symbolically expressed in mime and dance and its sequence is usually episodic.

This paper aligns with the view of scholars, some of whom are cited above, that the distinguishing factor of African theatrical performance is the inclusiveness of all the other genres of art vis-a-vis the verbal arts – proverbs, riddles, folktales, epigrams, the fine arts – painting, sculpture, carving, all forms of craft; the performance arts – dancing, singing, drumming, chanting, body movements, etc. to enhance audience participation, in any of the above forms of art, either separately or jointly, musical accompaniment is of utmost importance.

Traditional Theatrical Forms in Africa
Pre-colonial/Traditional/Residual Theatrical Forms

Prior to colonial encounter, the theatre of the indigenous people could be classified into two areas vis-à-vis sacred and the secular. The sacred has to do with communal worship. In this ritualistic theatre, use of drums takes a centre stage, largely because music has an esoteric contribution to worship. At the centre of these traditional forms of theatre are legendary figures, ancestors and deities who in one way or the other were adjudged larger than life during their earthly existence. Apart from use of music and theatrical elements that uniquely defined this performance mode, there were properties like carvings, totems, etc., that reinforced the belief of communities in their deities who participated in such activities albeit, invisibly, this traditional ritualistic performance has birthed many modern performance modes. The Edi festival at Ile–Ife provided the source material for *Moremi*, an Opera, by Kola Ogunmola.

Another traditional form of theatre that held sway during pre-colonial and colonial periods was the secular or profane form of performance. There were plays, though not necessarily ritualistic, but were performed during rituals, festivals, transitional periods/wedding/naming ceremonies etc. There were even days set-aside for satirical songs. The role of music in African theatrical performance is of utmost importance. Thematically, music and theatre are communicative agents. Messages are couched in gongs, drums, songs and imitation. During certain festivals, satires are used to deride unacceptable behaviours of errant members of the society. Hence Olusegun (2014:54) notes that:

> Yoruba satirical songs had been a useful instrument for combating deviant behaviour such as drunkenness, adultery, robbery, wayward and invitations women, lazy and coward folks, cheats and dubious character in a community.

These performances gained their fillip from the combination of music and theatre. Gbilekaa (1997: iii) asserts that:

> this theatre was practiced by the natives even during the colonial days because they found no meaning in the European concerts of 1870s and 1880s. This theatre eventually engendered the Yoruba operatic theatre or the "folk opera".

The Dominant Theatrical Forms

This embraces mostly what could be described as Nigerian Theatre in English expression. The works of dramatists and performance artists who have been to Europe and other climes but have come home to blend indigenous materials with foreign experience dominate this group. The use of language, especially the English Language, is the distinguishing factor in this type of plays.

Thematically, however, the plays here are related to residual performance arts. It is all about search for peace and harmony in this world and the cosmic realm. Examples are The gods are not to Blame (1975) by Ola Rotimi, *Death and the King's Horse Man* (2004) by Wole Soyinka.

Obafemi (2008:46) contends that "dramatists in this category are generally existentialist in their search for formal excellence, sometimes even to the detriment of content." On classification or identity, however, he avers that:

> ...playwrights in this category also take advantage of the "totality" of the myths-ritual indigenous theatre, using indigenous dramatic elements and weaving them with modern ones thus there is the use of cultural elements, the folkloric essence, the sayings, proverbs, songs, drumming, etc., all synthesized with western dramatic styles.

The Emergent Theatrical Forms

This group comprises mainly the "young" generation of performance artists who according to Obafemi (2008:46) "seek to break down societal problems in the light of real historical occurrences. Their ideology is materialist in description, perception and dialectical in approach". To this group, the problems of man originate from this world and should therefore be addressed here without any recourse to ancestors, deities or metaphysical phenomenon. The focus of this group is for a change of society from capitalist leaning and ideology to that of socialism. Obafemi (2008:46) continues "the argument is that an egalitarian set-up where all are workers and the wealth of the land is equally shared, will put an end to strife, hunger, violence, war, pestilence, etc., all of which are caused by want or capitalist greed".

Structurally, however the use of songs, dance, mime, riddles, and folkloric elements are freely used to embellish the plays. Thus, indigenous elements of music and dance structurally unite the different forms of indigenous performance art. In the same vein, the use of repetitions, variations and contrasts are useful in music and theatre. Repetition will enable the actors to know their lines off by heart, variation will help remove boredom in the trend of the play. Hence Olusegun (2010:38) concludes that:

> the basic forms are characterized by repetition, variation and contrast. Repetition keeps the music going and enables the participant to be acquainted with the content of the music when every participant is fully and actively involved. This is a common feature in the traditional music of the Yoruba and Elemure Music in particular. Changes in text may lead to a corresponding alternation in the melodic contour.

Christian Theatre and Accompaniment of Music in Nigeria

The genesis of Christian theatre could be traced to the colonial era when theatre became a means of reining in the 'natives' and evangelism. Foremost among the colonial arms was the Catholic Church. Gbilekaa (1997:6) asserts that:

> By far the greatest producer of drama in colonial Nigeria was the Catholic Church. This was ostensibly done to facilitate effective communication in the church among a predominantly Yoruba-speaking community and a Portuguese-speaking Brazilian community in English colony. Drama was also used to aid the teaching of language in schools.

However, the performances were mostly elitist in nature as the majority of audience comprised the freed slaves, colonial masters, missionaries, traders, etc. The elites of that period, irrespective of their political leanings, cultural affinity, etc., were white men in black skin.

The aforementioned idea of elitist theatre soon led to secessionist churches who were backed by cultural nationalists. Gbilekaa (1997:11)reports that the first of these churches to secede was the native Baptist Church founded in 1888, followed by United African church (UAC) in 1981.Gbilekaa (1997:11)goes on to report that:

> these churches started grafting and preserving aspects of African culture which they found convenient in their brand of Christianity. Gradually, African dance and music found their way into the church service. These attempts at exploiting indigenous modes of expression and communication in the worship of their God paved the way for authentic Nigerian drama.

Oriloye (2006:97) also reports that:

> about 1920, the Cherubim and Seraphim another truly indigenous independent church, was established in Lagos. This church did a lot to initiate and popularise the use of African folk tunes and musical instruments in their worship throughout Yorubaland.

Conclusion

The attempt to define or classify African theatre historically i.e. pre-colonial, colonial, post-colonial, formally – traditionally or modern, thematically – politically, socially, or structurally – having to do with arrangements, bring about avalanche of contradictions and inconclusive options from scholars. It is the position of this paper that theatrical performance in Africa is inclusive of all other arts – plastic, verbal and performing arts. The African dramatist synthesises traditional and cultural ideas to project a unique African aesthetic appeal. This aligns with the position of Adedeji (1960) cited in Ogunleye (2002:73) that:

> the verbal arts (proverbs, riddles, folktales, epigrams etc.) the fine arts (carving, painting etc.), the performing arts (dancing, singing, drumming and dramatizations)...are the basis of socialization and social control. But the theatre utilizes all three categories in synthesis.

If the yoke of colonialism is to be broken and Africa evolve a distinct canon in defining her own arts, then it is apt to consider the raging argument from different schools of thought surrounding the idea of total theatre: in total theatre, all other art forms feature in a given performance to present an authentic African aesthetic preference.

In Total Theatre, the use of music is preponderant. Such application could be structural. In the surreal play – *The Palm wine Drinkard* (1972) by

Kola Ogunmola, the use of songs dominates the communication among the characters. Also in *Death and the King's Horseman* (2004) by Wole Soyinka, music and dance take central positions. The use of proverbs, riddles, chants and mime make the play uniquely African.

In Yoruba festivals and ritual engagements, drums are used to evoke the presence of deities. It must be noted that individual deities have preference for different musical instruments, thus '*agogo* and *shekere*' are enamoured by Ogun. Alade and Olusegun (2011:2) note that:

> in traditional Yoruba society, there is music which is connected with rituals, liturgies and festivals; music for social activities such as puberty, marriage, funeral ceremonies and music connected with installation of chiefs and entertainment...nearly every Yoruba *orisa* also has his own special drum ensemble and often this drum group is said to be the group a particular deity enjoyed, danced or listened to during his earthly life.

The likes of Ogunde, Ladipo and Ogunmola make use of music both structurally and thematically. Even the Emergent dramatists borrow extensively from traditional music and dance to enable their works have the badge of authentic African art. The Christian churches also make use of music and dance to reach a higher audience in a bid to evangelize. The unifying idea behind all these performances is music in its various manifestations, i.e. singing, chanting, proverbs, riddles, drumming, etc.

Recommendations

It is recommended that scholars, artists and opinion movers, should come together and give unique identities to African arts and institutions. Universities and Colleges of Education offering Theatre Arts and Music as courses of study should incorporate other arts in their curricular so as to give depth and enable the students have knowledge of different areas of performance as this is what operates among typical indigenous African artistes.

References

Agawu, K. (2003). *Representing African Music: Post-colonial Notes, Queries and Positions*. New York: Routledge.

Ajewole, J.O. (2010). Foundation of Instrumental and Vocal Ensemble Music. Ibadan: Mercy-ken Services Ltd

Alade, L. B. & Olusegun, E.O. (2011). 'The Significance of Drums and their Liturgical Functions in Ceremonies'. *Journal of College of Education*, Ikere Ekiti (JOCEI) 1(1).

Dasylva, A. (2004). *Studies in Drama*. Ibadan. Stirling-Horden Publishers (Nig.) Ltd.

Ladipo D: Moremi. Ibadan: Macmillan Publishers.

Gbilekaa, E.T.S. (1997). *Radical Theatre in Nigeria*. Ibadan: Caltop Publications Nig. Ltd.

Nwanpa, O.N. (2016). 'Humanity and Humanities: Reconstructing Nigeria's indigenous knowledge Systems'. Abraka Humanities Review; 7(2)

Obafemi, O. (2008). *Politics and aesthetics: Essays in drama, theatre and performance*. Ilorin: Haytee Press and Publishing, co. Ltd.

Ogunleye, F. (2002). 'Preserving culture through Novel Forms: The Case of Duro Ladipo's Folkloric Theatre'. *Ife Journal of the Institute of Cultural Studies* (8).

Ogunmola, K. (1972). *The Palmwine Drunkard*. Ibadan: The Institute of African Studies, University of Ibadan.

Oriloye, S.A. (2006). 'The Emergence of Religious Folkmusic in Christian Worship in Yorubaland'. Catis: *Ikere Journal of Religious Studies*. 2(2).

Rotimi, O. (1975). *The gods are not to blame. London*: Oxford University Press.

Soyinka, W. (2004). *Death and the King's Horseman*. Ibadan: Spectrum Books Ltd.

Olusegun, E.O. (2010). 'The Role and Functions of Music at Yoruba Festival': *College of Education Book Series for Nigeria Certificate in Education*. Vol III pg 38.

Olusegun, E.O. (2014). 'Satirical Songs as a Social Control in Ogoye Festival in Igbara Oke': *Ondo Journal of Arts and Social Sciences* (OJASS) Vol XIII Pg 47.

Index

Abolagba, John Aideloje ; viii, xiii, xvii, 30, 35, 42, 52, 115, 131
Abraka Music School (AMS) ; xx, 11, 13, 15, 23, 24
Achinuvu, Kanu; 18
Adagbrassa-Ẹlumẹ; xviii
Adeboye, Pastor Enoch; 9
Adedeji, Professor 'Femi; vi, xi, xiii, xiv, xvi, 13, 14, 16, 27, 28, 75, 77, 87, 143, 148, 157, 173, 222, 223, 232, 238, 249, 250, 255, 265, 276, 281
Adegboyega, Ayodele Samuel; ix, xiii, xvii, 21,
African Music, concept of; 196
    Music Education; 197
African Total Theatre; ix, xvii, 276
Afro-beat; 50, 185
Afro-juju music; 48
Agu, Prof Dan; 14, 16, 19, 27, 42, 267
Agu, Prof C.C.; 2, 51
Akpabot, Samuel; 18
Akpakpan, Dr. Johnson James; vi
Akperi, Rev. Dr.Yemi; iii, v, vi, viii, ix, xi, xii, xvii, 8, 13, 42, 175, 178, 193
Aluede, Professor Charles; iii, v, vi-ix, xi, xii, xvi, 1-3, 6, 8, 13, 42, 75-77, 79, 86-88, 93, 95, 101, 116, 131, 232, 236, 239, 253
Amromare, Rev J. E.; 34
Amusan, Sam; 18
Anglican Communion; ix, xvii, 30, 35, 225, 229

Traditional Music in; 225
Need for Traditional Music; 227
Impact of traditional music; 235
Aniwene, Emmanuel; 18
Apala music; 48
Asaolu, OpeyemiAdeyinka; ix, xiv, xvii, 17
Associated Board of the Royal Schools of Music (ABRSM); xxiv, 3, 4, 33, 39
Association of Dance Practitioners of Nigeria (ADSPON); vi, xxvi, 41
Association of Nigerian Musicologists (ANIM); vi, xii, xiii, xxvi, 17, 27, 41, 57, 59, 158, 193, 194
Awobajo, Seun; 255, 259, 260, 261, 265, 266, 268
Bankole, Ayo (Jnr); 18, 208
Baptist High School, Orerokpe; xxiv, 3, 5, 17, 32, 39
Basic Schools' Music Programmes, Current State of; 176
Bata Music (Ogun-Ekiti); 133-144
    Instrumentation of Bata; 135
    Rhythmic Pattern; 138
    Functional Roles of; 140
Bendel Radio (BDR); xxiv, xxv, 39
Bethel Baptist Church, Sapẹlẹ; viii, xi, xvi, xviii, xxiv, 2, 3, 29, 30-36, 39
Bolaji, David; xiv
Brassine, Mrs; 18
Broadman Hymnal; 34
Chukwu, Dr. Sam; 17

Chukwuka, Chuma; 18
Church Music (Musician); vii, ix, xi, xiii-xv, xvii, xxii, xxiv, 2, 19, 29, 30-32, 34-36, 40, 195, 202, 203, 205, 208, 212-224, 238-241, 246, 252
  Levels of development; 216
  And Relations in Nigeria; 221
Church Music Composition, Bible as invaluable inspiration archive; 240
  Compositions with Bible passages; 241
  Compositions without Bible passages; 246
College of Education, Warri; xix, xxv, 1, 5, 6, 9, 17, 40, 42
Community Music; viii, xvii, 175, 176, 178-181, 188-194
Concert Music; 43-46, 50, 51
Conference of Music Educators in Nigeria (COMEN); vi, xiii, 17, 27, 39, 41
Council Primary School, Sapele; xxiv, 3, 16, 39
Cutliff, J.; 18
Dance of the Seven Spirit; xxvi, 10, 23, 41
Decline of Concert; 45
Delta State University (DELSU); xii, xiv, xv, xix, xx, xxii, xxv, 1, 2, 3, 5, 7, 8, 11, 12, 15, 17, 20, 23, 24, 40, 72, 101, 102, 131, 193
Dick-Duvwarovwo, Dr. Mrs. Ereforo; vi
Disease in African Cosmology; 77
Ecclesiastical Authority (Methodist) and Musical Creativity in Nigeria, tensions between; 213
  Ecclesiastical Authority and Artistic Expression; 218
Echezona, Wilberforce; 18
Edah, Mrs. Bridget Onome; 108

Efurhievwe, Margaret Akpevwoghene; viii, xiv, xvii, 8, 11, 42, 145, 151, 157
Ihi Ebo; 117
Ehigie, Sam; xxv, 40
Ekewenu, Bruno Dafe; vii, xi, xiv, xvi, 1, 8, 42
Eru, Lt. Col. Timothy; xviii, 2
Folk Music International; xxv, 40
From the Cotton Fields to the Concert Hall; xxv, 40
Fuchianga, Ijeoma; 18
Fuji music; 48
Full Gospel Businessmen's Fellowship International (FGBMF); 9
Furze, J., 18
Gomper, D.; 18
Gospel Bells Band; xxiv, 35, 39
Green, Victor L. D.; organist; xxiv, 2, 4, 13, 32, 33, 39, 71
Highlife music; 19, 20, 23, 27, 161-168, 170, 172
Ibude, Dr. Isaac; vi
Idamoyibo, Professor Ovaborhene; vi, 1, 13, 42, 51, 67, 72, 99, 101, 104, 136, 146, 148, 150, 153, 157
Idolor, Mus. Professor Emurobome G.; vi, vii, xi, xiii, xvi, xviii, xiii, xvi, xviii, 4, 5, 7, 16, 17, 24, 42, 46, 51, 52, 57-61, 65, 67, 69, 71-73, 104, 113, 120, 131, 193, 200
Ifionu, Azubuike; 18
Igbi, Oghenemudiakevwe; iii, iv, v, vi, vii, ix, xi, xii, xiii, xvi, 2, 4, 8, 15, 20, 27, 42, 43, 52, 116
Igue festival; 117
Institute of Continuous Education, Benin City; 4
Juju music; 43, 48-51
Living Faith Church, Winners' Chapel, Abraka; 9
Mereni, Anthony, 16, 85, 87, 88
Music, Role and Functions of in Odun-Isu; 91, 95

in Nigerian Festivals; 93
Song of Praise; 97
Closing Songs; 97
Music Education, National Development and Youths; 120
Music and Traditional Education System; 117
Music in Nollywood, relevance of; 269
   Music and Film; 270
   Application of Music in Nollywood; 271
Music Performance Hall; xx
Music therapy; xii, 75-77, 83, 85, 87-89, 101
Musical Nationalism, Rise of; 45
Musicians, some popular ones in Nigeria: 2000-2020; 181
National Universities Commission (NUC); xix, 11
   Benchmark; xx
Ndubuisi, Okechukwu; 18
New, L. J.; 18
Niger Delta; viii, xi, xvi, xxvi, 5, 40, 56, 71, 77, 146, 185
Niger Coast Constabulary Band of Calabar; 19, 20, 27
Niger Delta Development Commission; 191
Nigerian Art and Church Music; 195
Nigerian art music; viii, xi, xvi, 27, 37-52, 173, 212
Nigerian Baptist Convention (NBC); 31, 35, 8
Nigerian Highlife, applied theory of; 161
   Rhythm; 287
   Harmony; 164
   Orchestration; 166
   Melody and Vocalism Techniques; 171
   Lyrical Techniques; 172
Nigerian Musicology; 53
Nigerian Television Authority (NTA); xxiv, xxv, 3, 34, 39, 40

Nsukka Baptist Church (now Holy Ghost Baptist Church); x, xix, xxv, 39
Nwanbuoku, Dr. Emeka; 41
Nwankpa, Professor Onyee N.; vi, xi, 17, 180, 190, 194
Nwokedi, Sir Emeka; 18
Nzewi, Meki; 16, 18, 43, 50, 51, 76
Odogbor, Dr. Peter; vi, 8, 42, 52
Ofuani, Sunday; viii, xiv, xvii, xxii, 12, 30, 35, 42
Ogbeide, Mrs. Rebecca; vi, 42
Ogiedi; xviii
Ogigirigi, Mrs. Patricia; 6
Ogisi, Deacon Francis E.; xviii
Ogisi, Prof Dicta; 9, 12, 18
Ogisi, Dr. Arugha Aboyowa; v, vii, x, xviii, xii, xxi-xxiv, 3, 13, 31-36
Oguoma, Patience; 17
Ohwata, Madam Utọrọ; xviii
Oikelome, Dr. Albert; iii, iv, vi, ix, xi, xii, xvii,
Ojaide, Tanure; 107, 113
Okafor, Dr (Mrs.) Enoh; vi, vii, ix, xiv, xvii,
Okenrentie, R. P. I.; xxiv, 2- 4, 13, 41,
Okotie-Eboh Memorial Baptist Church, Sapele; xxiv, 33, 39
Okpẹ Disco; 55-74
Okpeki, Philo Igue; ix, xiv, xvii, 8, 20, 42, 189, 194
Okumbor, Mrs. Dora; vi
Okunade, Dr.Adeoluwa; vi, 134, 143
Ologundudu, Rotimi Peters; viii, xiv, xvi, xxiii, 7, 102
Olusegun, Edward Oluwagbemiga; ix, xv, xvii, 21, 42, 93, 102, 278, 280, 281, 282 -284
Omatsola, John; xxiv, 2, 4, 13, 33, 39
Omibiyi-Obidike, Prof Mosunmola Ayinke; 1, 13, 16, 18, 72, 102, 143, 178, 236
Omojola, Professor Bode; vi, ix, xi, xv, xvii, 15, 17, 23, 27, 38, 44, 57,

72, 94, 102, 162, 173, 203, 208, 212
Omuku, Precious; ix, xv, xvii, 14
Onyenye, Mrs. Peace; vi, viii, xi, xv, xvi, 8
Onyiuke, Young-Sook; 17
Opre, indigenous knowledge reconstruction; 145-158
   Transformation theory; 147
   Performance; 152
   Musical instruments; 153
   Lyrics; 153
Oral Performance; xii, 56, 58, 59, 62, 63, 70-72
Ordia, Cecilia; xxv, 40,
Osadebe, Chief Osita; 169
Ossaiga, Dr. Udoka Peace; v, vi, viii, xi, xv, xvi, 3, 42, 239, 253
Osunniyi, Akin Joseph; viii, xv, xvii, 10
Partum Opera; xxvi, 23, 41,
Peace, Rev, Dr. Udoka; v, vi, viii, xi,
Performance Arts and Societal Transformation; 255
   Footprints of David Academy; ix, xvii, 255, 257-259, 261, 266
   Inculcation of Moral Values; 263
   Communal Development and Interaction through the Arts; 265
Performance Style; 59, 60, 66
Peters, Sir Shina; 50
Phillips Ekundayo; ix, xi, xvii, 13, 15, 203-209, 211, 212, 230,
Popular Music; vii-xii, xvi, xvii, xxii, xxv, 7, 11, 18-23, 27, 33, 40, 43, 44, 46-51, 55-58, 72, 120, 159, 161, 162, 173, 177, 179, 181, 189, 194-196, 198-200, 216, 217, 219, 261
Popular Musicians; 181, 185, 188, 190, 192
Praise and worship songs; 19
Race, Tim; 18

Redeemed Christian Church of God (RCCG); Abraka; 9
Religious Music; viii, xvii, 115, 116-131, 213, 215, 230, 234, 235
Religious pop music; 19
Rocheska, Mrs.; 18
Royal Ambassador (RA); 31
Sacred Musicology; 24, 224, 226
Saint Luke Anglican Church Sapele; xxiv
Samuel, Dr. Kayode; vi, 13
Sapẹlẹ Baptist Association; xviii, 35,
Sapele Technical College, Sapele; xxiv, 3, 5, 39
Shyllon, Adepegba; 18
Society for Music Education (ISME); xxvi, 17, 41, 194,
Society of Music Educators of Nigeria (SOMEN); xxvi
Songs for living; 75
   Disease in African Cosmology; 77
Songs of the Wayfarers; xxvi, 41
Song-Texts and Healing in Nigeria; viii, xi, xvi, 75
   Healing Song Texts from Esan and Yoruba Cultures; 78
   Women in Labour Songs; 79
   Birth Songs; 81
   Satirical Songs; 82
   Work Songs; 84
   Healing Potentials of Dirges; 86
Sourcing Data in Popular Music Research in Nigeria; 49
Sowande, Prof Fela; 16, 72, 208
Students Industrial Work Experience Scheme (SIWES); 7
Sun Beam Band (SBB); 31
Tamuno, Prof Tekena.; 18
The Friends of Music; xxv, 40,
The Gospel Singers; xxv, 39,
The Touch of Magic; 6
Tofolon, Elsa; 18
Total Theatre; ix, xvii, 271, 276-278, 282

Towel, Chief James Edah; viii, xvi, 8, 104, 105, 108
Traditional music; ix, xvii, 23, 49, 57, 67, 75, 87, 93, 95, 101-106, 114, 119, 131, 133, 134, 141, 142, 145, 148, 156, 158, 180, 194, 196, 198, 200, 225-227, 229, 235, 281, 283
Traditional musician; 104, 106, 114,
Transformation Theory; 147, 148, 157
   Indigenous Music Knowledge Reconstruction; 148
   Extraction Approach; 150
   Interpretation Approach; 150
Udje Performance, Philosophical Aspects of; viii, xi, xvi, 103, 104-114
Udoh, Dr Isaac E. ; vi, xvii, 215,
Ugbege; xxiv, 39
Ugbuwangue; xxiv, 2, 16, 39
University of Nigeria, Nsukka; x, xii, xiii, xviii , xxiv, xxv, 1, 4, 5, 6, 9, 17, 33, 39, 40, 42, 194, 200, 203

Urhobo song-poetry; 107
Warri North Local Government Area; xxiv, 39
Warri South Local Government Area; 16, 39,
Western art music; x, 46, 47, 198
Yoruba Music, development and Ekundayo Phillips; 202
   Similarities between and European Medieval Musics; 203
   Rhythmic Development, Folk-Tune, and Dance; 205
   Part-Singing and Accompaniment; 206
   Form; 206
   Expression; 207
   Cadential Points; 204
Youth Fellowship (YF); 31, 50

www.ingramcontent.com/pod-product-compliance
Lightning Source LLC
Chambersburg PA
CBHW070809300426
44111CB00014B/2462